LONDON BUS FILE
1950-54

KEN GLAZIER

Capital Transport

INTRODUCTION

This is one of a series of handbooks, each of which contains a complete list of all buses and coaches owned by London Transport during a period of four or five years, together with a brief description and history of each type covered. Vehicles which either joined or left the fleet during the period under review are listed with an additional column showing the dates on which they were formally taken into or removed from stock. These refer to the dates on which ownership changed and, in the case of buses taken out of stock, do not necessarily coincide with the day on which a vehicle left London Transport's hands physically. Vehicles sold for scrap were often dispatched to the breaker's yard before the paperwork was completed and some vehicles were stored by London Transport for a time after being sold to other operators. Where a body was scrapped before the chassis, the date on which the chassis was scrapped is deemed to be the date the complete vehicle was written off.

For the years after 1942 dates 'into stock' for all but experimental buses refer to the day on which the completed vehicle was received from the body builder. The chassis will have been owned for some time before this, however, as the normal procedure was for chassis to be delivered formally to London Transport, either physically or as a book transaction, before being sent for bodying.

The present volume covers the period from 1st January 1950 to 31st December 1954 and therefore includes the delivery to completion of a large part of the RT family, and the whole of the RLH, RF, RFW and GS classes as well as the arrival on the scene of RM 1. Withdrawals include the bulk of the remaining pre-war vehicles in the ST, LT, STL, STD, T, C, Q, LTC, TF and CR classes, and the whole of the wartime fleet, both unfrozen and utility, of classes STD, STL, B, G and D. The last examples of the SRT class were taken into stock at the beginning of this period but all had gone again before the end, a dramatic illustration of their unfortunate fate.

These books would not have been possible without the generous help of Dr Andrew Gilks, from whose private collection the bulk of the information concerning dates has been derived. Others who have given assistance include Ken Blacker, Lawrie Bowles and Reg Westgate who have helped to fill the various gaps, and Les Stitson who has worked hard on checking the accuracy of the basic data and taken a leading part in preparing the text for production. Thanks are also due to Brian Bunker, John Gent, Malcolm Papes and Dave Ruddom for allowing me to raid their photographic collections for illustrations and to the photographers, who are acknowledged separately in the body of the book, for permitting the use of their work.

First published 1998
ISBN 185414 201 1
© Capital Transport Publishing, Harrow Weald, Middlesex

CONTENTS

Title page
RF 129 in Watford High Street in September 1952. *E J Smith*

Front cover
Cravens RT 1511 on Richmond Bridge. *A painting by Barry Pearce*

LT

The LT class was the first of three new models introduced by the LGOC in 1929 and became the company's standard bus for a time between 1930 and 1932.

LT 1-150 were the last LGOC buses to be built with open staircases and the last 272 (known as 'Bluebirds') the first with the upper deck extended over the driver's cab. The class was used as a test bed for developing oil engines and preselective transmission and most double-deckers were converted to oil engines between 1934 and 1939. Withdrawal of the oldest LTs should have started in 1940 but the embargo on new vehicle construction during the Second World War extended their lives by up to ten years. Apart from losses through enemy action, withdrawal of the double-deckers began in 1946, slowly at first, and the last were not taken out of service until January 1950. At this time examples of most types of LT were still in stock. A few continued in use as trainers until the beginning of March and the last double-decker in active service was LT 379, which was used as a tilt bus at Chiswick until the end of October 1950.

Chassis: AEC Renown 663.
Engine: AEC A145 6-cylinder 7.4 litre 110 bhp petrol (40-113); A161, A165 or A180 6-cylinder
    8.8 litre 110 bhp oil.
Transmission: AEC D124 4 speed crash; or Daimler D128 4-speed direct selection preselective
    with fluid flywheel (1374).
Bodywork: LGOC (Chiswick), Park Royal, Strachan or Short Bros.
Capacity: H32/28RO (40-113), H34/26R (966-995, 1262-1425) or H33/23R (others)
L.T. chassis code: 1/2LT (40-113); 4LT (750, 762): 7LT (1383, 1393); 1/7LT (1419, 1425); 8LT
    (1374); 11LT (966, 1262, 1270, 1276, 1318): 12 or 1/12LT (remainder).
L.T. body codes: LT2/1 (40-113); LT3/1, 3/3, 5/3, 5/5, 5/6, 5/7, 5/8 (153-933); LT6/2, 6/3, 6/4, 6/5
    (1262-1425).
Built: 1929-1932
Number built: 1227
Number in stock: 1.1.50: 74
               31.12.54: Nil

Facing Page **LT 468 was one of the survivors of the class which lasted in service until January 1950 at Upton Park garage, but is seen here outside Woolworth's in Brixton when operating on route 159 from Old Kent Road. It was a 1/12LT5/8 with a body whose general appearance was typical of the bulk of the class, but with the intermediate arrangement by which the destination box was housed in the cab roof.** F.W. Ivey

Above **The LT was the class on which most major technical developments took place in the early 1930s. LT 1419, a 1/7LT6/5 seen here at New Cross Gate, represents the apotheosis of the class in terms of body design, being one of 272 with 'Bluebird' bodies. It was one of nine fitted with Gardner oil engines when new but this was replaced by an AEC unit in 1947. It ran until January 1950, latterly at Upton Park garage.** F.W. Ivey

LT		Date out of stock	LT		Date out of stock	LT		Date out of stock
40	GC3907	16.1.50	344	GN4658	9.1.50	734	GT5174	12.1.50
59	GH3797	23.2.50	349	GN4660	2.3.50	737	GT5196	9.1.50
74	GH3795	23.2.50	366	GN4688	12.1.50	750	GT5144	2.1.50
91	GH3835	23.2.50	374	GN4710	5.1.50	762	GT7537	3.3.50
97	GH3868	24.2.50	379	GN4716	17.10.50	776	GT5184	5.1.50
113	GH3852	1.3.50	381	GN4712	23.2.50	781	GT5191	5.1.50
153	GK3167	5.1.50	382	GN4717	5.1.50	822	GT7426	12.1.50
158	GK3159	2.1.50	398	GN4721	12.1.50	859	GT7470	2.3.50
163	GK5317	1.3.50	404	GN4723	9.1.50	911	GT7533	12.1.50
165	GK5323	11.1.50p	409	GN4799	5.1.50	917	GT7543	5.1.50
173	GK5318	5.1.50	426	GO 608	5.1.50	931	GT7579	2.1.50
187	GK5340	5.1.50	468	GO7127	9.1.50	933	GT7569	2.1.50
190	GK5365	2.1.50	474	GO7132	5.1.50	966	GT7592	2.1.50
248	GN2074	9.1.50	533	GP3468	2.1.50	986	GW5827	2.1.50
258	GN2070	2.1.50	547	GP3504	9.1.50	995	GW5897	1.3.50
264	GN2078	3.2.50	611	GP3565	5.1.50	1262	GX5216	1.3.50
274	GN2100	5.1.50	619	GP3574	5.1.50	1270	GX5226	30.1.50
278	GN2102	1.3.50	628	GP3581	7.3.50	1276	GX5219	2.1.50
281	GN2121	12.1.50	634	GP3592	9.1.50	1318	GX5249	2.3.50
310	GN2149	5.1.50	660	GT5049	5.1.50	1374	GX5372	2.1.50
316	GN2169	12.1.50	664	GT5043	2.3.50	1383	GX5341	2.1.50
319	GN2170	3.3.50	672	GT5057	12.1.50	1393	GX5340	1.3.50
326	GN4662	5.1.50	673	GT7586	5.1.50	1419	GX5387	9.1.50
327	GN4616	9.1.50	711	GT5138	2.1.50	1425	GX5393	2.3.50
340	GN4626	12.1.50	718	GT5142	6.2.50			

p   Retained by London Transport for preservation

Almost all of the STs built for the LGOC were identical in appearance to ST 10, which was a Chiswick bodied 1ST1/1. It was almost the longest lived of the class, beaten only by ST 1, having been new in February 1930 and being one of those which remained in service until January 1950. F.W. Ivey

ST

The ST class was introduced by the LGOC at the end of 1929, following trial operation of a prototype (which later became ST 1139) by its subsidiary East Surrey Traction Co. Ltd. A total of 906 more or less identical buses were built, including those supplied to East Surrey and the National Omnibus & Transport Co. These were the first LGOC production buses to have an enclosed staircase and platform. The last twenty-three supplied to East Surrey in 1932 had a new style of bodywork based on the LT 'Bluebird' design. A further 191 purchased by Thomas Tilling Ltd had open staircases, as did the prototype ST 1139 and four others acquired by the LPTB from London Independents in 1933. Six of those supplied to National had forty-eight seat lowbridge bodywork by Short Bros, for operation on route 336, and two similar vehicles were purchased by Amersham & District for their share of the route.

The withdrawal of Tilling STs started in the summer of 1939 and this would normally have been followed by the remainder of the class but further withdrawals were delayed by the Second World War, although the Tillings saw little regular service after 1940. Apart from wartime losses, withdrawals did not resume until the end of 1946 and the highbridge version ran for the last time in January 1950, at which time examples of all main types were still in stock. Some STs continued in use as trainers for a while, the last to be withdrawn being ST 1062 on 2nd January 1951. This was the last operational petrol engined double-decker in the London Transport fleet. Because there was a shortage of the type, the eight lowbridge buses had to be retained in service until 1951/1952. They were therefore overhauled in 1949/1950 and fitted with oil engines salvaged from STLs. They were replaced by RLHs.

The six LGOC STs fitted with lowbridge bodywork by Short Bros and the two similar Amersham & District Strachan bodied buses had a number of minor modifications to the bodywork over the years and had their petrol engines replaced by oil units in 1949/1950. ST 140, at Staines West station after being displaced from Amersham by the first batch of RLHs, shows the final condition of the sub-class. Because of a need for additional lowbridge buses, some of these vehicles kept going until the end of 1952. F.G. Reynolds

ST 354 was a 1ST2 which had been withdrawn from service in October 1948 but survived in use until December 1950, first as a staff bus and finally as a trainer, in which guise it is seen at Streatham Hill leading a rehabilitated E1 class tram. F.W. Ivey

Chassis: AEC Regent 661
Engine: AEC A140 6-cylinder 6.1 litre 95bhp petrol; or AEC A171 95bhp oil
Transmission: AEC D124 4-speed crash
Bodywork: LGOC (Chiswick), Short Bros or Strachan (10-829, 1040-1073);
Ransomes Sims and Jefferies (1091-1129); Tilling (887); Short Bros (1089); Strachan (1090).
Capacity: H29/20R except ST 887 (H27/25RO), ST 1073 (H26/22R) and STs 136, 140, 141,
157, 162, 163, 1089, 1090 (L24/24R)
L.T. chassis code: 1 or 2/1ST except: 1/1ST (815, 816); 3/1ST (136, 140, 141, 157, 162, 163,
1089, 1090); 2ST (887); 3ST (1073).
L.T.body codes: ST1/1 or 2, except: ST2/1 (77, 459, 707); ST4 (1073); ST7 (887); ST9 (818,
821, 1040-1064, 1086, 1091-1138); ST9/1 (lowbridge except ST 1090); ST9/3 (ST 1090)
Built: 1929-1932   Number built: 1138 (plus one instruction chassis)
Number in stock: 1.1.50: 147 (plus ST 169 – instruction chassis) ;   31.12.54: Nil

ST		Date out of stock	ST		Date out of stock	ST		Date out of stock
10	GC3942	18.1.50	395	GK3047	18.1.50	680	GN4760	9.1.50
15	GC3944	16.2.50	400	GK3030	2.1.50	689	GN4757	16.1.50
34	GC3948	9.2.50	404	GK3052	19.1.50	692	GN4770	6.12.50
77	GF416	2.1.50	406	GK3115	18.1.50	694	GN4692	2.1.50
81	GC3994	7.12.50	410	GK3081	7.12.50	702	GN4696	9.1.50
83	GF406	31.1.50	416	GK3096	16.1.50	707	GN4622	5.12.50
90	GF417	19.1.50	417	GK3066	2.1.50	710	GN4611	18.1.50
101	GF412	5.1.50	421	GK3095	9.11.50	719	GN4634	2.1.50
102	GF415	3.2.50	427	GK3069	9.1.50	722	GN4645	2.1.50
110	GF429	18.1.50	428	GK3107	19.1.50	730	GN4788	2.1.50
136	GF7213	27.2.53	434	GK3105	12.1.50	735	GN4621	16.1.50
140	GF7214	26.3.53	435	GK3039	2.1.50	737	GN4668	19.12.50
141	GF7217	18.12.53	438	GK3128	3.2.50	750	GO610	16.1.50
148	GF458	28.11.50	440	GK3060	2.1.50	761	GO5108	2.1.50
157	GF7201	27.3.53	443	GK3051	6.12.50	778	GO5136	9.1.50
158	GF7205	6.2.50	445	GK3112	18.1.50	783	GO5122	3.2.50
160	GF464	19.12.50	459	GK3117	18.1.50	792	GO5144	19.1.50
161	GF460	2.1.50	469	GK3086	5.12.50	795	GO5139	22.3.50
162	GF7218	26.3.53	472	GK3142	12.1.50	803	GO5127	11.9.50c
163	GF7215	16.4.53	479	GK5303	19.1.50	814	GO5195	5.1.50
164	GF456	8.2.50	481	GK5312	18.1.50	815	GO7105	5.12.50
175	GF7206	19.1.50	482	GK5309	2.1.50	816	GO7106	6.2.50
181	GF7221	2.1.50	484	GK3136	18.1.50	817	GO7114	19.1.50
186	GF7230	2.1.50	485	GK3121	12.1.50	818	GN4614	31.1.50
189	GF7235	19.1.50	486	GK3104	18.1.50	821	GK3192	11.1.50p
210	GJ7953	19.1.50	488	GK3125	19.1.50	829	GN4624	23.3.50
218	GH547	30.11.50	490	GK3124	18.1.50	887	GJ2063	16.2.50
221	GH541	2.1.50	520	GK5332	5.1.50	1040	GN4699	6.6.50
230	GJ7960	12.1.50	524	GK5335	1.2.50	1041	GN4707	1.3.50
233	GJ7963	9.3.50	529	GK5350	5.12.50	1044	GN4726	6.2.50
237	GH542	20.6.50	531	GK5357	2.1.50	1055	GO698	19.12.50
238	GH551	22.2.50	533	GK5362	16.1.50	1057	GO5132	3.4.50
261	GJ7966	9.1.50	538	GK5370	12.1.50	1059	GO5152	19.12.50
265	GH579	16.1.50	548	GK5373	28.11.50	1062	GO5188	2.1.51
271	GH592	28.11.50	549	GK5368	19.1.50	1064	GO7108	1.6.50
295	GF7255	2.1.50	551	GK5372	2.2.50	1073	GX5317	19.12.50
314	GH8056	27.7.50c	562	GK5382	9.1.50	1089	KX4656	27.3.53
321	GH8059	18.1.50	566	GK5390	16.1.50	1090	KX5055	27.2.53
326	GH8067	18.1.50	572	GK5397	12.1.50	1091	PG7593	2.3.50
349	GK3001	19.1.50	582	GK5419	18.1.50	1092	PG7724	20.2.50
354	GK3007	7.12.50	608	GK5451	19.1.50	1095	PG7727	3.3.50
355	GK3031	19.12.50	609	GK5455	22.2.50	1100	PG7965	1.6.50
368	GK3024	19.1.50	613	GK5447	2.1.50	1114	PG7979	1.6.50
371	GK3011	9.1.50	620	GK5469	2.2.50	1117	PG7982	24.10.50
372	GK3032	31.1.50	623	GK5476	16.1.50	1121	PG7986	3.10.50
373	GK3025	19.1.50	628	GK5473	18.1.50	1126	PG7991	1.6.50
375	GK3155	22.2.50	636	GN2010	18.1.50	1129	PG7994	18.1.50
378	GK3035	18.1.50	655	GN2114	5.1.50	1136	UR5509	31.1.50
387	GK3120	19.1.50	668	GN4606	18.1.50	1138	UR7879	6.2.50

c - Chassis only, body scrapped earlier   p Retained by London Transport for preservation

Most of the lowest numbered STLs still running in 1950 had been modernised in 1939 to almost the same mechanical specification as the last batches of standard STLs, because of which they endured longer than many nominally younger vehicles. They were nicknamed 'sit-up-and-beg STLs' because the modifications gave them the uplifted front end which is clear in this view of STL 530 at Finsbury Pavement in May 1951, making a rare appearance on route 43. Alan B. Cross

STL

The STL was first introduced by Thomas Tilling Ltd and the London General Omnibus Company in 1932 to take advantage of new regulations which increased the maximum length of double-deckers from 25ft to 26ft. There were originally eighty Tillings and one hundred of the first General design, which was a sixty-seater based on the 'Bluebird' LT. In 1933, the LGOC decided to standardise on a capacity of fifty-six for double-deckers and this cleared the way for an improved design with a sloping front, which was applied to the next four hundred. At the end of 1934 this was improved further to produce the classic smoothly curved front profile which was the basic design applied to 1,903 of the class, London Transport's standard double-decker between 1933 and 1939. There were two main variants: the Country Bus department took 139 with doorless front entrances (STL 959-1043, 1056-1059 with Chiswick bodywork; 1464-1513 with Weymann metal framed bodywork); and forty had inward sloping roofs for operation through Blackwall Tunnel. From October 1936 all standard bodies, on a total of 994 buses, had roof route number boxes. Of these, 175 (STL 2014-2188) had metal framed bodywork by Park Royal. Thirty-nine of the last 132 were painted green, the first new rear entrance buses to be allocated to the Country department.

All STLs were built on the AEC Regent 661 or 0661 chassis. Apart from an experimental batch of eleven vehicles (STLs 342-352) all STLs numbered below 609 were originally fitted with petrol engines and there was a mixture of crash and preselective gearboxes. The experiment with STLs 342-352 proved successful and from 1934 onwards the standard specification was for oil engine and preselective gearbox. The chassis of the last 132 pre-war STLs (2516-2647; 15STL16) had an improved specification including the AEC A173 direct injection oil engine, which extensive trials had shown to be more economical and long lasting than the indirect injection type. The enhanced specification also included flexible engine mountings, automatic brake adjusters and automatic chassis lubrication. In the summer of 1939, all petrol engined STLs with preselective transmission were converted to oil, leaving 283 with petrol engines and crash gearboxes. The same flexibly mounted A173 engine was used and they were simultaneously fitted with automatic brake adjusters which brought them close to the same mechanical standard as the 15STLs.

There were twenty-two non-standard pre-war STLs. Twelve (STLs 1044-1055), always known as the 'Godstone' STLs, were lowbridge buses built in 1934 for operation by the Country Bus department on route 410. They had stock Weymann forty-eight seat metal framed bodywork and their chassis differed from standard in having crash gearboxes and the AEC 8.8 litre oil engine. Six (STLs 553-558) were acquired from Independents in 1933: and four (STLs 1260-1263) were special short wheelbase models fitted with bodies from DSTs. Only STLs 553 (now fitted with a standard body), 1260, 1262 (rebuilt to longer wheelbase with a standard body) and the 'Godstones' were in stock at the beginning of 1950.

In 1941 London Transport was authorised by the Ministry of War Transport to build twelve new bodies to replace some of those lost in the Blitz. These were built to resemble the latest pre-war design but to austerity standards, including unlined internal panelling, wooden framed seats and fewer opening windows. They were classified STL17 and were mounted on overhauled standard chassis. London Transport was later allocated thirty-four 'unfrozen' Regent chassis for which twenty lowbridge (STL19) and fourteen highbridge (STL17/1) austerity bodies were built at Chiswick. The highbridge bodies were similar to the STL17s but lacked a front route number box and rear indicator display. All of the lowbridge bodies and one of the highbridge version were fitted to standard chassis and eighteen of the new chassis received bodies of various pre-war types from the works float. Three received STL17 bodies. In 1946 a further twenty chassis of the post-war standard AEC design were purchased and these were fitted with Weymann's first post-war style of proprietary bodywork (STL 2682-2701). The 17STLs and the first three 18STL20s were painted red when new but all operated exclusively in the Country area and were later repainted green.

Fifty-seven STLs were lost through enemy action but the lives of many older vehicles were extended by wartime restrictions. Withdrawal of the petrol engined fleet did not begin until the spring of 1947. Only one petrol STL (43) was still in service at the beginning of 1950 and this was withdrawn on 12th January.

Because of the works float overhaul system used at Chiswick Works, many STLs exchanged bodies over the years and the different body types became thoroughly mixed throughout the numbering range. The neat division between Central and Country area batches was also broken up during the war when large numbers of red buses were transferred to the Country department to cover the prodigious increase in the requirements for double-deckers.

All but seven of the 15STL chassis and thirty-five of the most recent 4/9STL were modified in 1949 for use as SRT chassis. The best bodies from these buses were used to replace the Park Royal bodies which were in bad condition and had to be scrapped. Withdrawal of oil engined pre-war STLs started in 1949 and was completed on 1st September 1954, although some remained in use as staff and training buses. The 'unfrozen' buses were withdrawn from passenger service during 1952, the last on 1st November, but many were then used as staff buses. None of the pre-war nor wartime buses was in service at the end of 1954 but among those still in stock and awaiting disposal was the last survivor of the original batch of experimental oilers (STL 349) and no fewer than nineteen of those which originally had petrol engines. Ten of the 'tunnel' STLs, two of the forward entrance Country Bus version and twenty-four 'unfrozens' were also in stock. Among the latter were the two carrying bodies of the original LGOC design (STLs 2674, 2679: STL1/1s). All twenty post-war 18STL20 type were still in stock, seventeen of them licensed.

The first new double-deck design introduced by London Transport was the STL5, which revolutionised the appearance of the class by eliminating the angular front in favour of a gentle slope. The design became the basis of all subsequent standard STLs and is illustrated here by STL 915, a 1/9STL5 dating from 1935, seen at Greenford on route 105 from Hanwell garage, where it was withdrawn in June 1950.
Alan B. Cross

Below The STL11 body differed from the STL5 in a number of minor ways but most distinctively in having its front destination indicator box above the route number and intermediate point boxes. STL 1249 dated from March 1936 and was one of a number which had odd registrations (in this case BLT355) from a batch of unused ones cleared out by the LCC. The angle of the sunlight on Brixton Hill highlights the strapping which has been applied between the first and second bays to give added support to its worn out body. F.G. Reynolds

The first country bus version of the standard STL (10STL6) had an upper deck identical in appearance to the STL5 but was substantially modified below to accommodate a doorless forward entrance, which reduced the seating capacity to fifty-two. The angled bulkheads intended, without conspicuous success, to reduce draughts, are clearly shown in this view of STL 1025 at Dorking bus station in June 1950, six months before its withdrawal. Alan B. Cross

The rear of the STL6 body was distinctive, with its standard STL upper deck and a typical Chiswick-inspired centre emergency door on the lower deck. Unlike the rear entrance version, the lower deck staircase window was never panelled over. STL 1028 was withdrawn from passenger service in March 1950. F.G. Reynolds

The main external features which distinguished the Weymann batch of Country Bus forward entrance STL6/1s from their STL6 predecessors were the radiused corners of the front windows and the position of the destination box at the top of the front display. Under the skin they were fundamentally different, having patented Weymann metal framework. STL 1472, new in November 1936, was photographed at Sevenoaks bus station on 15th August 1950, just before its withdrawal.
Alan B. Cross

Left **The 'Godstone' STLs were different in almost all respects from the rest of the class, having crash gearboxes and 8.8 litre oil engines and Weymann's own design of forty-eight seat lowbridge bodywork. While working on home ground, they had the standard Country Bus arrangement of restricted blinds displayed by STL 1052 as it heads south out of Bromley.** F.G. Reynolds

Below **After being replaced at Godstone by RLHs and displaced STL19s, the 11STL7s saw further service in the Addlestone area, where the indicator masking was altered to fit the same type of blind as was being used on the RLHs. This view of STL 1046 shows the neater arrangement of the front entrance than on the STL6, with a sliding platform door which eliminates the need for space-wasting draught prevention measures. The presence of the autovac alongside the nearside sidelamp is noteworthy.**
F.G. Reynolds

Originally a 7STL3, STL 500 became a 2/16STL18 in the modification programme of 1939 and survived in this form until 1953. It was one of many which were painted green for use by the Country Bus department during and after the war and is seen in the 1950, mainly green, version of the livery operating on one of the former Eastern National routes taken over in September 1951. Alan B. Cross

The STL14 body appeared identical to the STL12, the hidden difference being a conventional rather than metal underframe. Many STLs which survived long enough after 1950 had full blind displays restored, as did STL 1763, seen at Gerrards Cross, which also received the plainer 1950 livery in its later years. F.G. Reynolds

From October 1936, all standard STL bodies were fitted with roof route number boxes, to improve the appearance of the advertisements. STLs 2255 and 1178, entering Parliament Square together in May 1950, provide a comparison of the roof box STL14 with the non-roof box STL11 body. Both are in the early post-war red and cream livery, introduced in 1946. Alan B. Cross

The reason for the classification STL14/1, applied to 245 bodies built in 1937, is unknown but certainly minor. As can be seen in this view of STL 2406, their appearance was identical to the STL14s. STL 2406 retained the pre-war red and white livery until it was withdrawn in May 1950, its latter days spent in Country Bus service at Watford High Street garage. F.G. Reynolds

The final standard STL body type was the STL16 of 1939, which differed externally only in having an opening lower section on the driver's windscreen. Internally there was an improved design of chair and a number of detailed changes, some of which anticipated the RT. Seen here at Rickmansworth near the end of its life, STL 2122 was one of 124 which received STL16 bodies in place of Park Royal units in 1948/1949, in which guise it became a 19STL16/2. Despite this, it was withdrawn as early as January 1950, still wearing the pre-war red and white colour scheme. F.G. Reynolds

The STL13, forty of which were built in 1937, was a modified version of the STL11 body with inward sloping upper deck pillars and arched roof, to give adequate clearance from the tight tubular profile of Blackwall Tunnel. These buses were also fitted with steel re-inforced tyres to protect them when rubbing against the kerbs in the narrow tunnel roadway. In this March 1953 view at Crystal Palace, the curved roof of STL 1891 stands out against the conventional shape of one of the standard RTLs which replaced the type at Athol Street garage. Ernie Roberts

Twenty of the 'unfrozen' chassis allocated to the Board in 1942 were intended to receive new low-bridge bodies of the STL19 type but overhauled standard 4/9STL chassis were used instead, to create this neat combination. Sixteen, including STL 2107 shown at Rayners Lane, were painted red when new, to replace single-deckers on routes 127 and 230.

The chassis of STL 2311 was new in 1937, when it carried an STL14/1 body. The lowbridge body was mounted in June 1943, when it was painted grey, and the bus was withdrawn in November 1952, by when it had been repainted in this special version of the 1950 livery. F.G. Reynolds

Fourteen new 'austerity' highbridge bodies were built at Chiswick in 1941/1942 for mounting on the balance of the 'unfrozens', although two were used on standard chassis. STL 2665 was one of the twelve 17STL17/1s, which shared the same basic body design as the pre-war vehicles but lacked route number boxes and opening front windows, had fewer side opening windows and had an interior finish conforming to austerity standards. Alan B. Cross

Twenty of the 17STLs were given bodies from the float, covering a fair cross-section of pre-war types. In this view at Amersham garage, STL 2679, on the left, has one of the earliest STL1 type (reclassified 1/1) dating from June 1933, while STL 2655 bears an STL11 (11/1) dating from June 1936. Their hybrid provenance is given away by the long 'provincial' style radiator shell, with slatted grille and the non-standard abbreviated nearside mudguards. F.W. Ivey

STL 2681 carried an STL3/2 body (reclassified in this form to 3/3) which had been new in December 1933. It retained the wartime style green and white livery until withdrawn in October 1952, creating an interesting combination with the full blind display which was restored at the latter end of its life. F.G. Reynolds

The last vehicles to be included in the STL class were twenty purely 'provincial' AEC Regents with Weymann bodywork, part of the early post-war 'stop-gap' intake. Originally allocated entirely to Watford High Street, some later went to Grays and Hertford. STL 2692 is seen at Watford. J. H. Aston

Although their design dated from 1934 as the STL3, many of the 'sloping bodied' STLs, outlived younger vehicles because their chassis specification was brought thoroughly up-to-date in 1939, when they were reclassified. STL 470, photographed on 1st March 1952 working from its last home at Alperton garage, was a 2/16STL18 and was withdrawn in July 1953. Alan B. Cross

Six 15STL16s evaded conversion to SRT, five of which were not withdrawn until 1953/1954. STL 2562, seen at Bulphan in the area taken over from Eastern National in 1951, remained in service until August 1953, being repainted into the 1950, mainly green, livery in the meantime. Over the years the 15STL16s lost the wheel disc trims and longer radiators which had added distinction to their appearance, leaving them barely distinguishable from other roof box vehicles. F.G. Reynolds

An unexpected development in May 1950 was the appearance of STL 2477 carrying a new experimental prefabricated body based on principles evolved by Arthur Sainsbury, foreman of the experimental shop at Chiswick Works. It quickly earned itself the nickname 'The Meccano Bus' and ran in service at Alperton until December 1953, followed by a spell as a staff bus. The absence of a route number box was one of its many curiosities. LTPS

In this rear view at Golders Green, the standard RT type emergency window underlines the odd mixture of old fashioned and modern features in STL 2477's body. Its distinctive lines were given added incongruity by the surprising use of the pre-war red and white livery. It is seen here at Haven Green. F.G. Reynolds

Chassis: AEC Regent 661 or 0661
Engine: AEC A140 6-cylinder 6.1 litre 95 bhp petrol (10-192, 553);
 AEC A145 6-cylinder 7.4 litre 110 bhp petrol (263, 299, 322, 357, 372-390);
 AEC A171 (indirect injection) or A173 (direct injection) 6-cylinder 7.7 litre 95 bhp oil (remainder).
Transmission: AEC D124 4 speed crash (10-192, 263, 299, 322, 344, 357, 372-390, 553, 2648-2701);
 or four speed direct selection preselective (D128 Daimler or D132 AEC) with fluid flywheel (remainder).
Chassis codes: 1STL (10, 27, 43); 2STL (159-192); 5STL (342-352), 6STL (263, 299, 322, 357, 372-390), 1/8STL (59, 75); 17STL (2648-2681); 18STL (2682-2701);
 remainder: 9, 1/9, 2/9, 3/9, 4/9, 15, 1/15, 16, 1/16, 2/16 or 19STL
Bodywork: LGOC or LPTB (Chiswick), or Park Royal (standard types); Weymann (1044-1055, 2682-2701 and STL6/1 type – see below);
Capacity: H30/26R except: 1044-1055 L26/22FD; STL6 type (see below) H29/23F;
 STL6/1 type (see below) H29/19F; STL13 type Tunnel buses (see fleet list) H30/25R;
 STL 19 lowbridge type (see list) L27/26R.
Body codes: STL1 (10, 27, 43), STL1/1 (2674, 2679), STL2/1 (2664), STL3 (299, 322, 334, 357-390), STL3/1 (342-352), STL3/2 (263), STL3/3 (2663, 2681), STL3/4 (2675), STL6 (959-974, 976-992, 994-1000, 1002, 1004-1007, 1010, 1012-1016, 1018-1020, 1024-1028, 1030-1034, 1036, 1037, 1040, 1043, 1057, 1058), STL6/1 (1466-1468, 1470-1476, 1478-1500, 1502, 1503, 1505-1513), STL7 (1044-1055), STL13 (tunnel buses – see fleet list), STL19 (Chiswick built lowbridge); STL20 (2682-2701); STL21 (2477); remainder – STL5, 5/2, 11, 11/1, 12, 12/1, 14, 14/1, 15, 16, 16/2, 17, 17/1 or 18
Built 1932-1946   Number built: 2679   Number in stock: 1.1.50: 2191   31.12.54: 262

STL		Date out of stock	STL		Date out of stock	STL		Date out of stock
10	JJ4361	23.2.50	235	AGX573	25.10.50	299	AUC555	1.6.50
27	GX5336	19.1.50	236	AGX590	15.1.51	322	AUC589	3.3.50
43	JJ4349	14.7.50†	239	AGX589	31.8.50	334	AXM607	27.6.50
59	YY5359	3.2.50	240	AGX582	1.3.50	342	AUC557	16.11.50
75	YY5375	24.2.50	242	AGX566	1.12.50	343	AUC591	10.5.54
159	JJ4376	6.9.50†	243	AGX567	10.2.50	344	AUC563	12.12.50
162	JJ4379	10.5.50†	244	AGX577	27.6.50	345	AUC581	20.12.50
164	AGX511	23.2.50	246	AGX580	6.3.50	346	AUC564	10.1.51
169	AGX520	2.1.50†	248	AGX586	22.11.50	347	AUC565	13.2.52
175	AGX517	15.2.50†	249	AGX593	30.5.50	348	AUC582	10.8.50
188	AGX531	22.2.50	250	AGX578	16.4.52c	349	AUC575	
192	AGX544	25.1.50†	251	AGX587	23.11.50	350	AUC576	20.3.51
203	AGX547	14.2.50	252	AGX579	14.11.50	351	AXM613	31.10.50
204	AGX557	17.10.50	254	AUC512	7.3.50	352	AXM654	14.1.54
205	AGX548	17.1.51	255	AUC539	29.11.50	357	AXM614	24.2.50
206	AGX552	7.9.50	256	AUC542	15.2.50	361	AXM622	23.2.50
207	AGX545	19.1.50	258	AUC544	29.5.53	372	AXM618	12.5.50†
209	AGX559	7.3.50	259	AUC538	27.7.50	377	AXM639	17.4.50†
210	AGX549	28.10.53	262	AUC510	14.7.53	381	AXM635	24.2.50
211	AGX556	15.2.50	263	AUC511	22.2.50	390	AXM649	24.3.50†
212	AGX554	16.11.50	264	AUC507	15.3.50	403	AXM666	13.12.54
213	AGX583	27.2.51	267	AUC533	17.8.50	404	AXM667	15.12.53
214	AGX584	15.1.51	268	AUC518	3.10.50	405	AXM655	29.3.50
217	AGX585	17.3.50	269	AUC514	11.10.50	406	AXM668	27.4.54
218	AGX551	5.1.50	270	AGX594	6.7.50	407	AXM657	14.10.53
220	AGX564	31.1.50	272	AGX599	9.2.50	408	AXM674	6.8.53
221	AGX561	17.2.50	273	AUC506	7.12.50	409	AXM663	21.5.53
222	AGX563	13.12.54	276	AUC516	10.10.50	410	AXM664	19.1.54
223	AGX562	24.8.50	277	AUC517	17.10.50	411	AXM673	19.3.53c
224	AGX553	16.11.53	279	AUC543	23.11.50	412	AXM675	18.11.53
226	AGX598	6.7.53	280	AUC520	12.1.54	413	AXM676	6.8.53
227	AGX588	2.1.51	281	AUC525	25.5.50	414	AXM669	15.6.53
228	AGX575	24.8.50	282	AUC536	5.2.53	415	AXM665	9.12.53
229	AGX568	29.6.50	284	AUC547	29.3.50	416	AXM672	23.4.52c
230	AGX571	24.2.50	285	AUC527	27.2.50	417	AXM671	11.6.53
231	AGX572	22.11.50	286	AUC532	24.5.50	418	AXM685	13.5.53
233	AGX592	9.6.50	288	AUC540	23.5.50	419	AXM681	27.4.53
234	AGX570	20.2.50	289	AUC545	21.11.50	420	AXM682	13.5.54

† Converted to service vehicle, see page 33
c Chassis only, body scrapped earlier

STL

STL	Reg	Date out of stock	STL	Reg	Date out of stock	STL	Reg	Date out of stock
421	AXM684	23.11.50	489	AYV650	13.11.53	570	AYV720	
422	AXM670	9.9.54	490	AYV648	27.3.53	571	AYV732	23.12.54
423	AXM680	27.7.53	491	AYV659	12.2.54	572	AYV733	
424	AXM683	20.7.50	493	AYV653	7.6.51	574	AYV724	31.12.54
425	AXM678	24.3.53	494	AYV654	3.11.53	575	AYV728	5.2.53
427	AYV610	30.11.53	495	AYV647	4.3.53	576	AYV743	28.12.50
428	AXM687	8.3.54	496	AYV666	27.3.53	578	AYV734	29.12.53
429	AXM688	7.5.53	497	AYV658	22.5.53	579	AYV738	27.6.50
430	AXM689	7.4.53	498	AYV670	10.9.53c	580	AYV729	7.11.50
431	AYV637	10.12.53	499	AYV656	21.12.53	581	AYV730	16.3.50
432	AXM690	11.3.53	500	AYV688	4.2.53	582	AYV731	3.3.50
433	AXM691	3.3.50	501	AYV678	14.4.53	583	AYV739	21.4.53
434	AXM686	4.12.53	502	AYV674	25.10.50	584	AYV740	8.6.50
435	AXM692	24.8.50	503	AYV669		585	AYV736	2.2.50
436	AXM697	25.2.53	504	AYV675	1.5.53	586	AYV760	3.10.50
437	AYV611		505	AYV686		587	AYV744	10.10.50
438	AYV608	1.12.53	506	AYV689	31.12.54	588	AYV751	1.6.50
439	AXM696	3.2.54	507	AYV690	3.8.50	589	AYV753	7.4.53
440	AXM699		508	AYV682	14.7.53	590	AYV749	30.8.50
441	AXM693	18.2.53n	509	AYV681	26.9.50	591	AYV737	2.1.50
442	AXM700	15.12.53	510	AYV697	8.2.54	593	AYV742	18.10.50
443	AXM695	24.2.54	511	AYV698		594	AYV765	25.4.50
444	AYV601	21.12.53	512	AYV657	12.1.54	596	AYV754	9.1.50
445	AXM694	5.10.50	514	AYV671	7.7.53	600	AYV746	25.4.50
446	AYV604	25.2.53	515	AYV660		601	AYV764	11.1.50
447	AYV602	4.5.53	516	AYV661	18.12.53	604	AYV762	15.3.50
448	AYV607	23.7.53	517	AYV662	13.2.53	605	AYV759	11.5.50
449	AYV612	20.7.53	518	AYV667	26.3.53	606	AYV757	31.10.50
450	AYV603	19.6.53	519	AYV663	24.7.53	607	AYV761	13.12.50
451	AYV605	13.2.53	520	AYV687	24.7.53	608	AYV763	16.5.50
452	AYV606	16.2.53	521	AYV664	22.10.53	609	AYV766	30.6.50
453	AYV633	8.6.53	522	AYV694	11.4.50	610	AYV772	9.4.53
454	AYV625	2.2.50	523	AYV676		611	AYV769	27.1.53
455	AYV619	20.8.53	524	AYV672	24.8.53	612	AYV774	20.2.50
456	AYV630	20.3.53	525	AYV668	3.8.50	613	AYV770	2.11.50
457	AYV614	2.2.54	526	AYV704	1.9.53	614	AYV775	10.12.53
458	AYV621	31.8.50	527	AYV701	11.6.53	615	AYV773	28.8.51
459	AYV613	1.6.53	529	AYV679	5.11.53	616	AYV779	
460	AYV609	22.9.53	530	AYV673	9.9.54	617	AYV787	20.7.53
461	AYV622	13.11.53	531	AYV685	6.7.53	618	AYV768	15.1.53
462	AYV617		532	AYV680	13.3.53	619	AYV767	17.6.53
463	AYV642	9.12.53	533	AYV677	21.8.53	621	AYV771	4.7.50
464	AYV620		534	AYV691	13.11.53	622	AYV788	2.1.50
465	AYV643	21.4.53	535	AYV725	10.4.53	625	AYV777	16.2.50
466	AYV618	22.5.53	536	AYV705		626	AYV780	13.2.50
467	AYV641	1.6.53	537	AYV706		627	BLH717	16.8.50
468	AYV628		538	AYV703	19.1.50	628	BLH711	9.5.50
469	AYV651	25.3.54p	539	AYV700	5.9.50	629	AYV789	2.7.51
470	AYV644	4.2.54	541	AYV716	23.3.50	630	AYV792	8.5.53
471	AYV649	11.3.53	542	AYV684	16.11.53	631	BLH703	20.2.53
472	AYV646	5.2.53	545	AYV708	25.2.54	633	BLH740	16.3.53
473	AYV624		546	AYV693	24.8.53	634	BLH716	16.11.50
474	AYV623	2.2.54	547	AYV714	28.8.51	635	AYV785	1.5.53
475	AYV645	18.12.53	548	AYV710		636	AYV793	2.7.51
476	AYV627	24.11.50	549	AYV699	10.11.53	637	AYV782	
477	AYV634	27.2.50	550	AYV702	18.5.54	640	BLH701	21.4.53
478	AYV632		552	AYV715	29.11.51c	641	BLH738	29.11.51c
479	AYV652	7.7.53	553	GW1744	22.2.50	642	AYV790	12.3.54
480	AYV655	6.8.53	559	AYV750	9.5.50	643	BLH709	24.3.50
481	AYV640	9.11.53	560	AYV719	7.7.53	644	AYV784	27.1.53
482	AYV626	23.3.53	561	AYV721	9.2.50	645	BLH712	8.6.50
483	AYV636	24.3.53	562	AYV727	13.11.53	646	AYV791	
484	AYV629	24.3.53	563	AYV712	3.8.50	647	BLH705	12.12.50
485	AYV639	23.12.53	564	AYV735		648	BLH733	
486	AYV631	7.4.53	565	AYV718	12.3.54	649	BLH706	5.2.53
487	AYV638	6.5.53	568	AYV726	17.3.50	650	BLH708	31.12.53
488	AYV635	6.11.53	569	AYV722	20.3.51	651	BLH704	16.11.54

c   Chassis only, body scrapped earlier   n   To Institut Van Den Auto Heindle, Netherlands
p   Retained by London Transport for preservation

STL

STL		Date out of stock	STL		Date out of stock	STL		Date out of stock
652	BLH707	2.3.50	729	BLH792	27.1.53	799	BXD469	21.4.53
653	BLH710	23.8.50	730	BLH788	8.10.53	800	BXD465	13.3.51
654	BLH715	18.1.50	731	BLH789	14.9.53	801	BXD459	10.4.53
655	BLH718	26.5.50	732	BXD408	31.10.50	802	BXD476	
656	BLH719	29.11.51c	733	BLH794	10.7.53	803	BXD467	7.12.54
658	BLH722	13.2.50	734	BXD421		804	BXD463	
659	BLH723	25.4.50	735	BXD404	1.5.53	805	BXD480	31.12.53
660	BLH732	28.4.53	737	BLH793	17.5.54	806	BXD474	1.3.54
661	BLH713	27.3.50	738	BXD402	20.1.53	807	BXD470	29.6.51
662	BLH714	9.5.50	739	BXD405	20.1.54	808	BXD489	
665	BLH741	29.11.51c	740	BXD403	10.12.53	809	BXD485	20.2.51
666	BLH729	27.2.50	741	BXD418	1.12.53	810	BXD471	14.4.53
667	BLH734	29.8.50	742	BXD451		811	BXD486	15.3.54
668	BLH721	16.1.53	743	BXD416	20.3.53	812	BXD511	22.7.53
669	BLH727	10.11.53	744	BXD417	24.8.54	813	BXD487	13.9.54
670	BLH760		746	BXD413	2.4.53	814	BXD477	
671	BLH731	29.1 54	747	BXD412	22.4.53	815	CGJ77	2.7.51
672	BLH730		748	BXD406	2.4.53	816	BXD493	7.4.53
674	BLH728	29.6.51	749	BXD409		817	BXD472	5.12.51c
675	BLH735	3.10.50	750	BXD411	7.9.54c	818	BXD507	6.3.51
676	BLH724	2.7.51	751	BXD415	5.1.54	819	BXD478	10.4.53
677	BLH745	12.1.50	752	BXD407	8.5.53	820	BXD494	20.7.50
678	BLH771	21.4.53	753	BXD410	4.11.53	821	BXD481	21.8.53
679	BLH739	17.12.53	754	BXD420	18.8.53	822	BXD510	18.11.53
680	BLH742	27.11.53	755	BXD422	27.7.53	823	BXD475	1.5.53
682	BLH737		756	BXD419	17.11.53	824	BXD495	16.5.50
683	BLH746	29.4.53	757	BXD424	23.3.53	825	BXD496	31.12.52
685	BLH748	30.3.53	758	BXD423	20.2.51	826	BXD479	21.12.53
686	BLH749	5.5.53	759	BXD425		827	BXD482	
688	BLH764		760	BXD441	30.11.50	828	BXD483	13.11.53
689	BLH750	8.12.53	761	BXD455	8.3.51	829	BXD497	9.11.53
690	BLH759	5.5.53	762	BXD426		830	BXD488	20.7.50
691	BLH752	16.12.53	763	BXD431	6.2.53	831	BXD518	24.10.50
692	BLH754	4.5.50	764	BXD443	20.3.51	832	BXD579	16.11.53
693	BLH751	24.2.50	765	BXD449	4.2.53	833	BXD509	10.5.54
694	BLH753	2.4.53	766	BXD444	18.7.50	834t	BXD499	20.7.53
695	BLH756	30.3.54	767	BXD437	4.12.53	835	BXD490	29.6.51
696	BLH758	12.6.50	768	BXD445	4.11.53	836	BXD505	13.2.51
697	BLH757	16.1.53	769	BXD473	2.7.51	837	BXD515	5.3.54
698	BLH755		770	BXD466	29.6.51	838	BXD610	18.11.53
699	BLH761	29.3.50	771	BXD442	14.4.53	839	BXD585	9.3.50
700	BLH768	24.2.50	772	BXD434	20.3.51	840	BXD491	27.3.50
701	BLH765	20.3.53	773	BXD432	5.10.53	841	BXD492	20.3.51
702	BLH763	9.12.53	774	BXD436	15.7.53	842	BXD512	7.12.54
703	BLH762	18.12.53	775	BXD435	23.4.53	843	BXD508	8.12.53
704	BLH770	17.3.53	776	BXD433	20.7.53	844	BXD498	20.3.51
705	BLH766	20.8.53	777	BXD430		845	BXD580	15.6.53
706	BLH767	8.1.54	778	BXD452	31.12.54	846	BXD506	3.4.51
707	BLH769	13.7.50	779	BXD438	1.5.51	847	BXD516	1.4.53
708	BXD414	5.3.54	780	BXD461	23.11.50	848	BXD519	5.4.54
709	BLH775	1.5.53	781	BXD439	3.4.51	849	BXD611	1.2.50
710	BLH772	28.5.52c	783	BXD446	20.2.51	850	BXD520	17.11.53
711	BLH773	27.6.50	784	BXD429	30.4.53	851	BXD514	12.4.54
712	BLH784		785	BXD428	23.4.53	852	BXD581	16.9.53
713	BLH776	15.12.50	786	BXD457	24.3.53	853	BXD592	4.7.50
715	BLH774	20.11.53	787	BXD456	6.2.51	854	BXD513	4.12.53
716	BLH782	6.11.51	788	BXD448	18.5.50	855	BXD591	22.6.50
717	BLH785	27.3.53	789	BXD450	1.12.53	856	BXD583	
718	BLH786	14.1.53	790	BXD462	30.4.54	857	BXD582	1.6.50
719	BLH778	14.1.54	791	BXD453	6.2.53	858	BXD517	18.8.53
720	BLH779	7.12.50	792	BXD447	1.5.51	859	BXD595	6.8.53
721	BLH790	30.11.53	793	BXD484	20.1.53	860	BXD598	29.6.51
723	BLH796	29.6.51	794	BXD468	4.7.50	861	CGJ20	
724	BLH780	1.12.53	795	BXD460	23.5.50	862	BXD603	29.12.53
725	BLH787	9.6.50	796	BXD458	3.11.53	863	BXD587	10.6.53
726	BLH781	9.3.50	797	BXD454	25.7.50	864	BXD597	7.11.50
727	BLH791	2.7.51	798	BXD464		865	CGJ11	29.12.53

c Chassis only, body scrapped earlier
t Tunnel body

STL

		Date out of stock
866	BXD590	7.4.53
867	BXD577	20.1.54
868	BXD594	
869	CGJ18	20.6.50
870	CGJ13	5.1.50
871	BXD578	6.11.51
872	BXD586	25.5.51c
873	BXD584	
874	CGJ15	16.1.51
875	BXD593	23.1.51
876	CGJ17	20.7.53
877	CGJ37	25.3.53
878	CGJ27	1.1.54
879	BXD609	4.2.54
880	CGJ32	12.9.50
881	CGJ21	13.1.54
882	BXD608	1.12.50
883	BXD612	7.6.51
884	BXD601	13.3.51
885	CGJ26	24.8.50
886	BXD600	20.7.53
887	CGJ29	22.3.50
888	CGJ23	17.3.50
889	BXD588	25.2.54
890	BXD589	4.5.53
891	BXD605	10.4.51
892	BXD616	23.10.50
893	BXD602	12.11.53
894	BXD618	10.1.51
895	BXD613	23.3.50
896	BXD604	10.7.53
897	BXD620	19.2.54
898	BXD596	4.7.50
899	BXD617	16.1.50
900	BXD607	
901	BXD621	20.2.51
902	CGJ43	6.2.50
904	CGJ22	18.4.50
905	CGJ28	
906	BXD606	12.1.50
907	CGJ30	20.7.50
908	CGJ44	2.4.54
909	CGJ14	21.8.52c
910	BXD599	21.4.53
911	CGJ34	19.1.50
912	CGJ51	1.2.50
913	BXD619	6.11.51
914	CGJ19	12.1.50
915	CGJ12	28.6.50
916	CGJ36	5.4.50
917	CGJ24	2.1.50
918	BXD615	29.6.51
919	CGJ33	
920	CGJ56	12.11.53
921	CGJ54	30.1.51
922	CGJ55	7.12.53
923	CGJ35	4.5.50
924	CGJ50	6.3.51
925	CGJ62	17.6.54
926	CGJ42	6.2.51
927	CGJ38	16.5.50
928	CGJ59	7.5.54
929	CGJ63	16.7.53
930	CGJ67	
931	CGJ16	6.8.53
932	CGJ69	
933	CGJ25	13.3.53

STL

		Date out of stock
934	CGJ52	8.5.53
935	CGJ74	
936	CGJ60	28.12.50
938	CGJ49	13.2.50
939	CGJ61	20.2.51
940	CGJ53	29.6.51
941	CGJ58	4.11.53
942	CGJ41	12.1.50
943	CGJ64	25.5.51
944	CGJ48	15.7.53
945	CGJ39	5.4.50
946	CGJ45	25.5.51
947	CGJ65	2.1.51
948	CGJ40	24.4.53
949	CGJ31	
950	CGJ46	31.12.53
951	CGJ47	
952	CGJ68	29.3.51
953	CGJ70	8.12.53
954	CGJ72	11.11.53
955	CGJ75	
956	CGJ66	10.10.50
957	CGJ71	13.2.51
958	CGJ73	18.11.53
959	BLH816	
960	BLH817	26.10.51
961	BLH830	6.3.51
962	BLH834	12.11.53
963	BLH826	29.6.51
964	BLH827	23.3.53
965	.BLH824	3.4.51
966	BLH831	10.4.51
967	BLH822	1.11.51
968	BLH835	16.10.53
969	BLH818	8.3.50
970	BLH823	6.11.51
971	BLH828	25.9.53
972	BLH819	14.9.53c
973	BLH820	31.12.51c
974	BLH832	25.9.53
975	BLH829	
976	BLH821	6.11.51
977	BLH825	3.4.51
978	BLH833	27.12.50
979	BLH836	7.6.51
980	BLH849	27.2.51
981	BLH837	20.1.50
982	BLH838	17.3.50
983	BLH839	2.7.51
984	BLH851	29.6.51
986	BLH859	
987	BLH847	12.10.53
988	BLH842	6.10.53
989	BLH843	10.7.50
990	BLH860	17.7.50
991	BLH850	12.10.53
992	BLH844	7.6.51
993	BLH845	8.10.53
994	BLH865	28.8.51
996	BLH848	1.11.51
997	BLH855	2.1.50
999	BLH852	27.12.50
1000	BLH846	28.8.51
1001	BLH854	7.6.51
1003	BLH857	7.12.54
1004	BLH862	5.12.50
1005	BLH863	25.5.51

STL

		Date out of stock
1006	BLH869	26.10.51
1007	BLH861	22.4.53
1008	BLH864	
1009	BLH868	16.10.53
1011	BLH870	
1012	BLH889	20.9.51
1013	BLH871	28.8.51
1014	BLH867	20.9.50
1015	BLH881	14.11.50
1016	BLH884	14.10.53
1017	BLH873	7.6.51
1018	BLH872	29.6.51
1019	BLH876	1.12.50
1020	BLH877	10.11.54
1021	BLH893	15.11.50
1022	BXD526	1.11.51
1023	BLH895	
1024	BLH878	6.11.51
1025	BLH879	14.12.50
1026	BLH874	5.10.53
1027	BLH880	27.2.51
1028	BLH892	27.4.50
1029	BLH896	
1031	BLH891	27.4.50
1032	BLH885	17.4.53
1033	BLH897	11.11.53
1034	BLH875	10.4.51
1035	BLH899	14.4.54
1036	BLH882	4.7.50
1037	BLH883	5.12.50
1038	BLH900	
1039	BLH886	12.1.53†
1040	BLH887	6.11.53
1041	BLH898	9.1.51
1042	BLH888	27.9.50
1043	BLH890	29.6.51
*1044	BPE221	18.3.53
*1045	BPF269	18.3.53
*1046	BPF270	17.3.53
*1047	BPF288	17.3.53
*1048	BPF289	4.3.53
*1049	BPF391	18.3.53
*1050	BPF397	23.1.53
*1051	BPF416	4.8.53
*1052	BPF417	27.7.53
*1053	BPF456	4.8.53
*1054	BPF457	23.1.53
*1055	BPF458	27.7.53
1056	BXD503	7.6.51
1057	BXD504	6.11.51
1058	BXD501	19.10.53
1059	BXD502	8.10.54
1060	CLE 37	
1062	CGJ138	19.10.50
1063	CGJ122	14.9.50
1064	CGJ78	28.8.51
1065	CGJ116	10.8.50
1066	CGJ84	14.2.50
1067	CGJ79	14.2.50
1068	CGJ80	5.12.50
1069	CGJ109	21.9.50
1070	CGJ83	8.6.50
1071	CGJ104	19.10.50
1072	CGJ134	16.8.50
1073	CGJ81	4.2.54
1074	CGJ89	20.6.50
1075	CGJ102	19.1.50

† Converted to service vehicle, see page 33   c Chassis only, body scrapped earlier
* Lowbridge bodywork

STL		Date out of stock	STL		Date out of stock	STL		Date out of stock
1076	CGJ85	8.3.50	1146	CLE14	29.6.51	1215	CLE58	15.3.50
1077	CGJ90	4.7.50	1147	CGJ141	17.3.50	1216	CLE72	6.9.50
1078	CGJ86	8.3.50	1148	CGJ154	14.2.50	1217	BLY145	21.8.52cs
1080	CGJ129	22.5.53	1149	CLE21	14.11.50	1218	BXB845	
1081	CLE30	9.3.50	1150	CGJ144	12.9.50	1219	CLE81	12.10.50
1082	CGJ127	7.2.50	1151	CGJ142	24.8.50	1220	BXH409	8.11.50
1083	CLE45		1152	CGJ148	26.9.50	1221	BXA711	6.3.50
1084	CGJ101	23.5.50	1153	CLE38	18.7.50	1222	BLD98	14.9.50
1085	CGJ117	6.2.50	1154	CGJ149	14.11.50	1223	CLE79	
1086	CGJ87	6.7.50	1155	CGJ155	6.9.50	1224	BUL279	20.9.50
1087	CGJ112	7.3.50	1157	CLE41	19.1.50	1226	CLE76	11.5.50
1088	CGJ91	15.1.51	1158	CGJ156	8.6.50	1227	BLN618	
1089	CGJ118	27.4.50	1159	CLE43	7.6.50	1228	BUC516	25.4.50
1090	CGJ82	25.10.50	1160	CLE15	8.3.50	1229	BUL48	27.7.50
1091	CGJ143	9.2.54	1161	CGJ151	21.11.50	1230	CLE91	5.10.50
1092	CLE20	1.5.50	1162	CGJ157	4.7.50	1231	BYM463	7.12.50
1093	CGJ137	16.8.50	1163	CLE42	11.7.50	1232	CLE95	30.8.50
1094	CGJ130	4.4.50	1164	CLE16	3.10.50	1233	CLE90	4.7.50
1095	CGJ123	20.9.50	1165	CLE18	14.2.50	1234	BUL347	
1096	CGJ93	6.3.50	1166	CLE44	16.5.50	1235	BUW595	3.10.50
1097	CGJ115	8.2.50	1167	CLE31	13.4.50	1236	BLO239	8.2.50
1098	CGJ88	1.2.50	1168	CLE32	6.9.50	1237	BLC45	26.9.50
1099	CGJ92	5.4.50	1169	CLE52	17.3.50	1238	BLN216	12.12.50
1100	CGJ146	13.2.50	1170	CLE24	7.2.50	1239	CLE92	27.6.50
1101	CGJ98		1171	CLE28	22.5.50	1240	BLC518	3.10.50
1102	CGJ103	8.6.50	1172	CLE40	16.2.50	1241	CLE89	13.7.50
1103	CGJ126	20.7.50	1173	CLE50	7.6.51	1242	BXX857	18.5.50
1104	CGJ111	16.8.50	1174	CLE27	24.8.50	1243	BXN283	9.6.50
1105	CGJ105	16.11.50	1175	CLE25	15.2.50	1244	BGF545	13.4.50
1106	CGJ94	16.5.50	1176	CLE73	29.6.51	1245	BXH468	13.3.51
1107	CGJ152	4.5.50	1177	CLE75	9.5.50	1246	BGO161	11.3.53
1108	CGJ97	11.10.50	1178	CLE60	28.9.50	1247	BXD992	5.10.50
1109	CGJ100	9.3.50	1179	CLE84	12.4.50	1248	BYE312	10.10.50
1110	CLE35	30.8.50	1180	CLE67	8.6.50	1249	BLT355	8.11.50
1111	CGJ99	19.1.50	1181	CLE88	1.6.50	1250	CLE96	29.11.50
1112	CGJ108	29.6.50	1182	CLE93	30.8.50	1251	BXH467	25.5.51
1113	CGJ107	9.5.50	1183	BXX973	8.3.50	1253	BXD965	19.7.50
1114	CGJ96	14.2.50	1184	CLE54	18.7.50	1254	BXL215	20.7.50
1115	CGJ106	29.6.50	1186	BXD401	16.1.50	1255	BUV785	14.12.50
1116	CLE85	20.9.50	1187	CLE55	9.5.50	1256	BUW576	19.7.50
1117	CGJ95	11.4.50	1188	CLE49	5.12.50	1257	BXA886	7.12.50
1118	CGJ133	22.2.50	1189	CLE53	23.5.50	1258	BXH603	7.6.51
1119	CGJ139	15.3.50	1190	CLE64	20.9.50	1259	BXF31	19.6.50
1120	CGJ113	4.7.50	1191	CLE86	22.11.50	1260	CLE33	19.1.50
1121	CGJ114	5.4.50	1192	CLE80	25.5.50	1262	CLE34	2.4.54
1122	CGJ124	12.11.53	1193	CLE61	18.8.53	1265	BXU721	14.9.50
1123	CGJ131	9.5.50	1194	CLE94	7.6.51	1266	BXO55	9.5.50
1124	CLE17	4.7.50	1195	CLE59	12.10.50	1267	BYH255	15.6.53
1125	CGJ150	24.2.50	1196	CLE56	4.7.50	1268	BXN540	8.6.50
1126	CGJ120	8.6.50	1197	CLE62	11.5.50	1269	BXN355	16.2.50
1127	CLE12	17.6.50	1198	CLE68	14.2.50	1270	CLX514	7.9.50
1128	CGJ110	17.2.50	1199	CLE51	5.4.50	1271	BXU722	23.5.50
1129	DGX216	1.5.53	1200	CLE47	7.3.50	1272	BXU715	11.10.50
1131	CLE13	31.8.50	1201	CLE63	7.11.50	1274	BXO54	7.3.51
1132	CLE29	4.5.50	1202	CLE57	1.8.50	1275	BXU752	5.1.54
1133	CLE26	8.2.50	1203	CLE70	20.6.50	1276	BYH256	9.3.50
1135	CGJ135	4.5.50	1204	CLE87	5.10.50	1277	BYH912	30.11.50
1136	CGJ121	1.3.50	1205	CLE82	9.1.50	1278	BYK791	12.10.50
1137	CLE11	8.3.50	1206	CLE83	15.1.51	1279	BYH679	9.2.50
1138	CGJ140	18.5.50	1207	BUW575	13.4.50	1280	BXW307	10.2.50
1139	CGJ153	11.7.50	1208	CLE69	11.7.50	1281	BYE589	16.11.50
1140	CLE46	22.3.50	1209	CLE78	10.2.50	1282	BXU800	19.1.50
1141	CGJ119	16.5.50	1210	CLE71	16.5.50	1283	BYH254	23.5.50
1142	CLE22	21.9.50	1211	BUW785	18.8.53	1284	BXV161	6.12.50
1143	CGJ132	22.9.54	1212	CLE65	12.1.50	1285	BYF360	14.11.50
1144	CGJ136	8.2.50	1213	CLE66	8.3.50	1286	BXW136	15.2.50
1145	CGJ145		1214	CLE77	17.10.50	1287	BYM557	9.2.50

c Chassis only, body scrapped earlier
s Sold to Royal Hospital Chelsea 24.3.50, returned to LT 25.6.52

STL

STL		Date out of stock	STL		Date out of stock	STL		Date out of stock
1288	BYL960	8.7.53	1358	CXX111	27.4.50	1430	CXX150	26.9.50
1289	CLX515	27.6.50	1359	CLX595	21.11.50	1431	CXX184	4.3.54
1290	BYM556	18.10.50	1360	CLX583	11.10.50	1433	CXX177	11.7.50
1291	BYM554	11.5.50	1361	CLX578	13.9.50	1434	CXX187	8.11.50
1292	BYN974	21.9.50	1362	CLX535	15.11.50	1435	CXX182	17.3.50
1293	BYN760	1.6.50	1363	CLX586	7.6.51	1436	CXX178	2.11.50
1294	BYO913	9.6.50	1364	CLX592	11.7.50	1437	CXX180	
1295	BYN920	13.2.50	1365	CLX589	21.4.54	1439	CXX185	12.12.50
1296	BYX961	27.4.50	1366	CLX584	20.6.50	1440	CXX183	14.2.50
1297	BYR802	9.6.50	1367	CLX541	13.9.50	1441	CXX188	31.8.50
1298	BYP4	20.6.50	1368	CLX538	13.6.50	1443	CXX192	15.2.50
1299	BYP480	14.11.50	1369	CLX576	7.12.50	1444	CXX196	18.2.54
1300	BYP481	16.5.50	1370	CXX130	22.11.50	1445	CXX191	2.7.51
1301	BYO986	24.11.50	1371	CLX585	12.1.50	1446	CXX190	20.7.50
1302	BYU319	7.6.50	1372	CXX106	17.8.50	1447	CXX193	
1303	BYU167	31.10.50	1373	CXX104	4.5.50	1448	CXX194	11.2.53
1304	BYU385	28.2.50	1374	CLX597	29.11.50	1449	CXX195	5.4.50
1306	BYU164	30.8.50	1375	CXX109	10.2.50	1450	CXX205	9.3.50
1307	CGC197	1.8.50	1376	CLX590	10.8.50	1452	CXX197	30.11.50
1308	BYU392	22.9.50	1377	CLX596	14.12.50	1453	CXX202	29.11.50
1309	BYU844	7.5.53	1378	CXX114	24.11.50	1454	CXX207	17.6.54
1310	BYU845	12.9.50	1379	CXX107	19.1.50	1455	CXX209	19.1.54
1311	CLF503	16.2.50	1380	CXX125	9.11.50	1456	CXX203	6.6.50
1312	BYV557	21.2.50	1381	CXX108	8.3.50	1457	CXX210	22.9.50
1313	BYY701	11.7.50	1382	CLX594	21.11.50	1458	CXX199	
1315	CGU762	7.11.50	1383	CLX588	23.4.52	1459	CXX198	23.11.50
1316	CGO129	11.7.50	1385	CXX101	10.2.50	1460	CXX200	27.4.54
1317	BYX39	19.7.50	1387	CXX118	15.2.50	1461	CXX211	15.6.50
1318	BYX979	11.7.50	1388	CXX115	5.7.50	1462	CXX204	4.5.50
1319	CGF536	7.12.50	1389	CXX103	8.7.53	1463	CXX212	7.11.50
1320	CGF540	7.9.50	1390	CXX116	2.7.51	1464	CXX451	10.7.50
1321	CLO39	8.6.50	1392	CXX110	3.3.50	1465	CXX452	1.5.53
1322	CLX511	20.2.50	1393	CXX112	5.12.50	1466	CXX453	29.6.51
1323	CLX512	1.5.50	1394	CXX120	29.8.50	1467	CXX454	19.10.53
1324	CLX516	21.11.50	1395	CXX119	20.1.54	1468	CXX455	28.8.51
1325	CLX513	5.12.50	1396	CXX105	18.10.50	1469	CXX456	12.10.50
1326	CLX530	7.6.50	1397	CXX124	14.11.50	1470	CXX457	1.3.53†
1327	CLX522	20.6.50	1398	CXX122	23.5.50	1471	CXX458	7.6.51
1328	CLX517	16.1.50	1399	CXX127	16.2.53	1472	CXX459	23.8.50
1329	CLX518	6.3.51	1400	CXX126	10.3.50	1473	CXX460	1.11.51
1330	CLX519	23.5.50	1401	CXX117	10.1.51	1474	CXX461	31.1.50
1331	CLX526	16.11.50	1402	CXX121	4.7.50	1475	CXX462	10.8.50
1332	CLX523	20.3.50	1403	CXX254	9.2.50	1476	CXX463	25.10.50
1333	CLX520	15.11.50	1404	CXX128	14.9.50	1477	CXX464	22.10.53
1334	CXX143	9.5.50	1405	CXX129	29.6.50	1478	CXX465	5.4.50
1335	CLX521	11.5.50	1406	CXX123	7.2.50	1479	CXX466	27.2.50
1336	CLX524	25.5.50	1407	CXX133	24.4.53	1480	CXX467	12.12.51c
1337	CLX527	5.4.50	1408	CXX131	15.11.50	1482	CXX469	31.5.50
1338	CLX525	21.1.50	1409	CXX132	28.4.54	1483	CXX470	27.9.50
1339	CLX528	5.9.50	1410	CXX134	2.6.50	1484	CXX471	1.8.50
1340	CLX577	1.6.50	1411	CXX135	2.7.51	1485	CXX472	25.9.53
1341	CLX529	6.12.50	1412	CXX141	11.10.50	1486	CXX473	19.10.53
1342	CLX531	25.10.50	1413	CLE209	15.12.50	1487	CXX474	1.3.51
1343	CLX591	11.7.50	1414	CLE210	31.5.50	1488	CXX475	20.7.51
1344	CLX532	29.11.50	1415	CXX140	18.10.50	1489	CXX476	1.3.51
1345	CLX542	18.7.50	1416	CXX147	21.11.50	1490	CXX477	7.6.51
1346	CLX533	22.11.50	1417	CXX179	16.11.50	1491	CXX478	20.10.53
1347	CLX587	8.11.50	1418	CXX144	30.3.50	1492	CXX479	8.11.50
1348	CLX582	21.12.50	1419	CXX137	27.2.50	1493	CXX480	20.10.53
1349	CLX580	10.1.51	1420	CXX208	14.4.53	1494	CXX481	27.3.53†
1350	CLX536	18.7.50	1421	CXX145	4.12.50	1495	CXX482	6.11.51
1351	CLX593	22.4.53	1422	CXX138	6.7.50	1496	CXX483	16.10.53
1353	CLX540	9.1.50	1424	CXX136	10.1.51	1497	CXX484	26.10.51
1354	CLX579	10.1.51	1425	CXX149	23.3.50	1498	CXX485	3.4.51
1355	CLX534	18.5.50	1426	CXX142	11.7.50	1500	CXX487	9.3.50
1356	CLX581	13.7.50	1427	CXX148	29.6.50	1501	CXX488	1.11.51
1357	CLX537	4.3.54	1429	CXX181	16.7.53	1502	CXX489	24.10.50

† Converted to service vehicle, see page 33
c Chassis only, body scrapped earlier

STL		Date out of stock	STL		Date out of stock	STL		Date out of stock
1503	CXX490	17.12.52†	1572	CXX285	27.4.53	1641	CXX347	23.10.53
1504	CXX491	20.9.50	1573	CXX281	11.3.53	1642	CXX366	
1505	CXX492	26.10.51	1574	CXX290	2.2.53	1643	CXX348	10.2.54
1506	CXX493	6.11.51	1575	CXX282	15.4.54	1644	CXX349	
1507	CXX494	23.10.53	1576	CXX293	10.2.54	1645	CXX365	3.10.50
1508	CXX495	2.7.51	1577	CXX283	15.7.53	1646	CLE19	10.4.53
1509	CXX496	19.10.53	1578	CXX287	22.9.53	1647	CXX363	26.2.53
1510	CXX497	6.11.51	1579	CXX299	22.7.53	1648	CXX372	
1511	CXX498	11.11.53	1580	CXX286	11.12.53	1649	CXX360	22.9.54
1512	CXX499	10.4.53†	1581	CXX292		1650	CXX356	25.2.53
1513	CXX500	30.10.51	1582	CXX302	20.1.53	1651	CXX350	5.11.53
1514	CXX225	12.2.53	1583	CXX291	21.4.54	1652	CXX358	
1515	CXX218	27.3.50	1584	CXX307	2.7.51	1653	CXX355	17.7.53
1516	CXX217	20.7.53	1585	CXX304	12.12.51c	1654	CXX368	15.11.54
1517	CXX213	19.9.50	1586	CXX322	27.7.53	1655	CXX362	22.3.50
1518	CXX216	1.2.50	1587	CXX288	10.12.53	1656	CXX354	16.7.53
1519	CXX226	10.1.51	1588	CXX294	2.4.54	1657	CXX367	25.3.53
1520	CXX219	22.5.53	1590	CXX295	13.2.53	1658	DGX196	8.7.53
1521	CXX221	18.9.53	1591	CXX300	29.1.54	1659	CXX357	
1522	CXX214		1592	CXX296	9.3.53	1660	DGX197	4.12.53
1523	CXX215	21.1.54	1593	CXX301	11.3.53	1661	CXX369	
1524	CXX224	31.10.50	1594	CXX289	17.4.54	1662	CXX364	24.4.53
1525	CXX227	8.12.53	1595	CXX308		1663	DLU172	24.8.50
1526	CXX223	2.3.50	1596	CXX309	20.3.53	1664	CXX353	28.7.53
1527	CXX220		1597	CXX325		1665	DGX198	13.9.50
1528	CXX222	4.6.53	1598	CXX323	8.5.53	1666	CXX373	21.6.50
1529	CXX235	1.9.52c	1599	CXX321	12.5.53	1667	DGX213	13.7.50
1531	CXX234	4.6.53	1600	CXX320	1.1.54	1668	CXX371	
1532	CXX238	20.5.53	1601	CXX297	20.4.53	1669	DGX199	6.10.54
1533	CXX239	17.3.50	1602	CXX310	5.4.54	1670	CXX370	
1534	CXX232	7.2.50	1603	ELP293		1671	DGX200	16.1.53
1535	CXX228	5.10.50	1604	CXX328		1672	DGX201	8.3.54
1536	CXX237	27.4.53	1605	CXX315	30.11.53	1673	DGX202	14.1.53
1538	CXX229	17.6.53	1606	CXX333	18.12.53	1674	DGX203	14.7.53
1539	CXX233	1.6.50	1607	CXX311		1675	DGX204	30.11.53
1540	CXX231	17.7.53	1608	CXX312		1676	DGX207	5.10.50
1541	CXX240	18.5.54	1609	CXX314	27.3.53	1677	DGX205	
1542	CXX236		1610	CXX313	30.4.52c	1678	DGX206	
1543	CXX241	29.11.51c	1611	CXX316	11.3.53	1679	DGX210	13.9.54
1544	CXX251	16.1.53	1612	CXX305	14.12.50	1680	DGX209	
1545	CXX246		1613	CXX324	13.2.53	1681	DGX217	
1546	CXX247	10.4.53	1614	CXX332	9.3.53	1682	DGX208	
1547	CXX252	18.7.50	1615	CXX329	21.12.53	1683	DGX211	8.12.53
1548	CXX253		1616	CXX326		1684	DGX212	7.10.54
1549	CXX245	4.2.53	*1617	CXX318	4.3.53	1685	CXX375	28.5.52c
1550	CXX266	16.2.50	1618	CXX317	20.8.53	1686	DGX193	10.11.50
1551	CXX255	24.3.53	1619	CXX319	21.5.53	1687	CXX376	15.7.53
1552	CXX260	9.1.53	1620	CXX327	29.12.53	1688	DGX254	
1553	CXX265	23.5.50	1621	CXX335	19.11.53	1689	CXX377	20.11.53
1554	CXX259	8.5.53	1622	CXX331		1690	CXX379	27.4.54
1555	CXX261	23.4.52c	1623	CXX334		1691	CXX378	18.11.53
1556	CXX262	14.5.53	1625	CXX330		1692	DGX191	9.9.54
1557	CXX263	27.7.53	1626	CXX338	13.9.54	1693	DGX192	
1558	CXX264	20.1.54	1627	CXX337	13.5.53	1694	DGX214	11.11.53
1559	CXX280	15.4.53	1628	CXX339	15.8.50	1695	CXX381	
1560	CXX274	17.2.53	1629	CXX336	11.4.51	1696	DGX215	5.11.53
1561	CXX268	8.5.53	1630	CXX340		1697	CXX380	6.11.53
1562	CXX284	14.1.53	1631	CXX351	19.3.53c	1698	DGX218	
1563	CXX267	1.5.50	1632	CXX342	22.10.53	1699	DGX194	19.3.53
1564	CXX269	9.3.50	1633	CXX361	18.3.53	1700	DGX219	25.2.54
1565	CXX279	17.2.53	1634	CXX343	19.6.53	1701	DGX250	4.6.52
1566	CXX275	29.3.51	1635	CXX344	15.11.50	1702	DGX195	12.3.54
1567	CXX276	13.12.54	1636	CXX352	13.7.50	1703	DGX245	23.10.53
1568	CXX277	22.11.50	1637	CXX374	22.9.54	1704	DGX246	2.4.53
1569	CXX278	12.1.54	1638	CXX345		1705	DGX247	23.11.53
1570	CXX306		1639	CXX346		1706	DGX248	
1571	CXX298	10.11.53	1640	CXX359	19.11.53	1707	DGX251	12.2.54

† Converted to service vehicle, see page 33   * Lowbridge bodywork
c Chassis only, body scrapped earlier

STL		Date out of stock	STL		Date out of stock	STL		Date out of stock
1708	DGX252	24.7.53	1775	DGX325		1845t	DLU211	15.3.54
1709	DGX249	23.2.54	1776	DGX330	24.2.54	1846t	DLU212	12.2.53
1710	DGX255	10.7.53	1777	DGX326		1847	DLU214	1.6.50
1711	DGX256	7.12.53	1778	DGX331	13.9.50	1848t	DLU218	16.7.53
1712	DGX265	6.3.51	1779	DGX332		1849t	DLU215	11.3.53
1713	DGX257	5.2.54	1780	DGX333	12.10.54	1850t	DLU219	
1714	DGX261	15.4.53	1781	DGX338		1851	DLU217	17.2.50
1715	DGX294		1782	DGX339		1852t	DLU224	
1716	DGX262		1783	DGX342		1853t	DLU225	22.2.54
1717	DGX323	15.2.54	1784	DGX340		1854	DLU221	
1718	DGX258	17.7.53	1785	DGX349	17.7.53	1855t	DLU232	
1719	DGX263	23.12.53	1786	DGX341	22.3.54	1856t	DLU222	17.3.54
1720	DGX264	14.4.53	1787	DGX345		1857t	DLU227	4.5.54
1721	DGX275	6.12.54	1788	DGX346		1858t	DLU226	23.12.54
1722	DGX259		1791	DGX358		1859	DLU220	28.8.51
1723	DGX266	16.2.53	1792	DGX356		1860t	DLU228	22.3.54
1724	DGX267	18.4.50	1793	DLU11	15.9.53	1861t	DLU229	5.2.53
1725	DGX268		1794	DLU14	18.3.54	1862	DLU223	24.8.50
1726	DGX269	23.3.53	1795	DLU16	22.4.53	1863	DLU239	12.4.54
1727	DGX270	26.5.53	1796	DGX360	18.3.53	1864t	DLU236	22.3.54
1728	DGX271		1797	DLU13	28.8.51	1865t	DLU230	
1729	DGX272	22.10.54	1798	DLU20	9.5.50	1866t	DLU237	
1730	DGX273		1799	DGX357	26.9.50	1867t	DLU235	30.4.54
1731	DGX276		1800	DLU15	5.2.54	1868t	DLU233	
1732	DGX277	10.4.53	1801	DLU32	28.11.50	1869	DLU252	26.2.53
1733	DGX278	29.5.53	1802	DLU29	29.4.53	1871t	DLU240	6.4.54
1734	DGX279	23.12.54	1803	DLU21		1872t	DLU238	18.2.54
1735	DGX280	7.1.54	1804	DLU17	15.2.54	1873	DLU268	
1736	DGX283	26.5.53	1805	DLU33	15.11.54	1874t	DLU241	
1737	DGX274	13.11.53	1806	DLU30		1875t	DLU234	
1738	DGX324	4.5.54	1807	DLU22	29.4.53	1876t	DLU243	
1739	DLU40	6.10.53	1808	DLU34	11.11.54	1877	DLU246	6.2.50
1740	DLU292	28.9.50	1809t	DLU48	10.5.54	1878	DLU289	18.5.50
1741	DGX281		1810	DLU36	29.6.51	1879	DLU284	10.1.51
1742	DGX284		1811	DLU31		1880	DLU248	16.8.50
1743	DGX282		1812	DLU41	9.1.51†	1881	DLU247	
1744	DGX286	17.5.54	1813	DLU35	24.2.53	1882	DLU259	19.9.50
1745	DGX287	17.2.54	1814t	DLU188	8.5.53	1883	DLU288	
1746	DGX285	22.2.54	1815	DLU44		1884t	DLU244	11.11.54
1747	DGX288	20.9.54	1816	DLU42	12.11.53	1885	DLU267	2.11.53
1748	DGX289		1817	DLU193	17.11.53	1886	DLU253	23.3.50
1749	DGX290		1818t	DLU189	5.4.54	1887	DLU245	8.2.50
1750	DGX291	20.3.51	1819	DLU195		1888	DLU280	10.2.50
1751	DGX292	18.1.54	1820	DLU194	2.7.51	1889	DLU266	25.1.54
1752	DGX293	23.12.54	1821	DLU49		1890	DLU251	
1753	DGX298	18.2.54	1822	DLU45	22.10.53	1891	DLU277	27.4.50
1754	DGX295	20.9.54	1823t	DLU190	30.4.54	1892	DLU249	1.4.53
1755	DGX296	16.12.53	1824	DLU205		1893	DLU285	23.5.50
1756	DGX297	19.10.53	1825t	DLU191	16.11.54	1894	DLU250	
1757	DGX299	20.10.53	1826	DLU197		1895	DLU272	9.3.50
1758	DGX301	21.5.53	1827t	DLU206		1896	DLU255	
1759	DGX302	1.10.53	1828t	DLU207	6.7.53	1897	DLU273	5.10.50
1760	DGX303		1829	DLU210	5.2.54	1898	DLU256	
1761	DGX304	27.1.53	1830t	DLU196	27.4.53	1899	DLU254	23.3.50
1762	DGX305		1831	DLU208		1900	DLU293	9.3.50
1763	DGX306	18.8.53	1832	DLU198		1901	DLU278	8.6.50
1764	DGX307	8.12.53	1833	DLU199		1902	DLU260	12.1.50
1765	DGX308	13.12.54	1834	DLU200		1903	DLU261	22.3.50
1766	DGX309		1835t	DLU201	3.3.54	1904	DLU274	27.9.50
1767	DGX310	28.8.51	1836	DLU202		1905	DLU258	13.12.54
1768	DGX311	4.7.50	1838	DLU204	23.12.53	1906	DLU296	15.11.50
1769	DGX312	1.6.50	1839	DLU50	4.9.53	1907	DLU263	8.6.50
1770	DGX313	5.11.53	1840	DLU192		1908	DLU275	28.8.51
1771	DGX314		1841t	DLU209	18.8.53	1909	DLU264	9.5.50
1772	DGX315	28.8.51	1842t	DLU242	29.12.53	1910	DLU279	23.5.50
1773	DGX316	4.12.53	1843t	DLU216	26.3.54	1911	DLU270	4.12.53
1774	DGX317		1844t	DLU213	21.4.54	1912	DLU265	29.6.51

† Converted to service vehicle, see page 33
t Tunnel body

STL

Date out
of stock

STL

Date out
of stock

STL

Date out
of stock

STL		Date out of stock	STL		Date out of stock	STL		Date out of stock
1913	DLU257	23.12.54	1980	CGW270	14.11.50	2049	DLU28	
1914	DLU262	6.12.50	1981	CLT303	19.7.50	2050	DLU46	16.5.50
1915	DLU294		1982	BYY149	13.2.50	2051	DLU47	1.12.50
1916	DLU308	8.12.53	1983	CGU628	14.2.50	2052	DLU53	29.6.51
1917	DLU298	8.3.50	1984	BYX384	1.6.50	2053	DLU54	5.1.50‡
1918	DLU276		1985	CGF772	13.3.51	2054	DLU51	8.2.50
1919	DLU290	24.8.53	1986	CGK953	29.6.50	2055	DLU52	27.12.50
1920	DLU269	10.8.50	1987	CLN408	27.2.50	2056	DLU55	
1921	DLU271	10.2.50	1988	CGX49	23.5.50	2058	DLU57	20.10.53
1922	DLU300		1989	CLM970	7.2.50	2059	DLU58	8.6.50
1923	DLU281	8.7.53	*1990	CGU38	25.2.53	2060	DLU59	21.8.51
1924	DLU301	10.2.50	1991	CGY212	15.1.51	2062	DLU61	
1925	DLU152	7.3.50	1992	CGW269	23.5.50	2063	DLU62	1.2.50
1926	DLU146	11.5.50	1993	CGX48	8.6.50	2064	DLU63	22.3.50
1927	DLU286		1994	CUV501	15.11.50	2065	DLU64	17.10.50
1928	DLU287	13.7.54c	1995	CLN413	15.1.51	2066	DLU65	5.10.53
1929	DLU282	8.6.50	1996	CXU346	20.6.50	2067	DLU66	16.6.53
1930	DLU306	2.2.50	1997	CGO914	7.11.50	2069	DLU68	28.11.50
1931	DLU302	12.10.50	1998	CLN740	20.9.50	2070	DLU69	22.9.54
1932	DLU283		1999	CGU222	7.6.51	2071	DLU70	
1933	DLU291	29.11.50	2000	CGY208	6.7.50	2072	DLU71	4.4.50
1934	DLU148	28.2.50	2001	CLO846	21.9.50	2073	DLU72	16.8.50
1935	DLU140	30.4.52c	2002	CLW777	15.3.50	2074	DLU73	26.4.54
1936	DLU299		2003	CGY607	23.5.50	2075	DLU74	6.1.50‡
1937	DLU145	29.6.50	2004	CLO847	9.5.50	2076	DLU75	25.2.54
1938	DLU139		2005	CLX700	23.8.50	2077	DLU76	22.3.50
1939	DLU141	5.10.50	2006	DYL846	20.2.50	2078	DLU77	20.12.50
1940	DLU295		2007	CGY428	22.8.50	2079	DLU78	11.5.50
1941	DLU304	20.9.54	2008	CGY663	12.1.50	2080	DLU79	7.11.50
1942	DLU159	29.6.50	2009	CLN401	9.5.50	2081	DLU80	
1943	DLU142	11.5.50	2010	CLU366	7.11.50	2082	DLU81	7.6.51
1944	DLU297	4.4.50	2011	CLX21	3.3.50	2083	DLU82	11.7.50
1945	DLU303	16.5.50	2012	CLW82	16.6.54	2084	DLU83	13.2.50
1946	DLU155	20.9.50	2013	CLF885		2085	DLU84	3.1.50‡
1947	DLU143	13.1.50	2014	DGX253	24.8.50	2086	DLU85	
1948	DLU147	6.9.50	2015	DGX300	8.2.51	2088	DLU87	24.2.54
1949	DLU307	12.10.50	2016	DGX319	8.10.54	2089	DLU88	19.6.50
1950	DLU305	28.12.50	2017	DGX320	20.3.53	2090	DLU89	2.1.50
1951	DLU138	21.2.50	2018	DGX321	28.8.51	2091	DLU90	5.4.50
1952	DLU150	29.4.53	2019	DGX318		2092	DLU91	16.5.50
1953	DLU151	5.10.50	2020	DGX322	17.12.53	2093	DLU92	
*1954	DLU144	19.2.53	2021	DGX327		2095	DLU94	29.3.51
*1955	DLU149	17.2.53	2022	DGX335	29.3.51	2096	DLU95	12.10.50
1956	DLU163	13.9.50	2023	DGX328	5.12.51c	2097	DLU96	5.1.50‡
1957	DLU153	31.1.50	2024	DGX329	29.3.51	2098	DLU97	26.11.53
1958	CGP272	13.2.50	2025	DGX337	7.7.53	2099	DLU98	22.6.50
*1959	DLU157	20.3.53	2026	DLU12	29.6.51	2100	DLU99	
1960	DLU161	24.2.50	2027	DGX351	18.10.50	2105	DLU104	23.12.54
1961	DLU160	7.11.50	2028	DGX343	11.1.50	2106	DLU105	
1962	DLU162	1.2.50	2029	DGX336	2.7.51	*2107	DLU106	20.3.53
1963	DLU154	16.1.50	2030	DGX344	21.2.51	2108	DLU107	
1964	DLU158	16.1.50	2031	DGX334	2.7.51	2109	DLU108	7.4.53
1965	DLU170		2032	DGX347		2110	DLU109	17.2.50
1966	DLU169	17.6.54	2034	DGX353	2.7.51	2111	DLU110	6.1.50‡
1967	DLU156	16.1.50	2035	DGX348	27.2.51	2112	DLU111	19.7.50
1968	DLU164	14.9.50	2036	DGX354	11.5.50	2113	DLU112	1.5.50
1969	BXT431	19.7.50	2037	DGX355	8.6.50	2114	DLU113	11.10.50
1970	DLU166	13.2.50	2038	DLU23		2115	DLU114	18.10.50
1971	DLU165	29.8.53	2039	DLU18	24.11.50	2116	DLU115	8.3.51
1972	DLU167	25.5.50	2040	DLU38	30.11.50	2117	DLU116	
*1973	DLU171	18.3.53	2041	DLU24	5.1.50‡	2118	DLU117	9.5.50
*1974	DLU168	19.2.53	2042	DLU25	6.1.50‡	2120	DLU119	
1975	BXU697	15.2.54	2043	DLU39	3.11.53	2121	DLU120	13.6.50
1976	BYR792	11.7.50	2044	DLU19	16.5.50	2122	DLU121	16.1.50
1977	BUW565	17.2.50	2045	DLU37	8.4.53	2123	DLU122	20.6.50
*1978	BXW938	20.3.53	2047	DLU43	22.6.50	2124	DLU123	
1979	CGK320	5.10.50	2048	DLU27	22.6.50	2125	DLU124	1.3.50

c   Chassis only, body scrapped earlier   *   Lowbridge body
‡   Converted to SRT

STL		Date out of stock	STL		Date out of stock	STL		Date out of stock
2126	DLU125		2196	CXO566	28.8.51	2265	DYL890	6.2.50
2128	DLU127	2.2.50	2197	CXR641	17.10.50	2266	DYL889	13.2.51
2129	DLU128	22.11.50	2198	CLX652	6.3.50	2267	DYL891	16.5.50
2130	DLU129	4.1.50‡	2199	CLR387	21.12.50	2268	DYL892	31.8.50
2131	DLU130	6.3.50	2200	CXO903	21.4.52c	2269	DYL893	24.11.50
2132	DLU131	2.11.53	2201	CXR251	27.6.50	2270	DYL894	24.8.50
2133	DLU132	21.12.50	2202	CXR254	16.5.50	2271	EGO332	13.9.50
2134	DLU133	1.5.53	2203	CYL465	8.6.50	2272	DYL898	9.3.50
2135	DLU134	26.1.54	2204	CYH783		*2273	DYL901	20.2.53
2136	DLU135	29.11.50	2205	CYT677	27.2.50	2274	EGO334	22.11.50
2137	DLU136	9.3.50	2206	CYF598	3.3.50	2275	DYL899	11.7.50
2138	DLU137	23.2.54	2207	CYL841	28.8.51	2276	DYL895	23.5.50
2139	DYL791	16.11.50	2208	CYT711	5.10.50	2277	DYL902	28.2.50
2140	DYL792	17.10.50	2209	CYT710	1.3.50	2278	DYL900	19.10.50
2141	DYL793	18.4.50	2210	CYR372		2279	DYL903	13.4.50
2142	DYL794	6.3.50	2211	DYL841	22.8.50	2280	DYL896	4.7.50
2143	DYL795	16.6.53	2212	CYU18	19.9.50	2281	EGO333	29.6.50
2144	DYL796	4.5.50	2213	CYU76	18.10.50	2282	EGO338	11.7.50
2145	DYL797	7.9.50	2214	CYU851	9.3.50	2283	EGO335	10.8.50
2146	DYL798	11.10.50	2215	DYL849	27.2.51	2284	EGO336	21.11.50
2147	DYL799	5.10.53	2216	DYL850	21.11.50	2285	EGO339	15.11.50
*2148	DYL800	5.2.53	*2217	DYL843	24.4.53	2286	EGO337	3.10.50
2149	DYL801	14.11.50	2218	DYL897	7.9.50	2288	EGO349	4.7.50
2150	DYL802	5.2.53	2219	DYL842	4.11.53	2289	EGO340	23.12.53
2151	DYL803	16.5.50	*2220	DYL853	6.2.53	2290	EGO341	27.4.50
2152	DYL804	18.7.50	2221	DYL848	23.5.50	*2291	EGO354	5.8.53
2153	DYL805	4.7.50	2222	DYL845	29.3.51	*2292	EGO343	10.8.53
2154	DYL806	28.8.51	2223	DYL847	30.3.50	2293	EGO347	2.1.50
2155	DYL807	6.1.50‡	2224	DYL844	16.5.50	2294	EGO350	8.6.50
2156	DYL808	28.8.51	2225	DYL851	19.10.50	2295	EGO345	31.1.50
2157	DYL809	21.11.50	2226	DYL854	12.1.50	2296	EGO348	9.5.50
2158	DYL810	15.6.50	2227	DYL858	7.6.51	2297	EGO370	6.3.50
2159	DYL811	17.2.54	2228	DYL852	22.11.50	2298	EGO344	27.9.50
2161	DYL813	19.7.50	*2229	DYL855	5.2.53	2299	EGO352	8.11.50
2162	DYL814	6.7.53	2230	DYL856	1.6.50	2300	EGO363	19.7.50
2163	DYL815	26.3.54	2231	DYL857	6.1.50‡	2301	EGO355	
2164	DYL816	25.4.50	*2232	DYL860	20.3.53	2302	EGO356	18.10.50
2165	DYL817	27.4.50	2233	DYL885	27.6.50	2303	EGO353	27.7.50
2166	DYL818		2235	DYL859	29.6.50	2305	EGO346	11.7.50
2168	DYL820	9.11.50	2236	DYL861	1.5.50	2306	EGO364	14.12.50
2169	DYL821	5.12.50	2237	DYL910	14.9.50	2307	EGO358	13.7.50
2170	DYL822	14.6.50	2238	DYL863	21.2.50	2308	EGO376	2.7.51
2171	DYL823	12.10.54	2240	DYL862	21.9.50	2309	EGO366	25.5.50
2172	DYL824	30.1.54	2241	DYL864	21.9.50	2310	EGO371	15.4.54
2173	DYL825	28.2.50	2242	DYL866	1.12.50	*2311	EGO367	24.4.53
2174	DYL826	5.10.50	2243	DYL870	3.10.50	2312	EGO357	4.7.50
2175	DYL827	19.2.54	2244	DYL869	23.5.50	2313	EGO420	31.8.50
2176	DYL828	27.7.50	2245	DYL865	21.9.50	2314	EGO405	6.12.50
2177	DYL829		2246	DYL871	9.3.50	2315	CLH173	20.2.51
2178	DYL830	13.2.51	2247	DYL880	1.6.50	2316	EGO359	3.10.50
2179	DYL831	10.8.50	2248	DYL868	17.10.50	2317	CLH861	17.8.50
2180	DYL832	15.8.50	2249	DYL882	29.6.50	2318	EGO391	11.7.50
2181	DYL833	8.11.50	2250	DYL874	22.4.53	2319	CLH885	15.3.50
2182	DYL834	23.3.50	2251	DYL875	24.7.53	2320	EGO369	3.10.50
2183	DYL835	13.12.54	2252	DYL872	16.8.50	2321	EGO365	10.10.50
2184	DYL836	6.12.50	2253	DYL876	7.2.50	2322	EGO384	8.3.50
2185	DYL837		2254	EGO331	16.5.50	2323	EGO379	13.12.50
*2186	DYL838	18.8.53	2255	DYL873	8.11.54	2324	EGO377	16.5.50
2187	DYL839	11.7.50	2256	DYL887	8.6.50	2325	EGO368	3.10.50
2188	DYL840	4.7.50	2257	DYL883	27.6.50	2326	EGO360	7.12.50
2189	CLF886	2.1.50	2258	DYL888	15.1.51	2327	EGO402	4.7.50
2190	CLH881	18.7.50	2259	DYL884	28.2.50	2328	EGO378	6.10.54
2191	CLL355	28.11.50	2260	DYL877	16.11.50	2329	EGO361	17.10.50
2192	CLN407	1.5.50	2261	DYL878	23.5.50	2330	EGO380	9.6.50
2193	CUU997	1.5.50	2262	DYL881	3.3.50	2331	EGO399	5.10.50
2194	CXR252		2263	DYL879	28.8.51	2332	EGO381	19.7.50
2195	CXL823	2.1.50	2264	DYL886	1.5.50	2333	EGO372	24.11.50

c   Chassis only, body scrapped earlier   *   Lowbridge body
‡   Converted to SRT

STL		Date out of stock	STL		Date out of stock	STL		Date out of stock
2334	EGO362	16.5.50	2402	EGO446	6.12.50	2474	ELP144	9.6.50
2335	EGO398	29.3.50	2403	EGO456	5.4.50	2475	ELP132	
2336	EGO373	21.9.50	2404	EGO450	31.10.50	2476	ELP142	8.6.50
2337	EGO382	9.5.50	2405	EGO453	6.1.50‡	2477	ELP154	
2338	EGO374	22.3.50	2406	EGO447	9.5.50	2478	ELP134	16.5.50
2339	EGO383	15.6.53	2407	EGO457	5.2.53	2479	ELP135	5.12.50
2340	EGO386	16.1.50	2408	EGO449	23.5.50	2480	ELP150	27.6.50
2341	EGO394	25.4.50	2409	EGO454	17.7.53	2481	ELP143	30.3.50
2342	EGO375	30.3.50	2410	EGO459	4.1.50‡	2482	ELP137	6.11.53
2343	EGO385	9.5.50	2411	EGO473	14.11.50	2483	ELP139	19.7.50
2345	EGO422	13.3.51	2412	EGO460	8.1.54	2484	ELP148	
2346	EGO400	20.7.50	2413	EGO455	25.5.50	2485	ELP147	1.8.50
2347	EGO390	11.10.50	2414	EGO469	5.4.51	2486	ELP151	28.12.50
2348	EGO397	23.11.53	2416	EGO461	30.11.50	2487	ELP141	5.6.50
2349	EGO387	13.7.50	2417	EGO470	14.4.50	2488	ELP140	17.2.50
2350	EGO389	15.11.50	2419	EGO467	20.2.50	2489	ELP146	24.11.50
2351	EGO396	7.3.50	2421	EGO474	12.12.50	2490	ELP152	11.5.50
2352	EGO403	31.10.50	2422	EGO472	22.11.50	2491	ELP145	1.6.50
2353	EGO388	6.3.50	2423	EGO475	9.6.50	2492	ELP168	17.8.50
2354	EGO413	16.11.50	2425	EGO480	27.4.50	2493	ELP156	27.6.50
2355	EGO401	20.9.54	2426	EGO476	18.12.53	2494	ELP167	14.12.50
2356	EGO392	29.6.50	2427	EGO478	1.12.50	2495	ELP162	3.4.50
2357	EGO393	4.5.50	2428	EGO464	10.3.50	2496	ELP153	6.7.50
2358	EGO429		2429	EGO479	20.6.50	2497	ELP165	8.6.50
2359	EGO404	13.7.50	2430	EGO483	9.6.50	2498	ELP157	19.10.50
2360	EGO406	19.7.50	2431	EGO465	22.3.50	2499	ELP164	13.12.50
2361	EGO407	9.1.50‡	2432	EGO487	3.8.50	2501	ELP163	
2362	EGO408	6.12.50	2433	EGO481	19.10.50	2502	ELP172	17.2.50
2363	EGO414	1.12.50	2434	EGO484	31.10.50	2503	ELP158	4.4.50
2364	EGO423	16.11.50	2436	EGO485	12.3.51	2504	ELP173	17.3.54
2365	EGO409	15.2.50	2437t	ELP108	8.12.53	2505	ELP159	
2366	EGO410	30.8.50	2438	EGO482	11.1.50‡	2506	ELP169	10.11.53
2367	EGO421	20.9.50	2439	ELP102	8.11.50	2507	ELP160	29.11.50
2368	EGO415	5.10.50	2440	EGO486	11.5.50	2508	ELP170	14.11.52c
2369	EGO428	6.12.50	2441	ELP103	17.3.50	2509	ELP149	30.8.50
2370	EGO411	16.1.50	2442	ELP104	11.5.50	2510	ELP161	1.6.50
2371	EGO416	23.11.50	2443	EGO489	20.4.51	2511	ELP166	31.5.50
2372	EGO439	8.11.50	2444	ELP114	3.10.50	2512	ELP155	29.11.51c
2373	EGO436	16.2.50	2445	ELP106	25.2.53	2513	ELP174	
2374	EGO412	20.6.50	2446	ELP109	9.3.50	2514	ELP176	10.12.54
2375	EGO433	13.7.50	2447	ELP107	13.12.50	2515	ELP175	7.5.53
2376	EGO425	20.6.50	2448	ELP101	28.8.51	2525	FJJ685	23.10.53
2377	EGO426	6.4.54	2449	ELP105	17.3.50	2543	FJJ703	15.9.53
2378	EGO417	7.2.50	2450	ELP112	19.6.50	2562	FJJ722	4.9.53
2379	EGO418	8.6.50	2451	ELP111	20.12.50	2584	FJJ744	15.10.54
2380	EGO419	29.11.50	2452	ELP115	23.6.50	2595	FJJ755	1.4.53
2381	EGO451	19.11.53	2453	ELP110	17.1.51c	2600	FJJ760	20.8.53
2382	EGO438	9.3.50	2454	ELP117	6.9.50	2621	FXT69	15.8.50
2383	EGO440	6.7.50	2455	ELP118	8.2.50	2648	FXT371	
2384	EGO458	28.8.51	2456	ELP120	19.7.50	2649	FXT372	21.7.52†
2385	EGO431	15.8.50	2457	ELP119	21.3.50	2650	FXT373	24.3.50
2386	EGO424	9.3.50	2458	ELP123	16.2.50	2651	FXT374	
2387	EGO432	9.2.50	2459	ELP113	1.5.53	2652	FXT375	16.5.50
2388	EGO430	9.2.54	2460	ELP116	21.6.50	2653	FXT376	15.3.50
2389	EGO427	11.8.53	2461	ELP121		2654	FXT377	
2390	EGO462	11.10.50	2462	ELP129	20.2.51	2655	FXT378	17.2.50
2391	EGO445	24.11.50	2463	ELP124	13.12.50	2656	FXT379	28.2.50
2392	EGO434		2464	ELP133	16.10.50	2657	FXT380	
2393	EGO441	21.11.50	2465	ELP126	4.1.50‡	2658	FXT381	
2394	EGO435	31.10.50	2466	ELP125	29.6.50	2659	FXT382	
2395	EGO437	21.2.51	2467	ELP138	4.6.53	2660	FXT383	1.11.50
2396	EGO443	14.11.50	2468	ELP128	10.2.50	2661	FXT384	27.9.54†
2397	EGO448	2.11.54c	2469	ELP122	13.12.50	2662	FXT385	
2398	EGO452	14.12.50	2470	ELP136	13.9.50	2663	FXT386	
2399	EGO442	15.1.51	2471	ELP127	12.12.50	2664	FXT387	2.4.52
2400	EGO444	20.7.53	2472	ELP130	16.5.50	2665	FXT388	19.9.52†
2401	EGO477	20.7.50	2473	ELP131	4.5.50	2666	FXT389	

c Chassis only, body scrapped earlier   t Tunnel body
‡ Converted to SRT

STL		STL		STL		STL		STL	
2667	FXT390	2674	FXT397	2681	FXT404	2688	HGC221	2695	HGC228
2668	FXT391	2675	FXT398	2682	HGC215	2689	HGC222	2696	HGC229
2669	FXT392	2676	FXT399	2683	HGC216	2690	HGC223	2697	HGC230
2670	FXT393	2677	FXT400	2684	HGC217	2691	HGC224	2698	HGC231
2671	FXT394	2678	FXT401	2685	HGC218	2692	HGC225	2699	HGC232
2672	FXT395	2679	FXT402	2686	HGC219	2693	HGC226	2700	HGC233
2673	FXT396	2680	FXT403	2687	HGC220	2694	HGC227	2701	HGC234

† These buses were converted to service vehicles on the dates shown, as follows:

STL 43	to 828J	STL 372	to 821J	STL 1503	to 969J
STL 159	to 833J	STL 377	to 811J	STL 1512	to 973J
STL 162	to 832J	STL 390	to 830J	STL 1812	to 952J
STL 169	to 738J	STL 1039	to 970J	STL 2649	to 963J
STL 175	to 739J	STL 1470	to 971J	STL 2661	to 1018J
STL 192	to 744J	STL 1494	to 972J	STL 2665	to 968J

971J was one of five Country Bus STLs converted to treeloppers between December 1952 and April 1953 by having their upper decks removed. As STL 1470, it last ran at Crawley and like the others was a metal-framed Weymann STL6/1. LTPS

The all-Leyland STDs were a product of the LPTB's need to place some of its 1937 body requirements with outside manufacturers. The STD1 body was a good copy of the contemporary Chiswick design for the STL but was based on standard Leyland metal framework and differed in detail, one notable feature being the smaller 'signalling' window in the staircase panel. STDs 76 and 91, passing the Royal Courts of Justice in Strand in November 1951, respectively bear the 1950 and 1946 versions of the Central Bus livery. STD 91 was one of the ten originally equipped with torque convertors. Alan B. Cross

STD

In 1937, London Transport placed a then record order for 786 buses and coaches, of which 672 were double-deckers. As the Board was barred by statute from building more than 527 bodies a year, it was necessary to find alternative suppliers for some of the work. Leyland was chosen to share the body contract and the opportunity was taken to purchase complete buses so that an alternative source for chassis could also be tested. The one hundred Titans (STD 1-100) were nominally based on the standard TD4 and TD4c model Titan chassis but they were modified to meet London Transport's requirements, notably in having STL type low geared steering and revised dumb-irons so that the towing arrangements could be interchangeable with the STL. Ninety were fitted with crash gearboxes (STD 1-90) and ten with torque convertors (STD 91-100). The bodywork was also the standard Leyland metal framed product modified in detail to resemble the latest style of roof-box STL. The torque converters were replaced by standard manual gearboxes at their first overhaul. The entire batch was allocated to Hendon garage, where the majority spent their whole lives, but some were transferred to Cricklewood and Victoria during the war and others spent their last couple of years at Enfield. The last of the pre-war STDs were withdrawn from passenger service on 14th June 1954.

STD 101-111 were part of London Transport's intake of non-standard vehicles during World War II. They were based on 'unfrozen' TD7 chassis, whose mechanical specification was broadly similar to the earlier Titans and were the first London buses to carry wartime austerity bodywork. They were allocated to Victoria garage, where they spent their entire operational career operating on most routes from that garage. They were withdrawn prematurely in March 1951 after drivers refused to drive them any longer. STD 112-176 were standard Leyland products, purchased by the LPTB as a stop-gap until the post-war standard models could go into production. The overall appearance of these buses was very similar to the pre-war version, particularly from the front aspect where a full set of route and destination indicators was fitted. No indicators of any kind were provided at the back, which was also more heavily curved than the earlier version. At first, they were distributed in small quantities around a number of garages: Victoria, Croydon, Potters Bar, Hanwell and Loughton, but those at Potters Bar and Croydon were soon replaced, followed by those at Hanwell in 1949. Leyton also received a small allocation and Victoria's were transferred to Stockwell in November 1953.

The 1STD chassis was based on the Titan TD4, modified to meet London Transport's specification. Externally this was most noticeable in the square section dumbirons designed to accommodate towing bars, which then became a standard feature on Leyland models right up to the PD3. STD 75 on the stand at 'The Red Lion' Pinner on 23rd January 1954, four months before it was withdrawn, stands alongside a later product from the same stable, a Mann Egerton TD. J.C. Gillham

The 3STD2 was the first bus to carry bodywork built to the full Ministry of Supply wartime specification. The chassis were 'unfrozen' Leyland Titan TD7s, broadly similar in specification to the pre-war STDs and the bodies were supplied by Park Royal Coachworks. STD 111, like the remainder, spent its entire service life at Victoria garage, and is seen at Victoria station in its final form with additional opening windows and glazed rear upper deck emergency door.
F.W. Ivey

The post-war 4STD3s were again all-Leyland products and their bodies were very similar in overall appearance to the pre-war version but with a more gracefully curved rear end. The chassis specification was substantially different, the engine being a new 7.4 litre unit developed during the war for use in tanks. STD 122 was still wearing the original 1946 livery when seen on 7th June 1952 crossing Vauxhall Bridge on a garage run from Victoria, one of the seven garages which operated the type between 1946 and 1955. Alan B. Cross

Chassis: Leyland Titan TD4 modified (1-100); TD7 (101-111); PD1 (112-176)
Engine: Leyland six cylinder 8.6 litre direct injection 94 bhp; or 7.4 litre 100 bhp (112-176)
Transmission: Leyland four speed crash or Leyland four speed constant mesh (112-176)
Bodywork: Leyland; or Park Royal (100-111)
L. T. codes: 1STD1 (1-90); 1STD1/1 (91-100); 3STD2 (101-111); 4STD3 (112-176)
Capacity: H30/26R (101-111 UH30/26R)
Built: 1937 (1-100); 1941 (101); 1942 (102-111); 1946 (112-176)
Number built: 176   Number in stock: 1.1.50: 176   31.12.54: 125

STD		Date out of stock	**STD**		Date out of stock	**STD**		
1	DLU311	11.12.53	60	DLU370		119	HGF997	
2	DLU312	22.9.54	61	DLU371	23.1.54	120	HGF998	
3	DLU313	7.12.53	62	DLU372		121	HGF999	
4	DLU314	20.9.54	63	DLU373	23.9.54	122	HLW51	
5	DLU315	20.9.54	64	DLU374	5.1.54	123	HLW52	
6	DLU316	22.12.54	65	DLU375	23.12.54	124	HLW53	
7	DLU317	20.9.54	66	DLU376		125	HLW54	
8	DLU318		67	DLU377	23.9.54	126	HLW55	
9	DLU319	20.9.54	68	DLU378		127	HLW56	
10	DLU320		69	DLU379	23.9.54	128	HLW57	
11	DLU321	2.12.54	70	DLU380		129	HLW58	
12	DLU322	14.12.53	71	DLU381		130	HLW59	
13	DLU323		72	DLU382	26.11.54	131	HLW60	
14	DLU324	28.9.54	73	DLU383	22.9.54	132	HLW61	
15	DLU325	22.9.54	74	DLU384		133	HLW62	
16	DLU326		75	DLU385	26.11.54	134	HLW63	
17	DLU327	5.1.54	76	DLU386	15.12.53	135	HLW64	
18	DLU328	28.9.54	77	DLU387		136	HLW65	
19	DLU329	20.9.54	78	DLU388		137	HLW66	
20	DLU330	28.9.54	79	DLU389		138	HLW67	
21	DLU331	26.11.54	80	DLU390		139	HLW68	
22	DLU332		81	DLU391		140	HLW69	
23	DLU333	14.12.53	82	DLU392		141	HLW70	
24	DLU334		83	DLU393		142	HLW71	
25	DLU335	15.12.53	84	DLU394		143	HLW72	
26	DLU336		85	DLU395		144	HLW73	
27	DLU337		86	DLU396	2.12.54	145	HLW74	
28	DLU338		87	DLU397		146	HLW75	
29	DLU339	20.9.54	88	DLU398		147	HLW76	
30	DLU340		89	DLU399		148	HLW77	
31	DLU341	13.12.54	90	DLU400		149	HLW78	
32	DLU342	14.12.53	91	DLU401		150	HLW79	
33	DLU343	28.9.54	92	DLU402		151	HLW80	
34	DLU344		93	DLU403	22.12.54	152	HLW81	
35	DLU345	23.12.54	94	DLU404		153	HLW82	
36	DLU346	1.1.54	95	DLU405		154	HLW83	
37	DLU347	28.9.54	96	DLU406		155	HLW84	
38	DLU348	22.9.54	97	DLU407		156	HLW85	
39	DLU349		98	DLU408		157	HLW86	
40	DLU350	28.9.54	99	DLU409		158	HLW87	
41	DLU351		100	DLU410		159	HLW88	
42	DLU352		101	FXT405		160	HLW89	
43	DLU353		102	FXT428		161	HLW90	
44	DLU354	5.1.54	103	FXT429		162	HLW91	
45	DLU355		104	FXT430		163	HLW92	
46	DLU356		105	FXT431		164	HLW93	
47	DLU357	23.12.54	106	FXT432	28.9.54	165	HLW94	
48	DLU358	1.1.54	107	FXT433		166	HLW95	
49	DLU359	23.9.54	108	FXT434	28.9.54	167	HLW96	
50	DLU360		109	FXT435		168	HLW97	
51	DLU361	28.9.54	110	FXT436		169	HLW98	
52	DLU362	2.12.54	111	FXT437	7.12.53	170	HLW99	
53	DLU363		112	HGF990		171	HLW100	
54	DLU364		113	HGF991		172	HLW101	
55	DLU365		114	HGF992		173	HLW102	
56	DLU366		115	HGF993		174	HLW103	
57	DLU367	23.9.54	116	HGF994		175	HLW104	
58	DLU368		117	HGF995		176	HLW105	
59	DLU369		118	HGF996				

Bristol supplied nine 'unfrozen' K5Gs to London Transport in 1942, their first of any type with Gardner five cylinder engines, also with MoS specification Park Royal bodywork. The Gardner engines were replaced by AEC 7.7 litre units in 1948/1949. The 1B1s spent their entire operational life at Hanwell (later renamed Southall) garage, mainly allocated to route 97, on which B 7 was photographed at Greenford terminus. The vehicle in the background is former Tilling ST 969 in use as staff canteen 689J. J.H. Aston

B

B 1-9 were the third group of 'unfrozen' vehicles allocated to London Transport by the Ministry of War Transport and, like the STDs, had bodywork to austerity specification by Park Royal. The chassis were standard pre-war specification Bristol K5Gs, whose Gardner 5LW engines were the first to be purchased by London Transport. Bristol was authorised to resume PSV production in 1945, using engines supplied by AEC, and twenty of the new K6A model mounted with Duple 'relaxed austerity' bodywork were allocated to the Board (B 10-29). All twenty-nine were always allocated to Hanwell (later renamed Southall) garage. After the war, the 'unfrozen' Bs had their bodywork upgraded in the same ways as the Guys and in 1949 their Gardner engines were replaced by AEC units salvaged from withdrawn STLs. Withdrawal from service of the Bristols began in June 1951, the first nine going by May 1952 and the remainder by April 1953. All were sold for further service with Tilling Group companies, although four were immediately sold on to Beeline Roadways of Hartlepool.

Twenty Bristols were allocated to London Transport in 1945, but these were K6As powered by the newly available AEC 7.7 litre engine and with a lower bonnet line which gave them a more modern look. They were classified 2B2. The Duple bodywork was to 'relaxed austerity' specification with more opening windows, a more rounded profile and, internally, improved seating. B 18, seen in the leafy 'Queen of the Suburbs' (Ealing), was withdrawn in April 1953 and was sold to Brighton Hove and District who ran it, re-bodied, until August 1965.
F.G. Reynolds

Chassis: Bristol K6A
Engine: AEC: A171 7.7 litre indirect injection 95 bhp oil (1-9); or A202 7.7 litre direct
  injection 95 bhp oil.
Transmission: Four speed crash.
Bodywork: Park Royal (1-9); Duple (10-29)
Capacity: UH30/26R
L.T. body and chassis codes: 1/1B1/1 (1-9); 2B2 (10-29).
Built: 1942 (1-9); 1945 (10-29).
Number built: 29
Number in stock: 1.1.50: 29
                 31.12.54: Nil.

B		Date out of stock	B		Date out of stock	B		Date out of stock
1	FXT419	16.1.53	11	HGC236	23.4.53	21	HGC246	23.4.53
2	FXT420	6.1.53	12	HGC237	9.1.53	22	HGC247	4.2.53
3	FXT421	14.1.53	13	HGC238	8.5.53	23	HGC248	9.1.53
4	FXT422	16.1.53	14	HGC239	8.5.53	24	HGC249	14.1.53
5	FXT423	11.3.53	15	HGC240	25.2.53	25	HGC250	22.1.53
6	FXT424	6.1.53	16	HGC241	8.5.53	26	HGC251	22.1.53
7	FXT425	11.3.53	17	HGC242	8.5.53	27	HGC252	9.1.53
8	FXT426	30.12.52	18	HGC243	12.5.53	28	HGC253	11.3.53
9	FXT427	30.12.52	19	HGC244	12.5.53	29	HGC254	13.5.53
10	HGC235	20.1.53	20	HGC245	20.1.53			

The first fully fledged wartime austerity vehicles in the LPTB fleet were a batch of Guy Arab Is with Park Royal bodywork, identical to that mounted on the STDs. Two distinguishing features helped identify the Park Royal version, the slight 'V' shape of the front dome and the ledge-like extension of the dash panel below the windscreen. G 11, a 1/2G2, is seen at Preston Road as modified after the war with additional opening windows and glazed emergency window. F.G. Reynolds

G

Once the supply of 'unfrozen' chassis had been exhausted in 1942, the Government authorised Guy Motors of Wolverhampton to build a limited number of new double-deck bus chassis to a strict austerity specification which required the use of substitute materials to economise on scarce resources such as aluminium alloys. The first five hundred chassis built in 1942, of which London Transport was allocated seventy-one, were designed to be powered by the Gardner 5LW engine but the specification was then changed and all subsequent examples had an extended bonnet to make them suitable for either the 5LW or 6LW engine. London Transport was allocated a total of 435 Guy Arab chassis, all of them with the 5LW engine, although from G 72 onwards they had the longer bonnet. Dispensation was given under Defence Regulations to allow these later Arabs to exceed the maximum permitted overall length of twenty-six feet, so that no adjustment to the body was needed and there was no loss of passenger capacity. Bodywork on Guys built before the middle of 1945 was also to strict austerity standards with no curves nor embellishments, no glazing in the rear upper deck emergency window, only two opening windows per deck and only one single aperture indicator box. Early deliveries had leather covered spring cushioned seats but material shortages later imposed the use of wooden slatted seats;

liveries also varied from standard red and white to various shades of brown with some being finished in overall grey. From G 137 onwards the specification was gradually relaxed to include rounded roof domes, more opening windows, improved seating and side indicator boxes. Gs 137 and 138 (Weymann) and 150 (Park Royal) were early prototypes for post-war production and had metal framed bodywork with a higher standard of finish.

Apart from one Duple body on G 43, Park Royal and Weymann were the main suppliers of bodywork until 1945 when first Massey then Northern Counties were added, both with distinctively different designs, and finally Northern Coach-builders who built twenty-six sub-contracted from Park Royal. Massey produced one of the most angular of the austerity designs, with no curves even on those bodies built under the relaxed specification. The Northern Counties version was metal-framed and had a smoother outline with a heavily curved rear upper deck almost giving it the appearance of a peacetime product. The Northern Coach-builders' bodies were identical to the Park Royal product. The Park Royal body of G 30 was destroyed by bombing in July 1944 and replaced by a new austerity Northern Coachbuilders body later that year. After the war, the earlier bodies were gradually brought up to the enhanced specification by the fitting of additional windows, ventilators at the front of the upper deck, side route indicator boxes and moquette upholstery.

The first Guys had gone into service at Tottenham garage on route 76 in December 1942 and they were eventually allocated to nine garages, mainly in east and north-east London, although the allocation to Victoria in 1945 was quickly abandoned. At the beginning of 1950 seven garages were still operating Guys and one, Hornchurch, had a complete double-deck allocation of Guys. The post-war fleet plan had envisaged that the wartime buses would not be replaced until 1953/1954, after the withdrawal of all pre-war buses, but the Guys in particular were unpopular with drivers and some of the class were taken out of service at Tottenham in 1950, starting modestly in March but more seriously from August, to replace STs in the training fleet. Others were used as temporary staff accommoda-tion at garages being rebuilt for the tram conversion and the chassis of G 99 did service as a fuel tanker at a temporary parking area for Brixton garage during January 1951. In April 1951 the vehicle replacement policy was changed and priority was given to removing the austerities, starting with the Guys which then disappeared rapidly. The last day of London service for the class was 24th December 1952, when only twelve were still licensed, all at Upton Park garage. At first all withdrawn Guys were scrapped but the change of government in 1951 brought about a new policy and from late 1951 they were sold for further service, notably to the Scottish Bus Group and the municipalities of Burton on Trent, Edinburgh and Lancaster. Many others were exported to Yugoslavia, Kenya, Southern Rhodesia, Ceylon, Spain and the Canary Islands.

In 1949, Guy Motors Ltd sought to enter the post-war London market by offering London Transport a version of their Arab chassis which could be adapted to take the standard RT body. G 436 was fitted with a 10.35 litre Meadows engine, a more powerful unit than the Gardner model. It also had an air operated preselective gearbox, bringing its specification up to or slightly beyond that of the RT. The chassis was otherwise a standard product and carried a Park Royal body of the type then being delivered in quantity to provincial operators. A second chassis was to have been ordered which would have been built to the same profile as the RTs and RTLs, so that LT designed bodywork, fully interchangeable between the different types, could be fitted. This order was either never placed or cancelled and the second bus was never built. G 436 was delivered to Chiswick in December 1949 and went into service at Old Kent Road garage on route 173 in January 1950. It later worked at Peckham, still on route 173, and latterly at Enfield on route 121.

Weymann supplied eighteen bodies on Arab I chassis, these having a flat dash panel, a shallower valance and a lower set destination blind box than the Park Royal. G 34, seen at North Wembley, started life in June 1943 at Tottenham and was withdrawn in October 1951. F.G. Reynolds

G 43 (classified 1/2G4) was the only Guy to be fitted with a Duple body and could be distinguished readily by the wide central pillar at the front of the upper deck. F.G. Reynolds

After the first 500 Arabs, seventy-one of which were allocated to the LPTB, the government authorised the supply of the larger 6LW Gardner engine to specified customers, which did not include London Transport. The bonnet was lengthened to make room for the longer engine and this revised version, known as the Arab II, was used for all subsequent wartime Arabs, whichever engine was fitted. The Park Royal bodies supplied for the 3G5s were identical to those on the earlier utilities but the bonnet projected beyond the front dash and the mudguards were extended forward in a reverse curve. G 109 was one of the few Guys to be painted in the 1950 livery style and is seen in Romford. Alan B. Cross

Two Guys delivered by Weymann in January and May 1945 had experimental metal-framed bodywork, with wind-down windows set in curved pans, laying the groundwork for return to peacetime practice. G 137, classified 3/3G6, was the first of these and although originally fitted with wooden slatted seats, presaged the move to 'relaxed austerity' bodywork on all subsequent vehicles. K.W. Glazier collection

Massey Bros of Wigan provided the most angular of wartime designs, even under the relaxed specification which applied to those supplied to London Transport. G 177, a 1/3G9 new in March 1945, was photographed on the old stand at Becontree Heath. F.G. Reynolds

The most handsome of the wartime bodies were those by the Northern Counties Motor Engineering Co Ltd. Its approach to the 'relaxed austerity' specification was to produce this nicely rounded and well proportioned design, enhanced by the rounded window pans which the company had been able to retain on all its utility bodies as it had secured dispensation to continue using its patented metal-framed construction throughout the war. G 171 was one of the 4/3G10s, which had opening front vents and no side destination box. The later G10/1s had no vents but did have side indicators. F.G. Reynolds

The two types of Northern Counties body, G 225 on the left and G 154, flank G 103, a Park Royal example, at New Road, Dagenham. F.W. Ivey

Chassis: Guy Arab I (1-71); Arab II (72-435); Arab III (436)

Engine: Gardner 5LW five-cylinder 7 litre 85 bhp oil; (436: Meadows 6DC430 6-cylinder 10.35 litre 130 bhp)

Transmission: Four speed sliding mesh crash with double plate clutch (1-435); Four speed air operated preselective with fluid flywheel (436).

Bodywork: Park Royal (1-29, 31, 51-136, 139-153, 194-218, 319-357, 431-435, 436); NCB (30); Weymann (32-42, 44-50, 137, 138, 369-430); Duple (43); Northern Counties (154-173, 219-257, 269-311); Massey (174-193, 258-268, 312-318, 358-368).

Capacity: UH30/26R (436: H30/26R)

L.T. chassis codes: 2G (1-10); 1/2G (11-71); 3G (72-138); 1/3G (139-435); 4G (436).

L.T. body codes: G2 (1-29, 31, 51-71), G3 (32-42, 44-50), G4 (43), G5 (72-136), G6 (137), G6/1 (138), G7 (30), G8 (139-149, 151-153, 194-205), G8/1 (206-218), G8/2 (319-357, 431-435), G9 (Massey), G10 (154-173), G10/1 (219-257, 269-311), G11 (369-430), G12 (150), G13 (436).

Built: 1942-1946 (436: 1949).

Number built: 436

Number in stock: 1.1.50: 436;
                  31.12.54: 1

G | | Date out of stock
G | | Date out of stock
G | | Date out of stock

#	Code	Date out of stock	#	Code	Date out of stock	#	Code	Date out of stock
1	GLF651	28.8.51	74	GLL574	4.4.52	147	GYE91	3.3.53
2	GLF652	25.5.51	75	GLL575	5.12.51	148	GYE92	5.3.53
3	GLF653	28.8.51	76	GLL576	14.11.52	149	GYE93	17.8.51
4	GLF654	29.6.51	77	GLL577	11.4.52	150	GYE94	10.3.53
5	GLF655	28.11.51	78	GLL578	21.11.51	151	GYE95	3.3.53
6	GLF656	4.4.52	79	GLL579	12.12.51	152	GYE96	5.3.53
7	GLF657	14.8.53	80	GLL580	1.4.53	153	GYE97	2.2.53
8	GLF658	16.11.51	81	GLL581	5.12.51	154	GYL293	30.6.52
9	GLF659	1.2.52	82	GLL582	12.12.51	155	GYL294	25.4.52
10	GLF660	4.4.52	83	GLL583	14.11.52	156	GYL295	30.6.52
11	GLF661	9.1.53	84	GLL584	9.4.52	157	GYL296	2.3.53
12	GLF662	23.10.51	85	GLL600	18.11.52	158	GYL297	4.7.52
13	GLF663	16.11.51	86	GLL585	4.4.52	159	GYL298	29.5.52
14	GLF664	23.10.51	87	GLL586	2.7.51	160	GYL299	11.3.53
15	GLF665	27.7.51	88	GLL587	12.12.51	161	GYL300	28.4.52
16	GLF666	16.11.51	89	GLL588	8.9.52	162	GYL301	29.5.52
17	GLF667	16.11.51	90	GLL589	9.4.52	163	GYL302	18.4.52
18	GLF668	27.7.51	91	GLL590	5.12.51	164	GYL303	25.4.52
19	GLF669	5.3.53	92	GLL591	4.5.51	165	GYL304	16.3.53
20	GLF670	28.8.51	93	GLL592	12.5.52	166	GYL305	25.4.52
21	GLF671	13.9.51	94	GLL593	5.9.52	167	GYL306	2.3.53
22	GLF672	27.12.51	95	GLL594	28.8.51	168	GYL307	5.12.51
23	GLF673	1.5.53	96	GLL595	30.12.52	169	GYL308	29.5.52
24	GLF674	28.8.51	97	GLL596	5.12.51	170	GYL309	4.3.53
25	GLF675	9.11.51	98	GLL597	7.6.51c	171	GYL310	21.11.51
26	GLF676	7.11.51	99	GLL598	29.6.51c	172	GYL311	4.7.52
27	GLF677	28.11.51	100	GLL599	18.7.52	173	GYL312	11.4.52
28	GLF678	28.11.51	101	GXE541	5.3.53	174	GYL313	20.12.51
29	GLF679	28.8.51	102	GXE542	8.9.52	175	GYL314	29.5.52
30	GLF680	29.12.52	103	GXE543	12.12.51	176	GYL315	11.6.52
31	GLF681	21.12.51	104	GXE544	21.4.52	177	GYL316	24.7.52
32	GLF682	29.6.51	105	GXE545	29.12.52	178	GYL317	18.12.52
33	GLF683	29.10.51	106	GXE546	26.5.52	179	GYL318	29.6.51
34	GLF684	2.3.53	107	GXE547	5.9.52	180	GYL319	25.5.51
35	GLF685	29.6.51	108	GXE548	12.12.51	181	GYL320	2.3.53
36	GLF686	5.12.51	109	GXE549	29.12.52	182	GYL321	28.8.51
37	GLF687	18.7.52	110	GXE550	15.4.53	183	GYL322	28.8.51
38	GLF688	28.11.51	111	GXE551	25.7.52	184	GYL323	17.4.52
39	GLF689	28.8.51	112	GXE552	28.11.51	185	GYL324	25.4.52
40	GLF690	28.8.51	113	GXE553	7.3.51c	186	GYL325	29.6.51
41	GLF691	17.12.51	114	GXE554	28.8.51	187	GYL326	4.5.51
42	GLF692	13.5.53	115	GXE555	29.6.51	188	GYL327	4.4.52
43	GLF693	18.7.52	116	GXE556	12.12.51	189	GYL328	10.4.52
44	GLF694	25.5.51	117	GXE557	24.2.53	190	GYL329	17.4.52
45	GLF695	29.12.52	118	GXE558	13.5.53	191	GYL330	28.8.51
46	GLF696	13.12.51	119	GXE559	23.4.52	192	GYL331	28.1.52
47	GLF697	17.12.51	120	GXE560	11.4.52	193	GYL332	2.3.53
48	GLF698	23.10.51	121	GXE561	25.4.52	194	GYL333	28.5.52
49	GLF699	5.12.51	122	GXE562	25.7.52	195	GYL334	12.8.53
50	GLF700	7.6.51	123	GXE563	5.9.52	196	GYL335	28.11.51
51	GLL551	28.11.51	124	GXE564	20.12.51	197	GYL336	28.4.52
52	GLL552	28.8.51	125	GXE565	23.12.52	198	GYL337	13.5.52
53	GLL553	5.11.51	126	GXE566	25.5.51	199	GYL338	29.6.51
54	GLL554	5.12.51	127	GXE567	3.5.51	200	GYL339	17.1.52
55	GLL555	5.12.51	128	GXE568	27.5.52	201	GYL340	28.11.51
56	GLL556	5.5.53	129	GXE569	18.12.52	202	GYL341	18.4.52
57	GLL557	5.5.53	130	GXE570	10.4.52	203	GYL342	28.1.52
58	GLL558	5.11.51	131	GXE571	24.7.52	204	GYL343	28.11.51
59	GLL559	28.8.51	132	GXE572	7.3.52	205	GYL344	28.4.52
60	GLL560	15.4.53	133	GXE573	17.1.52	206	GYL345	21.4.52
61	GLL561	5.12.51	134	GXE574	17.12.51	207	GYL346	28.8.51
62	GLL562	28.11.51	135	GXE575	17.7.52	208	GYL347	28.4.52
63	GLL563	13.12.51	136	GXE576	29.6.51	209	GYL348	17.1.52
64	GLL564	16.11.51	137	GXV793	30.12.52	210	GYL349	14.4.52
65	GLL565	29.10.51	138	GXV794	29.5.52	211	GYL350	5.12.51
66	GLL566	3.3.53	139	GYE83	3.3.53	212	GYL351	21.4.52
67	GLL567	7.11.51	140	GYE84	19.3.53	213	GYL352	21.4.52
68	GLL568	2.1.53	141	GYE85	13.3.53	214	GYL353	16.4.52
69	GLL569	1.4.53	142	GYE86	13.5.53	215	GYL354	23.4.52
70	GLL570	15.5.53	143	GYE87	16.2.53	216	GYL355	12.12.51
71	GLL571	26.10.51	144	GYE88	13.5.53	217	GYL356	12.12.51
72	GLL572	5.12.52	145	GYE89	13.4.53	218	GYL357	28.11.51
73	GLL573	7.3.51c	146	GYE90	5.3.53	219	GYL358	10.6.52

G		Date out of stock	G		Date out of stock	G		Date out of stock
220	GYL359	18.4.52	293	GYL433	19.3.53	366	HGC145	28.11.51
221	GYL360	11.3.53	294	GYL434	3.3.53	367	HGC146	28.11.51
222	GYL361	14.4.52	295	GYL435	4.5.52	368	HGC147	5.12.51
223	GYL362	11.4.52	296	GYL436	24.2.53	369	HGC148	21.11.51
224	GYL363	4.7.52	297	GYL437	19.3.53	370	HGC149	9.1.52
225	GYL364	4.7.52	298	GYL438	17.3.53	371	HGC150	21.11.51
226	GYL365	4.7.52	299	GYL439	17.3.53	372	HGC151	13.5.53
227	GYL366	16.4.52	300	GYL440	21.7.52	373	HGC152	12.12.51
228	GYL367	11.7.52	301	GYL441	17.3.53	374	HGC153	29.1.52
229	GYL368	11.7.52	302	GYL442	23.4.52	375	HGC154	5.12.51
230	GYL369	11.7.52	303	GYL443	4.5.52	376	HGC155	21.11.51
231	GYL370	16.4.52	304	GYL444	24.2.53	377	HGC156	30.4.52
232	GYL371	11.7.52	305	GYL445	4.5.52	378	HGC157	5.12.51
233	GYL372	11.7.52	306	GYL446	14.4.52	379	HGC158	21.11.51
234	GYL373	11.7.52	307	GYL447	13.9.51	380	HGC159	5.12.51
235	GYL374	4.3.53	308	GYL448	19.3.53	381	HGC160	5.12.51
236	GYL375	9.3.53	309	GYL449	19.3.53	382	HGC161	6.5.52
237	GYL376	11.7.52	310	GYL450	24.2.53	383	HGC162	29.6.51
238	GYL377	2.3.53	311	GYL451	17.3.53	384	HGC163	28.11.51
239	GYL378	28.4.52	312	GYL452	6.11.51	385	HGC164	9.1.52
240	GYL379	9.3.53	313	GYL453	9.4.52	386	HGC165	15.2.52
241	GYL380	4.3.53	314	GYL454	4.5.52	387	HGC166	28.11.51
242	GYL381	21.11.51	315	GYL455	29.6.51	388	HGC167	6.5.52
243	GYL382	21.11.51	316	GYL456	4.3.53	389	HGC168	21.3.52
244	GYL383	28.11.51	317	GYL457	17.4.52	390	HGC169	28.8.51
245	GYL384	10.6.52	318	GYL458	29.6.51	391	HGC170	29.1.52
246	GYL385	10.6.52	319	GYL459	2.2.53	392	HGC171	13.5.53
247	GYL386	30.4.52	320	GYL460	22.1.52	393	HGC172	2.7.51
248	GYL387	10.6.52	321	HGC100	4.5.52	394	HGC173	7.6.51
249	GYL388	17.6.52	322	HGC101	13.9.51	395	HGC174	2.3.53
250	GYL389	30.4.52	323	HGC102	27.3.53	396	HGC175	15.2.52
251	GYL390	30.4.52	324	HGC103	5.2.53	397	HGC176	15.2.52
252	GYL391	4.3.53	325	HGC104	7.1.52	398	HGC177	21.4.52
253	GYL392	2.3.53	326	HGC105	26.3.53	399	HGC178	20.3.52
254	GYL393	2.3.53	327	HGC106	15.5.53	400	HGC179	5.12.51
255	GYL394	16.4.52	328	HGC107	1.4.53	401	HGC180	1.11.51
256	GYL395	11.3.53	329	HGC108	12.12.51	402	HGC181	14.4.52
257	GYL396	4.3.53	330	HGC109	13.5.53	403	HGC182	18.4.52
258	GYL397	30.4.52	331	HGC110	9.3.53	404	HGC183	9.1.53
259	GYL398	3.5.51	332	HGC111	17.1.52	405	HGC184	1.10.51
260	GYL399	28.8.51	333	HGC112	13.4.53	406	HGC185	5.12.51
261	GYL400	17.1.52	334	HGC113	21.11.51	407	HGC186	12.12.51
262	GYL401	19.9.51c	335	HGC114	12.8.53	408	HGC187	16.12.52
263	GYL402	31.12.52	336	HGC115	4.9.53	409	HGC188	21.11.51
264	GYL403	23.4.52	337	HGC116	10.3.53	410	HGC189	14.8.53
265	GYL404	2.5.52	338	HGC117	9.3.53	411	HGC190	28.11.51
266	GYL405	7.1.52	339	HGC118	10.3.53	412	HGC191	21.11.51
267	GYL406	28.1.52	340	HGC119	13.5.53	413	HGC192	15.2.52
268	GYL407	7.6.51	341	HGC120	28.11.51	414	HGC193	28.11.51
269	GYL409	17.6.52	342	HGC121	13.4.53	415	HGC194	5.2.53
270	GYL410	2.5.52	343	HGC122	12.12.51	416	HGC195	7.1.52
271	GYL411	17.6.52	344	HGC123	5.12.51	417	HGC196	3.3.52
272	GYL412	2.5.52	345	HGC124	16.4.52	418	HGC197	21.11.51
273	GYL413	9.3.53	346	HGC125	2.2.53	419	HGC198	11.4.52
274	GYL414	17.6.52	347	HGC126	13.5.53	420	HGC199	21.11.51
275	GYL415	6.5.52	348	HGC127	1.4.53	421	HGC200	18.4.52
276	GYL416	17.6.52	349	HGC128	13.5.53	422	HGC201	14.8.53
277	GYL417	30.6.52	350	HGC129	13.5.53	423	HGC202	21.11.51
278	GYL418	30.6.52	351	HGC130	1.4.53	424	HGC203	12.12.51
279	GYL419	30.6.52	352	HGC131	29.12.52	425	HGC204	26.3.53
280	GYL420	2.5.52	353	HGC132	14.4.52	426	HGC205	15.5.53
281	GYL421	9.3.53	354	HGC133	9.3.53	427	HGC206	14.5.53
282	GYL422	11.3.53	355	HGC134	6.5.53	428	HGC207	12.3.53
283	GYL423	11.3.53	356	HGC135	13.5.53	429	HGC208	21.11.51
284	GYL424	16.3.53	357	HGC136	13.3.53	430	HGC209	23.4.52
285	GYL425	2.5.52	358	HGC137	23.4.52	431	HGC210	14.3.52
286	GYL426	21.7.52	359	HGC138	15.5.53	432	HGC211	13.5.53
287	GYL427	16.3.53	360	HGC139	12.12.51	433	HGC212	14.3.52
288	GYL428	16.3.53	361	HGC140	28.11.51	434	HGC213	4.3.53
289	GYL429	16.3.53	362	HGC141	29.6.51	435	HGC214	29.12.52
290	GYL430	9.3.53	363	HGC142	12.12.51	436	KGK981	
291	GYL431	17.3.53	364	HGC143	28.11.51			
292	GYL432	24.2.53	365	HGC144	5.12.51			

The first Daimlers received by London Transport were six lowbridge vehicles with bodywork by Duple Motor Bodies of Hendon, delivered in the spring of 1944. The mechanical specification of the CWA6, with preselective gearbox, fluid flywheel and AEC 7.7 litre oil engine very nearly matched that of the pre-war STL. They were allocated to Merton garage for route 127, thus determining the home for all 181 austerity Daimlers. A further four with relaxed austerity bodywork (2/1D1/1), as shown by D 129, completed the number needed for route 127. Alan B. Cross

D

Daimler resumed production of PSVs at a temporary factory in Wolverhampton from the end of 1942, standardising at first on the Gardner 5LW engine in the CWG5 model and retaining the pre-war Daimler specification of preselective gearbox and fluid transmission. It was therefore the least austerity of the wartime models. No CWG5s were allocated to London Transport who were able to wait for the new CWA6 which became available when AEC was authorised to resume production of engines during 1943. The Board was eventually allocated 281 CW chassis, 181 of which had austerity bodywork by either Brush or Duple the development of whose specification followed the same course as the Guys. The first six (D 1-6), which went into service in April and May 1944, had Brush lowbridge bodywork, for use on route 127 from Merton garage. A further four lowbridge examples (D 128-131), this time with Duple 'relaxed austerity' bodywork, went into service at the end of 1945. Twelve of the final batch with Duple bodywork had a modified chassis incorporating the new Daimler 8.6 litre CD6 engine and also a new Daimler rear axle. They were classified CWD6. Most of the austerity Daimlers were allocated to Merton garage but thirty-seven of those licensed at the beginning of 1946 were finished in Green Line colours and went to Romford garage for the post-war resumption of Green Line operation.

Duple also supplied over half the highbridge bodies for the wartime Daimlers, the first forty-eight of which were 1/1D2 or 2/1s, like D 89, to full austerity specification. J.H. Aston

The last hundred Ds had Park Royal bodywork of a transitional design based on utility framework but with a more curved rear end and with various items of trim, including radiused window pans, which softened the design. Interior trim was also closer to normal peacetime standards, including standard LT moquette. These were the first vehicles to have provision for full indicator displays since the STL17s and RT2s, although they were never used. They were allocated to Sutton garage and remained there until withdrawn.

The Green Line Daimlers were replaced by standard RTs in August 1950 and remained unused for several months before being returned to service at Merton garage, at first still painted green but with standard 'London Transport' fleet names. Because of their superior specification, the Daimlers were the last austerity vehicles to be taken out of service. Final withdrawal started in August 1952 more or less simultaneously at both Merton and Sutton. The last days of operation were 18th December 1952 for the lowbridge type and 8th January 1953 for both highbridge types. All 281 were sold for further service, significant numbers going to Belfast Corporation (100), Southend Corporation (13), Samuel Ledgard of Leeds (30), Trimdon Motor Services (10), Beeline Roadways of Hartlepool (8) and overseas to the South Western Omnibus Company in Colombo, Ceylon (83). The remainder went to various independent operators in Scotland and the north of England.

Distinguishing features of the Brush bodies which graced seventy-three Daimlers were the series of slanting vents above the lower deck saloon windows and the more raked front end. Despite the advertisement carried by D 98 (a 1/1D3/1) on the approach to Morden, it was not one of the 100 which eventually found their way to Belfast. F.G. Reynolds

D 160 was originally a CWD6 with Duple 'relaxed' austerity bodywork (2D2/2) but, like the remainder, had its Daimler engine replaced by an AEC 7.7 litre taken from a withdrawn STL in April 1950. F.G. Reynolds

Thirty-seven of the final batch of 'relaxed' Duple bodied Daimlers, all CWA6s, were set aside for operation on the Romford Green Line services when they restarted in 1946, the only concession to their unique role being their livery. They were replaced by RTs in 1950 and were transferred later to Merton, where they were eventually repainted red. D 174 is seen in original condition at Aldgate. K.W. Glazier collection

The last hundred CWA6s received Park Royal bodywork of an even more relaxed standard, with windows set in pans, half-drop opening windows at the front, a more curved rear dome and a high standard of interior trim. They also had a full set of indicators, front side and rear, but these were never used. All went to Sutton garage, where they became the sole type for a time. D 205 is at Belmont towards the end of its life alongside a new RF and sharing the stand with staff canteen 693J, formerly and latterly ST 922. J.H. Aston

Chassis: Daimler CWA6 (or CWD6 - code 2D)
Engine: AEC A173 direct injection 7.7 litre 95 bhp oil; or Daimler CD6 8.6 litre 100 bhp oil (code 2D)
Transmission: Daimler four speed preselective with fluid flywheel.
Bodywork: Duple (1-34, 74-92, 128-181); Brush (35-73, 93-127); Park Royal (182-281).
Capacity: UH30/26R (1-6 and 128-131: UL27/28R); or H30/26R (182-281)
L.T. chassis code: 1D (1-6); 1/1D (7-115; 2/1D 116-126, 132-137, 141, 143-149, 151-154, 156-159, 161, 164-170, 172-179); 3/1D (182-281); 2D (127, 138-140, 142, 150, 155, 160, 162, 163, 171, 180, 181).
L.T. body codes: D1 (1-6); D1/1 (128-131); D2 (7-34); D2/1 (74-92); D2/2 (132-181); D3 (35-61); D3/1 (62-73); D3/2 (93-115); D3/3 (116-126); D3/4 (127); D4 (182-281).
Built: 1944-1946
Number built: 281
Number in stock: 1.1.50: 281   31.12.54: Nil

D		Date out of stock	D		Date out of stock	D		Date out of stock
1	GXE578	7.1.53	49	GXV780	25.11.53	97	GYL262	11.5.53
2	GXE579	22.12.52	50	GXV781	24.11.53	98	GYL263	21.5.53
3	GXE580	29.12.52	51	GXV782	7.9.53	99	GYL264	3.9.53
4	GXE581	7.1.53	52	GXV783	27.1.54	100	GYL265	22.12.52
5	GXE582	29.12.52	53	GXV784	29.1.54	101	GYL266	15.5.53
6	GXE583	29.12.52	54	GXV785	7.9.53	102	GYL267	24.11.53
7	GXE584	18.11.52	55	GXV786	27.11.53	103	GYL268	15.9.53
8	GXE585	15.5.53	56	GXV787	15.10.53	104	GYL269	15.10.53
9	GXE586	22.12.52	57	GXV788	25.11.53	105	GYL270	3.9.53
10	GXE587	15.5.53	58	GXV789	4.9.53	106	GYL271	14.10.53
11	GXE588	11.9.53	59	GXV790	14.10.53	107	GYL272	16.10.53
12	GXE589	14.9.53	60	GXV791	15.5.53	108	GYL273	19.1.54
13	GXE590	14.9.53	61	GXV792	27.11.53	109	GYL274	30.11.53
14	GLX900	7.1.53	62	GYE51	11.9.53	110	GYL275	15.10.53
15	GLX901	7.9.53	63	GYE52	10.9.53	111	GYL276	14.9.53
16	GLX902	11.9.53	64	GYE53	11.9.53	112	GYL277	3.9.53
17	GLX903	7.9.53	65	GYE54	28.10.53	113	GYL278	14.10.53
18	GLX904	7.9.53	66	GYE55	14.9.53	114	GYL279	14.10.53
19	GLX905	16.10.53	67	GYE56	14.9.53	115	GYL280	14.10.53
20	GLX906	14.9.53	68	GYE57	30.11.53	116	GYL281	18.1.54
21	GLX907	30.11.53	69	GYE58	18.1.54	117	GYL282	2.12.53
22	GLX908	14.9.53	70	GYE59	7.12.53	118	GYL283	8.9.53
23	GLX909	11.9.53	71	GYE60	27.1.54	119	GYL284	15.10.53
24	GLX910	25.11.53	72	GYE61	14.9.53	120	GYL285	18.1.54
25	GLX911	25.11.53	73	GYE62	18.1.54	121	GYL286	18.1.54
26	GLX912	30.11.53	74	GYE64	10.9.53	122	GYL287	1.12.52
27	GLX913	11.3.53	75	GYE65	14.10.53	123	GYL288	25.11.53
28	GLX914	14.10.53	76	GYE66	10.9.53	124	GYL289	8.9.53
29	GLX915	30.12.52	77	GYE67	9.9.53	125	GYL290	7.9.53
30	GLX916	20.10.53	78	GYE68	9.9.53	126	GYL291	11.5.53
31	GLX917	9.9.53	79	GYE69	8.9.53	127	GYL292	26.11.53
32	GLX918	4.9.53	80	GYE70	8.12.53	128	HGC255	24.12.52
33	GLX919	25.11.53	81	GYE71	10.9.53	129	HGC256	22.12.52
34	GLX920	8.9.53	82	GYE72	7.12.53	130	HGC257	30.12.52
35	GLX921	27.11.53	83	GYE73	25.11.53	131	HGC258	30.12.52
36	GLX922	27.11.53	84	GYE74	11.5.53	132	HGC259	15.10.53
37	GLX923	14.9.53	85	GYE75	1.12.53	133	HGC260	19.1.54
38	GLX924	25.11.53	86	GYE76	11.5.53	134	HGC261	15.1.54
39	GXV770	1.12.52	87	GYE77	7.9.53	135	HGC262	16.10.53
40	GXV771	10.9.53	88	GYE78	1.12.53	136	HGC263	29.1.54
41	GXV772	20.10.53	89	GYE79	7.9.53	137	HGC264	14.1.54
42	GXV773	4.9.53	90	GYE80	10.9.53	138	HGC265	11.9.53
43	GXV774	24.11.53	91	GYE81	28.10.53	139	HGC266	16.10.53
44	GXV775	25.11.53	92	GYE82	15.10.53	140	HGC267	3.9.53
45	GXV776	8.9.53	93	GYE98	14.9.53	141	HGC268	19.1.54
46	GXV777	24.11.53	94	GYE99	14.10.53	142	HGC269	14.10.53
47	GXV778	25.11.53	95	GYE100	16.2.54	143	HGC270	2.12.53
48	GXV779	10.9.53	96	GYL261	21.5.53	144	HGC271	1.12.53

D		Date out of stock	D		Date out of stock	D		Date out of stock
145	HGC272	26.11.53	191	HGF868	4.9.53	237	HGF914	26.1.54
146	HGC273	3.9.53	192	HGF869	8.9.53	238	HGF915	28.5.53
147	HGC274	15.1.54	193	HGF870	3.9.53	239	HGF916	24.2.53
148	HGC275	30.11.53	194	HGF871	8.9.53	240	HGF917	6.3.53
149	HGC276	11.5.53	195	HGF872	15.10.53	241	HGF918	24.2.53
150	HGC277	14.9.53	196	HGF873	9.9.53	242	HGF919	19.2.53
151	HGC278	15.1.54	197	HGF874	15.10.53	243	HGF920	24.12.52
152	HGC279	27.3.53	198	HGF875	1.12.53	244	HGF921	22.12.52
153	HGC280	27.3.53	199	HGF876	12.1.54	245	HGF922	22.12.52
154	HGC281	3.9.53	200	HGF877	13.10.53	246	HGF923	31.3.53
155	HGC282	26.11.53	201	HGF878	14.1.54	247	HGF924	23.12.52
156	HGC283	16.10.53	202	HGF879	5.1.54	248	HGF925	11.12.52
157	HGC284	15.9.53	203	HGF880	8.12.53	249	HGF926	31.12.52
158	HGC285	3.12.52	204	HGF881	7.12.53	250	HGF927	14.1.54
159	HGC286	14.5.53	205	HGF882	7.12.53	251	HGF928	24.12.52
160	HGC287	3.12.52	206	HGF883	30.11.53	252	HGF929	3.12.52
161	HGC288	27.3.53	207	HGF884	7.12.53	253	HGF930	3.12.52
162	HGC289	16.10.53	208	HGF885	7.12.53	254	HGF931	14.1.54
163	HGC290	16.10.53	209	HGF886	30.11.53	255	HGF932	30.12.52
164	HGC291	26.11.53	210	HGF887	11.1.54	256	HGF933	23.12.52
165	HGC292	27.3.53	211	HGF888	27.1.54	257	HGF934	31.12.52
166	HGC293	30.12.52	212	HGF889	27.11.53	258	HGF935	22.12.52
167	HGC294	31.3.53	213	HGF890	11.1.54	259	HGF936	13.1.54
168	HGC295	29.12.52	214	HGF891	27.1.54	260	HGF937	13.4.53
169	HGC296	1.4.53	215	HGF892	14.1.54	261	HGF938	13.4.53
170	HGC297	22.12.52	216	HGF893	7.12.53	262	HGF939	22.12.52
171	HGC298	24.12.52	217	HGF894	20.1.54	263	HGF940	17.3.53
172	HGC299	20.5.53	218	HGF895	7.12.53	264	HGF941	18.11.52
173	HGF800	11.5.53	219	HGF896	13.1.54	265	HGF942	3.12.52
174	HGF801	26.11.53	220	HGF897	6.3.53	266	HGF943	24.12.52
175	HGF802	16.3.53	221	HGF898	20.1.54	267	HGF944	23.12.52
176	HGF803	16.3.53	222	HGF899	7.12.53	268	HGF945	11.5.53
177	HGF804	16.4.53	223	HGF900	8.12.53	269	HGF946	8.12.53
178	HGF805	15.4.53	224	HGF901	15.1.54	270	HGF947	19.2.53
179	HGF806	20.3.53	225	HGF902	30.12.52	271	HGF948	14.4.53
180	HGF807	23.12.52	226	HGF903	14.1.54	272	HGF949	13.4.53
181	HGF808	29.12.52	227	HGF904	18.2.53	273	HGF950	11.12.52
182	HGF859	10.9.53	228	HGF905	16.2.54	274	HGF951	25.2.53
183	HGF860	8.9.53	229	HGF906	30.12.52	275	HGF952	10.3.53
184	HGF861	10.9.53	230	HGF907	26.1.54	276	HGF953	16.4.53
185	HGF862	10.9.53	231	HGF908	27.1.54	277	HGF954	13.3.53
186	HGF863	15.10.53	232	HGF909	3.12.52	278	HGF955	20.2.53
187	HGF864	4.9.53	233	HGF910	27.1.54	279	HGF956	17.4.53
188	HGF865	3.9.53	234	HGF911	24.2.53	280	HGF957	20.3.53
189	HGF866	11.9.53	235	HGF912	22.12.52	281	HGF958	13.4.53
190	HGF867	11.9.53	236	HGF913	20.2.53			

The bodywork of the 2RT2s established the basic design used for the post-war model but showed its late 1930s provenance in the curved driver's cab window and windscreen, both hallmarks of the stream-lining craze of the period. Other external recognition features were the position of the destination blind above the 'via' box and the seven inlet grilles for the cab ventilator on the dash. Although not visible in this photograph of RT 71 at Morden station in December 1951, a roof route number box was also fitted at the rear. The vertical route number plate holder on the nearside bulkhead pillar, added to those allocated to Putney Bridge in 1946, fell into disuse in later years. Alan B. Cross

RT

The RT was a development of the AEC Regent chassis as used in the STL class but with an engine design strongly influenced by Leyland practice, following London Transport's successful operation of the one hundred 1937 Leyland Titans. At the end of the 1930s London Transport adopted a policy of having large engines, with a derated power output to improve fuel economy and engine life and the engine chosen for the RT was the AEC A185 9.6 litre unit, which developed 100 bhp at 1,800 rpm. The well tried Wilson type preselective gearbox and fluid flywheel were of the type used on the STL class but were actuated by compressed air, as were the brakes. Other features of the design were flexible engine mountings, improved and lighter steering, automatic chassis lubrication, automatic brake adjusters and a low bonnet and radiator. The prototype chassis first operated in service from Hanwell garage (HW) on route 18C between 13th July and 31st December 1938 with the number ST 1140, under a six year old

Six 2RT2s were fitted experimentally with quarter drop windows in 1947–1949, anticipating their adoption as standard on the RF class. RT 121 was one of eighteen drafted into New Cross garage for the final tram conversion in July 1952 and is seen at Woolwich soon afterwards. Alan B. Cross

fifty-six seat Dodson open staircase body originally carried by TD 111. A revolutionary new design of metal framed body, built at Chiswick Works, was then fitted and the vehicle numbered RT 1. The new body was of four bay construction and notable for its graceful curves, including the combined bulkhead and front wing assembly. Roof route number boxes were carried at both front and rear. RT 1 went into service on 9th August 1939.

Meanwhile an order had been placed for a production batch of 150, subsequently increased to 338 and the intention was to manufacture up to 527 a year from 1940 onwards. Following the outbreak of war on 3rd September 1939, government restrictions were placed on the construction of chassis for civilian use and the order for the last 188 was suspended. The 2RT2s (2-151) differed from RT 1 in having composite bodywork but only minor changes were made to the design and the mechanical specification was the same. Although often referred to incorrectly as 'pre-war' RTs, the RT2s were all built during the war, starting at the end of 1939, and the first did not enter service until 2nd January 1940 at Chelverton Road. Others went to Putney Bridge and Victoria. Towards the end of the programme deliveries slowed down and the last did not enter service until 1st February 1942.

In 1945 the chassis of RT 19 was remodelled as the prototype for the post-war version. This was similar to the 2RT but had a new engine, the A204, with toroidal cavity pistons and an increased power output of 125 bhp at 1,800 rpm (derated by LT to 115 bhp). The extension behind the rear axle was omitted as the platform on the new bodies was to be self-supporting. The only variations from this standard during the entire production run were those modified for Green Line (1/3RT). The RT3 bodies were also very similar in appearance to the RT2 but without a rear route number box and without the downward curve of the windscreen. Technically the bodies were more advanced, being metal framed and designed for complete interchangeability of all parts. The RT3 was a transient design as the standard body was intended to have no roof route number box at the front and an illuminated route number box under the canopy. The last hundred Park Royal (RT 752-851) and fifty Weymann (RT 962-1011) RT3s had an interim modification incorporating a route number plate under the canopy and trafficator housings and were also made suitable for mounting on both AEC and Leyland chassis. These were recoded RT10 in about 1951. The final modified design was coded RT3/1 and appeared from October 1948, after 450 Park Royal and 300 Weymann bodied buses had been built. The trafficator housing on these and the RT10s was plated over and the equipment was not fitted to·most vehicles, although 135 RT3/1s (and sixty-five RTLs) were fitted with them experimentally for a time from November 1949. These vehicles were also fitted with driver's cab heaters, a feature which was eventually extended to the whole class. From February 1949 modifications were made to the body mountings to make them compatible with the SRT class for which a new code RT8 was allocated. Later Green Line versions were coded RT8/1 and bodies built after December 1952 had a modified bulkhead and were classified RT8/2.

Delivery of chassis from AEC began at the end of March 1946 but there were serious delays in the manufacture of bodies by Park Royal and Weymann and the first 3RT3 (RT 402) did not go into service until 10th May 1947, at Leyton garage. Because of these delays, London Transport ordered additional bodies, 300 from the Saunders Engineering and Shipyard Company of Beaumaris, Anglesey and 120 from Cravens Ltd of Sheffield. The Saunders bodies (classified RT3/3) were virtually identical to the RT3, the distinguishing feature being their offside route number plate which was further back; but the Cravens (RT3/4) were stock products with five bay construction, a more upright front and more curved back but with a standard indicator layout, including a roof route number box. The Saunders were delivered between September 1948 and February 1951 and the Cravens between September 1948 and April 1950. Other odd men out were RTs 2116-2121 which received second hand bodies recovered from the works float when new in 1950. A late arrival, also in 1950, was RT 657 (KLB712) whose original body and registration number had been appropriated for proto-type RTL 501 in 1948. Another registration oddity was RT 4668, which was fitted with the body of RTL 1337 when that bus returned from MIRA in 1953 and, unusually, also took the registration reserved for it (MXX40). Twenty-two float bodies were built altogether, fifteen being the last RT bodies built by Park Royal, which were stored on redundant SRT chassis at New Cross garage until required for the new overhaul system at Aldenham.

Right **This nearside view of RT 155 at Victoria shows the route number plate in the nearside front bulkhead pillar which was incorporated as a transitional stop-gap until the design could be changed to incorporate an illuminated blind under the canopy.** F.G. Reynolds

Superficially the 3RT3 differed little from the 2RT2, although the straight line of the cab windows, the reduced size of the cab ventilator grille and the absence of a rear roof number box gave it a cleaner and more modern look. Underneath it was significantly different, having jig-built metal framed bodywork and self-supporting platform. RT 406, outside South Africa House in November 1951, typifies the appearance of the class in the early 1950s, the vehicle having received full blinds at its first overhaul. Alan B. Cross

During the period under review a number of RTs were used for overseas trade promotion visits, the first being RTs 1692, 1702, 3070 and 3114 which made a grand tour of continental Europe in 1950, covering about 4,000 miles, on loan to the Festival of Britain authorities. In 1952 RTs 2775 and 2776, in company with RTL 1307, were hired by the British Travel and Holidays Association to make a 12,000 mile tour of north America. RT 2776 was used to give rides, for which duty it was equipped with additional ventilators to combat the heat of the southern States. Two were fitted in the front dome in the form of semi-circular grilles and a third under the canopy. Other trips were made by RT 3710 (with RTL 1459) to Zurich and Malmô in 1953 and RT 4760 (the last red RT from Weymann) to Maastricht in 1954. All these vehicles retained their GB plates and their individual identity when overhauled.

Post-war RT deliveries continued until November 1954, when the number of RTs in stock reached its maximum of 4820, the last into stock being Weymann RT 4794. Eighty-one of the new green RTs did not enter service immediately but went straight into store at Loughton garage, as there was no immediate use for them. They were RTs 4543-4556, 4747-4759 and 4761-4794.

Withdrawal of RTs had started as early as 1946 when the chassis of RT 1 was scrapped, its body being used on post-war prototype RT 19 indirectly replacing that of RT 66 which was destroyed during the war. RT 22 overturned in icy conditions on Wimbledon Hill in 1951 and was a write-off. RT 97 was converted to RTC 1 in 1949 and RT 85 was destroyed by fire while in service on route 74 in May 1949. RT 19, still with the body of RT 1, was transferred to the Miscellaneous vehicle fleet in September 1954 as an instruction chassis and renumbered 1020J. RT 3995 was withdrawn from service in March 1951, soon after being licensed, and became a permanent test bed for the Chiswick Works experimental shop.

The first green RT3s, identical to the Central Bus version, went into service at Tring and Two Waters garages in July 1948. The layout of their livery was the same as the red version except that the mudguards were green, not black. Route number plates were carried at first but that soon came to an end because of the complications of Country Bus scheduling. Weymann RT 618, one of Two Waters's inaugural twenty-three, is seen at Hemel Hempstead. Alan B. Cross

An interim stage towards the standard body design was applied to the last one hundred Park Royal and fifty Weymann RT3s, later classified RT10, on which a route number plate was installed under the canopy. Another new feature introduced with this type of body was the housing for semaphore trafficators, the nearside one of which was attached in a vertical oblong box to the corner pillar of the front bulkhead, as seen on green RT 962, the first Weymann of the type. They were never used and remained plated over. F.G. Reynolds

London Transport decided in October 1946 that the standard post-war RT body would not have a roof route number box but the design, coded RT3/1, did not appear until the autumn of 1948. RT 1083 was one of the early Weymann examples, first licensed in December 1948, but by the time it was photographed at St Mary's Square, Hitchin, it had been repainted into the 1950 livery and received a full blind display. F.G. Reynolds

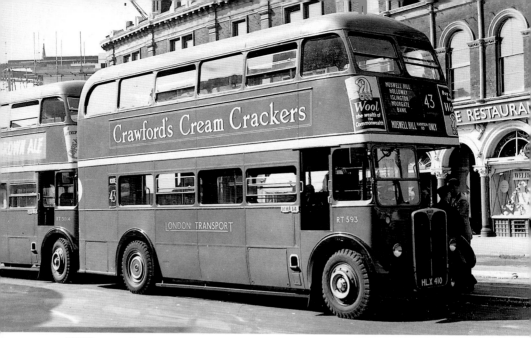

RT 593, seen at London Bridge station after being overhauled, was one of six which exchanged their original RT3 bodies for new 3/1s in 1948, to create a small float of bodies to cover repairs. One of the purposes of this design was to put the number indicator nearer the kerb so that intending passengers could see it more clearly. F.G. Reynolds

From February 1949 the body mountings on the RT were altered to enable full interchangeability with SRTs and the body code was altered to RT8. There was no visible difference and this photograph of RT 2474, a 3RT8, at Old Town, Clapham Common, shows how both the RT3/1 and early RT8 bodies looked when new, with cream upper deck window surrounds and restricted blinds. Just visible is the amended design of nearside wing, incorporating a rubber section inserted between the main body and the mudguard, to counteract cracking at the junction between the bulkhead and the wing assembly.
F.G. Reynolds

The other new feature introduced with the RT3/1 was an illuminated route number blind under the canopy, which can be seen shining out in this photograph of RT 2227 (a 3RT8) at Armoury Way, Wandsworth. J.H. Aston

Full blind displays were restored to new green RTs from May 1950, during a delivery to Godstone garage, five months before they returned to Central Area buses. RT 3138, parked at Reigate garage, was the second bus so treated. F.G. Reynolds

The Saunders Engineering & Shipyard Company made such an excellent job of copying the RT3 design that the only external clue was the position of the offside route number plate, midway along the staircase panel, although they were structurally quite different. The company's performance earned them a repeat order for fifty (RT 4218-4267). RT 4229 was one of a batch allocated to Victoria for route 137, but was photographed in July 1952 working the Sunday-only allocation on route 134. When they appeared in the autumn of 1950, these were the only new vehicles still being built with roofboxes. Alan B. Cross

Unlike Saunders, the Cravens Railway Carriage & Wagon Company Ltd made little attempt to modify its standard product to resemble the standard design, producing instead this distinctive product with an indicator layout based on the later RT3. The first twenty-seven were allocated to the Country Bus department and were concentrated at Watford (High Street) and Windsor garages. RT 1406 was in its original condition when photographed on route 351.

The frontal curve of the Cravens body was flatter than the standard version and they were the only RTs built with five bay bodywork, but the rear was more rounded and the overall effect was attractive. Central Buses did not single out the Cravens for special treatment and they were scattered around the fleet in small numbers. RT 1442 is the example illustrated. S. A. Newman

Although given the new code 3RT8/1, the Green Line version of the RT which took to the road in August 1950, was identical to the bus variety except for its livery and the metal 'Green Line' bullseyes attached to the upper deck side panels. RT 3259, in familiar surroundings at Aldgate, carries the orange-on-green route and destination blinds with which the RTs were originally supplied.
F.G. Reynolds

RT 2775 was one of three buses which toured north America in 1952 on behalf of the British Travel and Holiday Association, when it had the dual roles of crew quarters (upstairs) and mobile workshop. Like many such celebrities, it saw service on the Circular Tour of London, on which it is seen in Buckingham Palace Road on a day the BTHA might prefer not to advertise. F.G. Reynolds

RT 2776 was the second RT on the 1952 north American tour and was used to give rides to the locals. It was equipped with additional ventilators to combat the intense heat of the southern summer and these were retained for the rest of its life. Its first home on return to the UK was Forest Gate garage, where it was allocated when photographed in South Street, Romford. B.A. Jenkins

Newly delivered RTs nearly always appeared without external commercial advertising, as exemplified by Weymann bodied RT 3562 at Golders Green station soon after it went into service at Alperton garage in July 1952. Although there is no apparent difference, this is an early example of an RT8/2, a new code which was applied to vehicles with a re-designed and strengthened front bulkhead. F.G. Reynolds

The bodies of the SRTs were transferred to new RT chassis when the hybrid class was withdrawn, the resulting vehicles being distributed between Central, Country and Green Line. Twickenham's RT 4443, in the old unwidened Euston Road, was an example of the Central Bus allotment. Alan B. Cross

Chassis: AEC Regent III 0661 (2-151); AEC Regent 3RT 0961 (remainder)

Engine: AEC A185 (2-151) 100 bhp or A204 9.6 litre direct injection oil 125 bhp (derated to 115 bhp)

Transmission: AEC D140 4-speed air operated preselective with fluid flywheel

Bodywork: LPTB (2-151); Park Royal (originally 152-401, 652-961, 1522-2115, 2117-2121, 2522-3041, 4268-4556, 4569-4684, 4795-4825); Weymann (originally 402-651, 962-1151, 2116, 2122-2521, 3042-4217); Saunders (1152-1401, 4218-4267); Cravens (1402-1521)

Capacity: H30/26R

L.T. chassis code: 3RT (3224-3259, 4489-4509: 1/3RT)

L.T. Body codes: RT3: 152-656, 658-851, 962-1011, 2116-2121: first post-war roof-box design (752-851 and 962-1011 with canopy route number plate and trafficator housings.)

RT3/1: 852-945, 1012-1111: first design without roof-box.

RT3/3: 1152-1401, 4218-4267: Roof-box bodies built by Saunders Engineering and Shipyard, similar to RT 752 etc.

RT3/4: 1402-1521 non-standard roof box bodies built by Cravens Railway Carriage & Wagon.

RT8: 657, 946-961, 1112-1151, 1522-2829, 3042-3223, 3260-3527, 3842-4217, 4397-4556: as RT3/1 but with modified mountings for interchangeability with SRT class.;

RT8/1: 3224-3259: as RT8 but modified for Green Line service, including saloon heaters.

RT8/2: 2830-3041, 3528-3841, 4268-4396, 4557-4825: improved version of RT8, including revised front bulkhead.

RT10: Code applied to last 150 RT3 bodies (RT 752 etc) when mountings modified to allow use on RTL chassis.

Built: 1939-1942 (2-151); 1947-1954 (rest)

Number built: 4825

Number in stock: 1.1.50: 1812

31.12.54: 4820

RT		RT		RT		RT		RT	
2	FXT177	70	FXT245	139	FXT314	206	HLW193	273	HLX90
3	FXT178	71	FXT246	140	FXT315	207	HLW194	274	HLX91
4	FXT179	72	FXT247	141	FXT316	208	HLW195	275	HLX92
5	FXT180	73	FXT248	142	FXT317	209	HLW196	276	HLX93
6	FXT181	74	FXT249	143	FXT318	210	HLW197	277	HLX94
7	FXT182	75	FXT250	144	FXT319	211	HLW198	278	HLX95
8	FXT183	76	FXT251	145	FXT320	212	HLW199	279	HLX96
9	FXT184	77	FXT252	146	FXT321	213	HLW200	280	HLX97
10	FXT185	78	FXT253	147	FXT322	214	HLW201	281	HLX98
11	FXT186	79	FXT254	148	FXT323	215	HLW202	282	HLX99
12	FXT187	80	FXT255	149	FXT324	216	HLW203	283	HLX100
13	FXT188	81	FXT256	150	FXT325	217	HLW204	284	HLX101
14	FXT189	82	FXT257	151	FXT326	218	HLW205	285	HLX102
15	FXT190	83	FXT258	152	HLW139	219	HLW206	286	HLX103
16	FXT191	84	FXT259	153	HLW140	220	HLW207	287	HLX104
17	FXT192	86	FXT261	154	HLW141	221	HLW208	288	HLX105
18	FXT193	87	FXT262	155	HLW142	222	HLW209	289	HLX106
†19	FXT194	88	FXT263	156	HLW143	223	HLW210	290	HLX107
20	FXT195	89	FXT264	157	HLW144	224	HLW211	291	HLX108
21	FXT196	90	FXT265	158	HLW145	225	HLW212	292	HLX109
23	FXT198	91	FXT266	159	HLW146	226	HLW213	293	HLX110
24	FXT199	92	FXT267	160	HLW147	227	HLW214	294	HLX111
25	FXT200	93	FXT268	161	HLW148	228	HLW215	295	HLX112
26	FXT201	94	FXT269	162	HLW149	229	HLW216	296	HLX113
27	FXT202	95	FXT270	163	HLW150	230	HLW217	297	HLX114
28	FXT203	96	FXT271	164	HLW151	231	HLW218	298	HLX115
29	FXT204	98	FXT273	165	HLW152	232	HLW219	299	HLX116
30	FXT205	99	FXT274	166	HLW153	233	HLW220	300	HLX117
31	FXT206	100	FXT275	167	HLW154	234	HLW221	301	HLX118
32	FXT207	101	FXT276	168	HLW155	235	HLW222	302	HLX119
33	FXT208	102	FXT277	169	HLW156	236	HLW223	303	HLX120
34	FXT209	103	FXT278	170	HLW157	237	HLW224	304	HLX121
35	FXT210	104	FXT279	171	HLW158	238	HLW225	305	HLX122
36	FXT211	105	FXT280	172	HLW159	239	HLW226	306	HLX123
37	FXT212	106	FXT281	173	HLW160	240	HLW227	307	HLX124
38	FXT213	107	FXT282	174	HLW161	241	HLW228	308	HLX125
39	FXT214	108	FXT283	175	HLW162	242	HLW229	309	HLX126
40	FXT215	109	FXT284	176	HLW163	243	HLW230	310	HLX127
41	FXT216	110	FXT285	177	HLW164	244	HLW231	311	HLX128
42	FXT217	111	FXT286	178	HLW165	245	HLW232	312	HLX129
43	FXT218	112	FXT287	179	HLW166	246	HLW233	313	HLX130
44	FXT219	113	FXT288	180	HLW167	247	HLW234	314	HLX131
45	FXT220	114	FXT289	181	HLW168	248	HLW235	315	HLX132
46	FXT221	115	FXT290	182	HLW169	249	HLW236	316	HLX133
47	FXT222	116	FXT291	183	HLW170	250	HLW237	317	HLX134
48	FXT223	117	FXT292	184	HLW171	251	HLW238	318	HLX135
49	FXT224	118	FXT293	185	HLW172	252	HLW239	319	HLX136
50	FXT225	119	FXT294	186	HLW173	253	HLW240	320	HLX137
51	FXT226	120	FXT295	187	HLW174	254	HLW241	321	HLX138
52	FXT227	121	FXT296	188	HLW175	255	HLW242	322	HLX139
53	FXT228	122	FXT297	189	HLW176	256	HLW243	323	HLX140
54	FXT229	123	FXT298	190	HLW177	257	HLW244	324	HLX141
55	FXT230	124	FXT299	191	HLW178	258	HLW245	325	HLX142
56	FXT231	125	FXT300	192	HLW179	259	HLW246	326	HLX143
57	FXT232	126	FXT301	193	HLW180	260	HLW247	327	HLX144
58	FXT233	127	FXT302	194	HLW181	261	HLW248	328	HLX145
59	FXT234	128	FXT303	195	HLW182	262	HLW249	329	HLX146
60	FXT235	129	FXT304	196	HLW183	263	HLW250	330	HLX147
61	FXT236	130	FXT305	197	HLW184	264	HLX81	331	HLX148
62	FXT237	131	FXT306	198	HLW185	265	HLX82	332	HLX149
63	FXT238	132	FXT307	199	HLW186	266	HLX83	333	HLX150
64	FXT239	133	FXT308	200	HLW187	267	HLX84	334	HLX151
65	FXT240	134	FXT309	201	HLW188	268	HLX85	335	HLX152
66	FXT241	135	FXT310	202	HLW189	269	HLX86	336	HLX153
67	FXT242	136	FXT311	203	HLW190	270	HLX87	337	HLX154
68	FXT243	137	FXT312	204	HLW191	271	HLX88	338	HLX155
69	FXT244	138	FXT313	205	HLW192	272	HLX89	339	HLX156

† Converted to service vehicle 1020J on 9.8.54

RT		RT		RT		RT		RT	
340	HLX157	407	HLX224	474	HLX291	541	HLX358	608	HLX425
341	HLX158	408	HLX225	475	HLX292	542	HLX359	609	HLX426
342	HLX159	409	HLX226	476	HLX293	543	HLX360	610	HLX427
343	HLX160	410	HLX227	477	HLX294	544	HLX361	611	HLX428
344	HLX161	411	HLX228	478	HLX295	545	HLX362	612	HLX429
345	HLX162	412	HLX229	479	HLX296	546	HLX363	613	HLX430
346	HLX163	413	HLX230	480	HLX297	547	HLX364	614	HLX431
347	HLX164	414	HLX231	481	HLX298	548	HLX365	615	HLX432
348	HLX165	415	HLX232	482	HLX299	549	HLX366	616	HLX433
349	HLX166	416	HLX233	483	HLX300	550	HLX367	617	HLX434
350	HLX167	417	HLX234	484	HLX301	551	HLX368	618	HLX435
351	HLX168	418	HLX235	485	HLX302	552	HLX369	619	HLX436
352	HLX169	419	HLX236	486	HLX303	553	HLX370	620	HLX437
353	HLX170	420	HLX237	487	HLX304	554	HLX371	621	HLX438
354	HLX171	421	HLX238	488	HLX305	555	HLX372	622	JXC430
355	HLX172	422	HLX239	489	HLX306	556	HLX373	623	JXC431
356	HLX173	423	HLX240	490	HLX307	557	HLX374	624	JXC432
357	HLX174	424	HLX241	491	HLX308	558	HLX375	625	JXC433
358	HLX175	425	HLX242	492	HLX309	559	HLX376	626	JXC434
359	HLX176	426	HLX243	493	HLX310	560	HLX377	627	JXC435
360	HLX177	427	HLX244	494	HLX311	561	HLX378	628	JXC436
361	HLX178	428	HLX245	495	HLX312	562	HLX379	629	JXC437
362	HLX179	429	HLX246	496	HLX313	563	HLX380	630	JXC438
363	HLX180	430	HLX247	497	HLX314	564	HLX381	631	JXC439
364	HLX181	431	HLX248	498	HLX315	565	HLX382	632	JXC440
365	HLX182	432	HLX249	499	HLX316	566	HLX383	633	JXC441
366	HLX183	433	HLX250	500	HLX317	567	HLX384	634	JXC442
367	HLX184	434	HLX251	501	HLX318	568	HLX385	635	JXC443
368	HLX185	435	HLX252	502	HLX319	569	HLX386	636	JXC444
369	HLX186	436	HLX253	503	HLX320	570	HLX387	637	JXC445
370	HLX187	437	HLX254	504	HLX321	571	HLX388	638	JXC446
371	HLX188	438	HLX255	505	HLX322	572	HLX389	639	JXC447
372	HLX189	439	HLX256	506	HLX323	573	HLX390	640	JXC448
373	HLX190	440	HLX257	507	HLX324	574	HLX391	641	JXC449
374	HLX191	441	HLX258	508	HLX325	575	HLX392	642	JXC450
375	HLX192	442	HLX259	509	HLX326	576	HLX393	643	JXC451
376	HLX193	443	HLX260	510	HLX327	577	HLX394	644	JXC452
377	HLX194	444	HLX261	511	HLX328	578	HLX395	645	JXC453
378	HLX195	445	HLX262	512	HLX329	579	HLX396	646	JXC454
379	HLX196	446	HLX263	513	HLX330	580	HLX397	647	JXC455
380	HLX197	447	HLX264	514	HLX331	581	HLX398	648	JXC456
381	HLX198	448	HLX265	515	HLX332	582	HLX399	649	JXC457
382	HLX199	449	HLX266	516	HLX333	583	HLX400	650	JXC458
383	HLX200	450	HLX267	517	HLX334	584	HLX401	651	JXC459
384	HLX201	451	HLX268	518	HLX335	585	HLX402	652	JXC15
385	HLX202	452	HLX269	519	HLX336	586	HLX403	653	JXC16
386	HLX203	453	HLX270	520	HLX337	587	HLX404	654	JXC17
387	HLX204	454	HLX271	521	HLX338	588	HLX405	655	JXC18
388	HLX205	455	HLX272	522	HLX339	589	HLX406	656	JXC19
389	HLX206	456	HLX273	523	HLX340	590	HLX407	* 657	KLB712
390	HLX207	457	HLX274	524	HLX341	591	HLX408	658	JXC21
391	HLX208	458	HLX275	525	HLX342	592	HLX409	659	JXC22
392	HLX209	459	HLX276	526	HLX343	593	HLX410	660	JXC23
393	HLX210	460	HLX277	527	HLX344	594	HLX411	661	JXC24
394	HLX211	461	HLX278	528	HLX345	595	HLX412	662	JXC25
395	HLX212	462	HLX279	529	HLX346	596	HLX413	663	JXC26
396	HLX213	463	HLX280	530	HLX347	597	HLX414	664	JXC27
397	HLX214	464	HLX281	531	HLX348	598	HLX415	665	JXC28
398	HLX215	465	HLX282	532	HLX349	599	HLX416	666	JXC29
399	HLX216	466	HLX283	533	HLX350	600	HLX417	667	JXC30
400	HLX217	467	HLX284	534	HLX351	601	HLX418	668	JXC31
401	HLX218	468	HLX285	535	HLX352	602	HLX419	669	JXC32
402	HLX219	469	HLX286	536	HLX353	603	HLX420	670	JXC33
403	HLX220	470	HLX287	537	HLX354	604	HLX421	671	JXC34
404	HLX221	471	HLX288	538	HLX355	605	HLX422	672	JXC35
405	HLX222	472	HLX289	539	HLX356	606	HLX423	673	JXC36
406	HLX223	473	HLX290	540	HLX357	607	HLX424	674	JXC37

* Date into stock 27.1.50

RT		RT		RT		RT		RT	
675	JXC38	742	JXC105	809	JXN187	876	JXN254	943	JXN343
676	JXC39	743	JXC106	810	JXN188	877	JXN255	944	JXN345
677	JXC40	744	JXC107	811	JXN189	878	JXN256	945	JXN346
678	JXC41	745	JXC108	812	JXN190	879	JXN257	946	KGK917
679	JXC42	746	JXC109	813	JXN191	880	JXN258	947	KGK918
680	JXC43	747	JXC110	814	JXN192	881	JXN259	948	KGK919
681	JXC44	748	JXC111	815	JXN193	882	JXN260	949	KGK920
682	JXC45	749	JXC112	816	JXN194	883	JXN261	950	KGK921
683	JXC46	750	JXC113	817	JXN195	884	JXN262	951	KGK922
684	JXC47	751	JXC114	818	JXN196	885	JXN263	952	KGK923
685	JXC48	752	JXC115	819	JXN197	886	JXN264	953	KGK924
686	JXC49	753	JXC116	820	JXN198	887	JXN265	954	KGK925
687	JXC50	754	JXC117	821	JXN199	888	JXN266	955	KGK926
688	JXC51	755	JXC118	822	JXN200	889	JXN267	956	KGK927
689	JXC52	756	JXC119	823	JXN201	890	JXN268	957	KGK928
690	JXC53	757	JXC120	824	JXN202	891	JXN269	958	KGU232
691	JXC54	758	JXC121	825	JXN203	892	JXN270	959	KGU233
692	JXC55	759	JXC122	826	JXN204	893	JXN271	960	KGU234
693	JXC56	760	JXC123	827	JXN205	894	JXN272	961	KGU235
694	JXC57	761	JXC124	828	JXN206	895	JXN273	962	JXC490
695	JXC58	762	JXC125	829	JXN207	896	JXN274	963	JXC491
696	JXC59	763	JXC126	830	JXN208	897	JXN275	964	JXC492
697	JXC60	764	JXC127	831	JXN209	898	JXN276	965	JXC493
698	JXC61	765	JXC128	832	JXN210	899	JXN277	966	JXC494
699	JXC62	766	JXC129	833	JXN211	900	JXN278	967	JXC495
700	JXC63	767	JXC130	834	JXN212	901	JXN279	968	JXC496
701	JXC64	768	JXC131	835	JXN213	902	JXN280	969	JXC497
702	JXC65	*769	JXC132	836	JXN214	903	JXN281	970	JXC498
703	JXC66	770	JXC133	837	JXN215	904	JXN282	971	JXC499
704	JXC67	771	JXC134	838	JXN216	905	JXN283	972	JXC500
705	JXC68	772	JXC135	839	JXN217	906	JXN284	973	JXN1
706	JXC69	773	JXC136	840	JXN218	907	JXN285	974	JXN2
707	JXC70	774	JXC137	841	JXN219	908	JXN286	975	JXN3
708	JXC71	775	JXC138	842	JXN220	909	JXN287	976	JXN4
709	JXC72	776	JXC139	843	JXN221	910	JXN288	977	JXN5
710	JXC73	777	JXC140	844	JXN222	911	JXN289	978	JXN6
711	JXC74	778	JXC141	845	JXN223	912	JXN290	979	JXN7
712	JXC75	779	JXC142	846	JXN224	913	JXN291	980	JXN8
713	JXC76	780	JXC143	847	JXN225	914	JXN292	981	JXN9
714	JXC77	781	JXC144	848	JXN226	915	JXN293	982	JXN10
715	JXC78	782	JXC145	849	JXN227	916	JXN294	983	JXN11
716	JXC79	783	JXC146	850	JXN228	917	JXN295	984	JXN12
717	JXC80	784	JXC147	851	JXN229	918	JXN296	985	JXN13
718	JXC81	785	JXC148	852	JXN230	919	JXN297	986	JXN14
719	JXC82	786	JXC149	853	JXN231	920	JXN298	987	JXN15
720	JXC83	787	JXC150	854	JXN232	921	JXN299	988	JXN16
721	JXC84	788	JXC151	855	JXN233	922	JXN300	989	JXN17
722	JXC85	789	JXC152	856	JXN234	923	JXN301	990	JXN18
723	JXC86	790	JXC153	857	JXN235	924	JXN302	991	JXN19
724	JXC87	791	JXC154	858	JXN236	925	JXN303	992	JXN20
725	JXC88	792	JXC155	859	JXN237	926	JXN304	993	JXN21
726	JXC89	793	JXC156	860	JXN238	927	JXN305	994	JXN22
727	JXC90	794	JXC157	861	JXN239	928	JXN306	995	JXN23
728	JXC91	795	JXC158	862	JXN240	929	JXN307	996	JXN24
729	JXC92	796	JXC159	863	JXN241	930	JXN308	997	JXN25
730	JXC93	797	JXC160	864	JXN242	931	JXN309	998	JXN26
731	JXC94	798	JXC161	865	JXN243	932	JXN310	999	JXN27
732	JXC95	799	JXC162	866	JXN244	933	JXN311	1000	JXN28
733	JXC96	800	JXC163	867	JXN245	934	JXN312	1001	JXN29
734	JXC97	801	JXC164	868	JXN246	935	JXN325	1002	JXN30
735	JXC98	802	JXN180	869	JXN247	936	JXN326	1003	JXN31
736	JXC99	803	JXN181	870	JXN248	937	JXN327	1004	JXN32
737	JXC100	804	JXN182	871	JXN249	938	JXN328	1005	JXN33
738	JXC101	805	JXN183	872	JXN250	939	JXN329	1006	JXN34
739	JXC102	806	JXN184	873	JXN251	940	JXN330	1007	JXN35
740	JXC103	807	JXN185	874	JXN252	941	JXN331	1008	JXN36
741	JXC104	808	JXN186	875	JXN253	942	JXN332	1009	JXN37

* Date into stock 15.2.51

RT		RT		RT		RT		RT		Date into stock
1010	JXN38	1077	JXN105	1144	JXN172	1211	KGK680	1278	KLB527	
1011	JXN39	1078	JXN106	1145	JXN173	1212	KGK681	1279	KLB528	
1012	JXN40	1079	JXN107	1146	JXN174	1213	KGK682	1280	KLB529	
1013	JXN41	1080	JXN108	1147	JXN175	1214	KGK683	1281	KLB530	
1014	JXN42	1081	JXN109	1148	JXN176	1215	KGK684	1282	KLB531	
1015	JXN43	1082	JXN110	1149	JXN177	1216	KGK685	1283	KLB532	
1016	JXN44	1083	JXN111	1150	JXN178	1217	KGK686	1284	KLB533	
1017	JXN45	1084	JXN112	1151	JXN179	1218	KGK687	1285	KLB534	
1018	JXN46	1085	JXN113	1152	JXC460	1219	KGK688	1286	KLB535	
1019	JXN47	1086	JXN114	1153	JXC461	1220	KGK689	1287	KLB536	
1020	JXN48	1087	JXN115	1154	JXC462	1221	KGK690	1288	KLB537	
1021	JXN49	1088	JXN116	1155	JXC463	1222	KGK691	1289	KLB538	
1022	JXN50	1089	JXN117	1156	JXC464	1223	KGK692	1290	KLB539	
1023	JXN51	1090	JXN118	1157	JXC465	1224	KGK693	1291	KLB540	
1024	JXN52	1091	JXN119	1158	JXC466	1225	KGK694	1292	KLB541	
1025	JXN53	1092	JXN120	1159	JXC467	1226	KGK695	1293	KLB542	
1026	JXN54	1093	JXN121	1160	JXC468	1227	KGK696	1294	KLB543	
1027	JXN55	1094	JXN122	1161	JXC469	1228	KGK697	1295	KLB544	
1028	JXN56	1095	JXN123	1162	JXC470	1229	KGK698	1296	KLB545	
1029	JXN57	1096	JXN124	1163	JXC471	1230	KGK699	1297	KLB546	6.1.50
1030	JXN58	1097	JXN125	1164	JXC472	1231	KGK700	1298	KLB547	6.1.50
1031	JXN59	1098	JXN126	1165	JXC473	1232	KGK701	1299	KLB548	6.1.50
1032	JXN60	1099	JXN127	1166	JXC474	1233	KGK702	1300	KLB549	6.1.50
1033	JXN61	1100	JXN128	1167	JXC475	1234	KGK703	1301	KLB550	13.1.50
1034	JXN62	1101	JXN129	1168	JXC476	1235	KGK704	1302	KLB551	12.1.50
1035	JXN63	1102	JXN130	1169	JXC477	1236	KGK705	1303	KLB552	13.1.50
1036	JXN64	1103	JXN131	1170	JXC478	1237	KGK706	1304	KLB553	13.1.50
1037	JXN65	1104	JXN132	1171	JXC479	1238	KGK707	1305	KLB554	19.1.50
1038	JXN66	1105	JXN133	1172	JXC480	1239	KGK708	1306	KLB555	20.1.50
1039	JXN67	1106	JXN134	1173	JXC481	1240	KGK709	1307	KLB556	20.1.50
1040	JXN68	1107	JXN135	1174	JXC482	1241	KGK710	1308	KLB557	27.1.50
1041	JXN69	1108	JXN136	1175	JXC483	1242	KGK711	1309	KLB558	27.1.50
1042	JXN70	1109	JXN137	1176	JXC484	1243	KGK712	1310	KLB559	27.1.50
1043	JXN71	1110	JXN138	1177	JXC485	1244	KGK713	1311	KLB560	3.2.50
1044	JXN72	1111	JXN139	1178	JXC486	1245	KGK714	1312	KLB561	3.2.50
1045	JXN73	1112	JXN140	1179	JXC487	1246	KGK715	1313	KLB562	3.2.50
1046	JXN74	1113	JXN141	1180	JXC488	1247	KGK716	1314	KLB563	10.2.50
1047	JXN75	1114	JXN142	1181	JXC489	1248	KGK717	1315	KLB564	10.2.50
1048	JXN76	1115	JXN143	1182	KGK651	1249	KGK718	1316	KLB565	10.2.50
1049	JXN77	1116	JXN144	1183	KGK652	1250	KGK719	1317	KLB566	10.2.50
1050	JXN78	1117	JXN145	1184	KGK653	1251	KGK720	1318	KLB567	17.2.50
1051	JXN79	1118	JXN146	1185	KGK654	1252	KLB501	1319	KLB568	17.2.50
1052	JXN80	1119	JXN147	1186	KGK655	1253	KLB502	1320	KLB569	17.2.50
1053	JXN81	1120	JXN148	1187	KGK656	1254	KLB503	1321	KLB570	24.2.50
1054	JXN82	1121	JXN149	1188	KGK657	1255	KLB504	1322	KLB571	24.2.50
1055	JXN83	1122	JXN150	1189	KGK658	1256	KLB505	1323	KLB572	24.2.50
1056	JXN84	1123	JXN151	1190	KGK659	1257	KLB506	1324	KLB573	3.3.50
1057	JXN85	1124	JXN152	1191	KGK660	1258	KLB507	1325	KLB574	3.3.50
1058	JXN86	1125	JXN153	1192	KGK661	1259	KLB508	1326	KLB575	3.3.50
1059	JXN87	1126	JXN154	1193	KGK662	1260	KLB509	1327	KLB576	3.3.50
1060	JXN88	1127	JXN155	1194	KGK663	1261	KLB510	1328	KLB577	10.3.50
1061	JXN89	1128	JXN156	1195	KGK664	1262	KLB511	1329	KLB578	10.3.50
1062	JXN90	1129	JXN157	1196	KGK665	1263	KLB512	1330	KLB579	10.3.50
1063	JXN91	1130	JXN158	1197	KGK666	1264	KLB513	1331	KLB580	17.3.50
1064	JXN92	1131	JXN159	1198	KGK667	1265	KLB514	1332	KLB581	17.3.50
1065	JXN93	1132	JXN160	1199	KGK668	1266	KLB515	1333	KLB582	17.3.50
1066	JXN94	1133	JXN161	1200	KGK669	1267	KLB516	1334	KLB583	24.3.50
1067	JXN95	1134	JXN162	1201	KGK670	1268	KLB517	1335	KLB584	24.3.50
1068	JXN96	1135	JXN163	1202	KGK671	1269	KLB518	1336	KLB585	24.3.50
1069	JXN97	1136	JXN164	1203	KGK672	1270	KLB519	1337	KLB586	24.3.50
1070	JXN98	1137	JXN165	1204	KGK673	1271	KLB520	1338	KLB587	31.3.50
1071	JXN99	1138	JXN166	1205	KGK674	1272	KLB521	1339	KLB588	31.3.50
1072	JXN100	1139	JXN167	1206	KGK675	1273	KLB522	1340	KLB589	31.3.50
1073	JXN101	1140	JXN168	1207	KGK676	1274	KLB523	1341	KLB590	6.4.50
1074	JXN102	1141	JXN169	1208	KGK677	1275	KLB524	1342	KLB591	6.4.50
1075	JXN103	1142	JXN170	1209	KGK678	1276	KLB525	1343	KLB592	6.4.50
1076	JXN104	1143	JXN171	1210	KGK679	1277	KLB526	1344	KLB593	14.4.50

RT		Date into stock	RT		RT		Date into stock	RT		Date into stock
1345	KLB594	14.4.50	1411	JXC174	1477	KGK736		1543	KGU412	
1346	KLB595	21.4.50	1412	JXC175	1478	KGK737		1544	KGU413	
1347	KLB596	21.4.50	1413	JXC176	1479	KGK738		1545	KGU414	
1348	KLB597	21.4.50	1414	JXC177	1480	KGK739		1546	KGU415	
1349	KLB598	21.4.50	1415	JXC178	1481	KGK740		1547	KGU416	
1350	KLB599	28.4.50	1416	JXC179	1482	KGK741		1548	KGU440	
1351	KLB600	28.4.50	1417	JXC180	1483	KGK742		1549	KGU441	
1352	KXW451	28.4.50	1418	JXC181	1484	KGK743		1550	KGU442	
1353	KXW452	5.5.50	1419	JXC182	1485	KGK744		1551	KGU443	
1354	KXW453	5.5.50	1420	JXC183	1486	KGK745		1552	KGU444	
1355	KXW454	5.5.50	1421	JXC184	1487	KGK746		1553	KGU445	
1356	KXW455	12.5.50	1422	JXC185	1488	KGK747		1554	KGU446	
1357	KXW456	12.5.50	1423	JXC186	1489	KGK748		1555	KGU447	
1358	KXW457	12.5.50	1424	JXC187	1490	KGK749		1556	KGU448	
1359	KXW458	12.5.50	1425	JXC188	1491	KGK750		1557	KGU449	
1360	KXW459	19.5.50	1426	JXC189	1492	KGK751		1558	KGU450	
1361	KXW460	19.5.50	1427	JXC190	1493	KGK752		1559	KLB631	
1362	KXW461	19.5.50	1428	JXC191	1494	KGK753		1560	KLB632	
1363	KXW462	2.6.50	1429	JXC192	1495	KGK754		1561	KLB633	
1364	KXW463	2.6.50	1430	JXC193	1496	KGK755		1562	KLB634	
1365	KXW464	2.6.50	1431	JXC194	1497	KGK756		1563	KLB635	
1366	KXW465	2.6.50	1432	JXC195	1498	KGK757		1564	KLB636	
1367	KXW466	2.6.50	1433	JXC196	1499	KGK758		1565	KLB637	
1368	KXW467	2.6.50	1434	JXC197	1500	KGK759		1566	KLB638	
1369	KXW468	9.6.50	1435	JXC198	1501	KGK760		1567	KLB655	
1370	KXW469	9.6.50	1436	JXC199	1502	KGK761		1568	KLB656	
1371	KXW470	9.6.50	1437	JXC200	1503	KGK762		1569	KLB657	
1372	KXW471	16.6.50	1438	JXC201	1504	KGK763		1570	KLB658	
1373	KXW472	16.6.50	1439	JXC202	1505	KGK764		1571	KLB659	
1374	KXW473	16.6.50	1440	JXC203	1506	KGK765		1572	KLB660	
1375	KXW474	23.6.50	1441	JXC204	1507	KGK766		1573	KLB661	
1376	KXW475	23.6.50	1442	JXC205	1508	KGK767		1574	KLB662	
1377	KXW476	23.6.50	1443	JXC206	1509	KGK768		1575	KLB663	
1378	KXW477	30.6.50	1444	JXC207	1510	KGK769		1576	KLB664	
1379	KXW478	30.6.50	1445	JXC208	1511	KGK770	3.1.50	1577	KLB665	
1380	KXW479	30.6.50	1446	JXC209	1512	KGK771	6.1.50	1578	KLB666	
1381	KXW480	30.6.50	1447	JXC210	1513	KGK772	10.1.50	1579	KLB667	
1382	KXW481	7.7.50	1448	JXC211	1514	KGK773	17.1.50	1580	KLB668	
1383	KXW482	7.7.50	1449	JXC212	1515	KGK774	17.1.50	1581	KLB669	
1384	KXW483	7.7.50	1450	JXC213	1516	KGK775	19.1.50	1582	KLB670	
1385	KXW484	14.7.50	1451	JXC214	1517	KGK776	9.2.50	1583	KLB671	
1386	KXW485	14.7.50	1452	JXC215	1518	KGK777	16.2.50	1584	KLB672	
1387	KXW486	14.7.50	1453	JXC216	1519	KGK778	3.3.50	1585	KLB673	
1388	KXW487	21.7.50	1454	JXC217	1520	KGK779	3.4.50	1586	KLB674	
1389	KXW488	21.7.50	1455	JXC218	1521	KGK780	19.4.50	1587	KLB675	
1390	KXW489	21.7.50	1456	JXC219	1522	KGU236		1588	KLB676	
1391	KXW490	28.7.50	1457	JXC220	1523	KGU237		1589	KLB677	
1392	KXW491	28.7.50	1458	JXC221	1524	KGU238		1590	KLB678	
1393	KXW492	28.7.50	1459	JXC222	1525	KGU239		1591	KLB713	26.1.50
1394	KXW493	4.8.50	1460	JXC223	1526	KGU240		1592	KLB714	27.1.50
1395	KXW494	4.8.50	1461	JXC224	1527	KGU241		1593	KLB715	30.1.50
1396	KXW495	4.8.50	1462	KGK721	1528	KGU242		1594	KLB716	30.1.50
1397	KXW496	4.8.50	1463	KGK722	1529	KGU243		1595	KLB717	30.1.50
1398	KXW497	18.8.50	1464	KGK723	1530	KGU290		1596	KLB718	27.1.50
1399	KXW498	18.8.50	1465	KGK724	1531	KGU291		1597	KLB719	30.1.50
1400	KXW499	18.8.50	1466	KGK725	1532	KGU292		1598	KLB720	1.2.50
1401	KXW500	1.9.50	1467	KGK726	1533	KGU293		1599	KLB721	1.2.50
1402	JXC165		1468	KGK727	1534	KGU294		1600	KLB722	2.2.50
1403	JXC166		1469	KGK728	1535	KGU295		1601	KLB723	2.2.50
1404	JXC167		1470	KGK729	1536	KGU296		1602	KLB724	2.2.50
1405	JXC168		1471	KGK730	1537	KGU297		1603	KLB725	3.2.50
1406	JXC169		1472	KGK731	1538	KGU298		1604	KLB726	3.2.50
1407	JXC170		1473	KGK732	1539	KGU299		1605	KLB727	3.2.50
1408	JXC171		1474	KGK733	1540	KGU300		1606	KLB728	3.2.50
1409	JXC172		1475	KGK734	1541	KGU410		1607	KLB729	6.2.50
1410	JXC173		1476	KGK735	1542	KGU411		1608	KLB730	6.2.50

RT		Date into stock	RT		Date into stock	RT		Date into stock
1609	KLB731	6.2.50	1675	KXW321	27.3.50	1741	KYY579	17.5.50
1610	KLB732	6.2.50	1676	KXW322	27.3.50	1742	KYY580	18.5.50
1611	KLB733	7.2.50	1677	KXW323	29.3.50	1743	KYY581	18.5.50
1612	KLB734	8.2.50	1678	KXW324	31.3.50	1744	KYY582	19.5.50
1613	KLB735	9.2.50	1679	KXW325	31.3.50	1745	KYY583	18.5.50
1614	KLB736	8.2.50	1680	KXW326	31.3.50	1746	KYY584	19.5.50
1615	KLB737	9.2.50	1681	KXW327	31.3.50	1747	KYY585	19.5.50
1616	KLB738	16.2.50	1682	KXW328	31.3.50	1748	KYY586	19.5.50
1617	KLB739	10.2.50	1683	KXW329	31.3.50	1749	KYY587	19.5.50
1618	KLB740	10.2.50	1684	KXW330	31.3.50	1750	KYY588	19.5.50
1619	KLB741	10.2.50	1685	KXW331	1.4.50	1751	KYY589	19.5.50
1620	KLB742	10.2.50	1686	KXW332	3.4.50	1752	KYY590	23.5.50
1621	KLB743	13.2.50	1687	KXW333	4.4.50	1753	KYY591	24.5.50
1622	KLB744	13.2.50	1688	KXW334	1.4.50	1754	KYY592	23.5.50
1623	KLB745	13.2.50	1689	KXW335	4.4.50	1755	KYY593	24.5.50
1624	KLB746	15.2.50	1690	KXW336	4.4.50	1756	KYY594	25.5.50
1625	KLB747	14.2.50	1691	KXW337	6.4.50	1757	KYY595	25.5.50
1626	KLB748	15.2.50	1692	KXW338	5.4.50	1758	KYY596	26.5.50
1627	KLB749	21.2.50	1693	KXW339	4.4.50	1759	KYY597	24.5.50
1628	KLB750	16.2.50	1694	KXW340	5.4.50	1760	KYY598	26.5.50
1629	KXW251	17.2.50	1695	KXW341	5.4.50	1761	KYY599	26.5.50
1630	KXW252	17.2.50	1696	KXW342	13.4.50	1762	KYY600	26.5.50
1631	KXW253	17.2.50	1697	KXW343	6.4.50	1763	KYY601	26.5.50
1632	KXW254	17.2.50	1698	KYY525	21.4.50	1764	KYY602	31.5.50
1633	KXW255	17.2.50	1699	KYY526	27.4.50	1765	KYY603	31.5.50
1634	KXW256	20.2.50	1700	KYY527	19.4.50	1766	KYY604	26.5.50
1635	KXW257	20.2.50	1701	KYY528	19.4.50	1767	KYY605	31.5.50
1636	KXW258	20.2.50	1702	KYY529	21.4.50	1768	KYY606	2.6.50
1637	KXW259	20.2.50	1703	KYY530	21.4.50	1769	KYY607	31.5.50
1638	KXW260	21.2.50	1704	KYY531	21.4.50	1770	KYY608	2.6.50
1639	KXW261	22.2.50	1705	KYY532	20.4.50	1771	KYY609	7.6.50
1640	KXW262	23.2.50	1706	KYY533	21.4.50	1772	KYY610	2.6.50
1641	KXW263	22.2.50	1707	KYY534	21.4.50	1773	KYY611	2.6.50
1642	KXW264	22.2.50	1708	KYY535	21.4.50	1774	KYY612	2.6.50
1643	KXW265	23.2.50	1709	KYY536	21.4.50	1775	KYY613	2.6.50
1644	KXW266	24.2.50	1710	KYY537	21.4.50	1776	KYY614	6.6.50
1645	KXW267	27.2.50	1711	KYY538	21.4.50	1777	KYY615	7.6.50
1646	KXW268	24.2.50	1712	KYY539	26.4.50	1778	KYY616	8.6.50
1647	KXW269	3.3.50	1713	KYY540	25.4.50	1779	KYY617	8.6.50
1648	KXW270	27.2.50	1714	KYY541	27.4.50	1780	KYY618	8.6.50
1649	KXW271	28.2.50	1715	KYY542	28.4.50	1781	KYY619	9.6.50
1650	KXW272	28.2.50	1716	KYY543	5.5.50	1782	KYY620	8.6.50
1651	KXW273	1.3.50	1717	KYY544	26.4.50	1783	KYY621	9.6.50
1652	KXW274	1.3.50	1718	KYY545	26.4.50	1784	KYY622	9.6.50
1653	KXW275	1.3.50	1719	KYY546	28.4.50	1785	KYY623	9.6.50
1654	KXW276	1.3.50	1720	KYY547	27.4.50	1786	KYY624	9.6.50
1655	KXW301	16.3.50	1721	KYY548	28.4.50	1787	KYY625	9.6.50
1656	KXW302	17.3.50	1722	KYY549	28.4.50	1788	KYY626	13.6.50
1657	KXW303	16.3.50	1723	KYY550	28.4.50	1789	KYY627	14.6.50
1658	KXW304	16.3.50	1724	KYY551	28.4.50	1790	KYY628	15.6.50
1659	KXW305	17.3.50	1725	KYY552	2.5.50	1791	KYY629	14.6.50
1660	KXW306	17.3.50	1726	KYY553	4.5.50	1792	KYY630	15.6.50
1661	KXW307	31.3.50	1727	KYY554	4.5.50	1793	KYY631	16.6.50
1662	KXW308	20.3.50	1728	KYY555	4.5.50	1794	KYY632	15.6.50
1663	KXW309	20.3.50	1729	KYY556	5.5.50	1795	KYY650	23.6.50
1664	KXW310	20.3.50	1730	KYY557	10.5.50	1796	KYY651	23.6.50
1665	KXW311	21.3.50	1731	KYY569	10.5.50	1797	KYY652	28.6.50
1666	KXW312	22.3.50	1732	KYY570	10.5.50	1798	KYY653	27.6.50
1667	KXW313	22.3.50	1733	KYY571	10.5.50	1799	KYY654	28.6.50
1668	KXW314	24.3.50	1734	KYY572	12.5.50	1800	KYY655	30.6.50
1669	KXW315	24.3.50	1735	KYY573	12.5.50	1801	KYY656	29.6.50
1670	KXW316	24.3.50	1736	KYY574	12.5.50	1802	KYY657	29.6.50
1671	KXW317	24.3.50	1737	KYY575	12.5.50	1803	KYY658	30.6.50
1672	KXW318	24.3.50	1738	KYY576	12.5.50	1804	KYY659	30.6.50
1673	KXW319	24.3.50	1739	KYY577	16.5.50	1805	KYY660	30.6.50
1674	KXW320	24.3.50	1740	KYY578	16.5.50	1806	KYY661	5.7.50

RT		Date into stock	RT		Date into stock	RT		Date into stock
1807	KYY662	30.6.50	1873	LLU759	16.8.50	1939	LUC19	12.10.50
1808	KYY663	30.6.50	1874	LLU760	17.8.50	1940	LUC20	13.10.50
1809	KYY664	30.6.50	1875	LLU761	17.8.50	1941	LUC21	13.10.50
1810	KYY665	30.6.50	1876	LLU762	18.8.50	1942	LUC22	13.10.50
1811	KYY666	3.7.50	1877	LLU763	18.8.50	1943	LUC29	19.10.50
1812	KYY667	6.7.50	1878	LLU764	18.8.50	1944	LUC30	19.10.50
1813	KYY668	4.7.50	1879	LLU765	18.8.50	1945	LUC31	19.10.50
1814	KYY669	6.7.50	1880	LLU766	18.8.50	1946	LUC32	19.10.50
1815	KYY670	6.7.50	1881	LLU767	18.8.50	1947	LUC33	20.10.50
1816	KYY671	7.7.50	1882	LLU768	23.8.50	1948	LUC34	20.10.50
1817	KYY672	7.7.50	1883	LLU769	23.8.50	1949	LUC35	20.10.50
1818	KYY673	7.7.50	1884	LLU770	23.8.50	1950	LUC36	24.10.50
1819	KYY674	7.7.50	1885	LLU771	24.8.50	1951	LUC37	24.10.50
1820	KYY675	7.7.50	1886	LLU794	6.9.50	1952	LUC38	20.10.50
1821	KYY676	7.7.50	1887	LLU795	6.9.50	1953	LUC39	23.10.50
1822	KYY677	7.7.50	1888	LLU796	7.9.50	1954	LUC40	27.10.50
1823	KYY678	11.7.50	1889	LLU797	8.9.50	1955	LUC44	25.10.50
1824	KYY679	21.7.50	1890	LLU798	8.9.50	1956	LUC45	26.10.50
1825	KYY680	12.7.50	1891	LLU799	8.9.50	1957	LUC46	25.10.50
1826	KYY681	12.7.50	1892	LLU800	8.9.50	1958	LUC47	25.10.50
1827	KYY682	12.7.50	1893	LLU801	8.9.50	1959	LUC48	27.10.50
1828	KYY683	13.7.50	1894	LLU802	8.9.50	1960	LUC49	27.10.50
1829	KYY684	13.7.50	1895	LLU803	8.9.50	1961	LUC50	26.10.50
1830	KYY685	14.7.50	1896	LLU804	13.9.50	1962	LUC51	27.10.50
1831	KYY686	13.7.50	1897	LLU805	13.9.50	1963	LUC52	27.10.50
1832	KYY687	14.7.50	1898	LLU806	13.9.50	1964	LUC53	27.10.50
1833	KYY688	25.7.50	1899	LLU807	13.9.50	1965	LUC54	31.10.50
1834	KYY689	14.7.50	1900	LLU808	21.9.50	1966	LUC55	30.10.50
1835	KYY690	14.7.50	1901	LLU809	13.9.50	1967	LUC56	31.10.50
1836	KYY691	14.7.50	1902	LLU810	15.9.50	1968	LUC57	2.11.50
1837	KYY692	19.7.50	1903	LLU811	15.9.50	1969	LUC58	3.11.50
1838	KYY693	20.7.50	1904	LLU812	15.9.50	1970	LUC59	31.10.50
1839	KYY694	14.7.50	1905	LLU813	22.9.50	1971	LUC60	1.11.50
1840	KYY695	19.7.50	1906	LLU814	20.10.50	1972	LUC61	1.11.50
1841	KYY696	19.7.50	1907	LLU815	15.9.50	1973	LUC62	3.11.50
1842	KYY697	20.7.50	1908	LLU816	22.9.50	1974	LUC63	1.11.50
1843	KYY698	20.7.50	1909	LLU817	15.9.50	1975	LUC64	3.11.50
1844	KYY699	20.7.50	1910	LLU818	22.9.50	1976	LUC65	3.11.50
1845	KYY700	21.7.50	1911	LLU831	5.10.50	1977	LUC66	6.11.50
1846	KYY701	21.7.50	1912	LLU832	29.9.50	1978	LUC67	6.11.50
1847	KYY702	21.7.50	1913	LLU833	29.9.50	1979	LUC80	14.11.50
1848	KYY703	21.7.50	1914	LLU834	29.9.50	1980	LUC81	10.11.50
1849	KYY704	21.7.50	1915	LLU835	4.10.50	1981	LUC82	13.11.50
1850	KYY716	2.8.50	1916	LLU836	29.9.50	1982	LUC83	15.11.50
1851	KYY717	8.8.50	1917	LLU837	28.9.50	1983	LUC84	15.11.50
1852	KYY718	28.7.50	1918	LLU838	29.9.50	1984	LUC85	16.11.50
1853	KYY719	2.8.50	1919	LLU839	4.10.50	1985	LUC86	15.11.50
1854	KYY720	3.8.50	1920	LLU840	29.9.50	1986	LUC87	15.11.50
1855	LLU741	3.8.50	1921	LUC1	6.10.50	1987	LUC88	16.11.50
1856	LLU742	3.8.50	1922	LUC2	29.9.50	1988	LUC89	16.11.50
1857	LLU743	3.8.50	1923	LUC3	2.10.50	1989	LUC90	17.11.50
1858	LLU744	4.8.50	1924	LUC4	6.10.50	1990	LUC91	17.11.50
1859	LLU745	4.8.50	1925	LUC5	6.10.50	1991	LUC92	17.11.50
1860	LLU746	8.8.50	1926	LUC6	6.10.50	1992	LUC93	20.11.50
1861	LLU747	9.8.50	1927	LUC7	11.10.50	1993	LUC94	17.11.50
1862	LLU748	10.8.50	1928	LUC8	6.10.50	1994	LUC95	20.11.50
1863	LLU749	10.8.50	1929	LUC9	6.10.50	1995	LUC96	20.11.50
1864	LLU750	10.8.50	1930	LUC10	6.10.50	1996	LUC97	22.11.50
1865	LLU751	11.8.50	1931	LUC11	6.10.50	1997	LUC98	20.11.50
1866	LLU752	17.8.50	1932	LUC12	6.10.50	1998	LUC99	21.11.50
1867	LLU753	11.8.50	1933	LUC13	10.10.50	1999	LUC100	24.11.50
1868	LLU754	16.8.50	1934	LUC14	11.10.50	2000	LUC226	22.11.50
1869	LLU755	11.8.50	1935	LUC15	12.10.50	2001	LUC227	22.11.50
1870	LLU756	11.8.50	1936	LUC16	11.10.50	2002	LUC228	23.11.50
1871	LLU757	15.8.50	1937	LUC17	13.10.50	2003	LUC229	23.11.50
1872	LLU758	16.8.50	1938	LUC18	13.10.50	2004	LUC230	23.11.50

RT		Date into stock	RT		Date into stock	RT	
2005	LUC231	24.11.50	2071	LYF9	22.1.51	2137	KGK946
2006	LUC232	24.11.50	2072	LYF10	23.1.51	2138	KGK947
2007	LUC233	27.11.50	2073	LYF11	24.1.51	2139	KGK948
2008	LUC234	27.11.50	2074	LYF12	24.1.51	2140	KGK949
2009	LUC235	27.11.50	2075	LYF13	24.1.51	2141	KGK950
2010	LUC236	28.11.50	2076	LYF14	24.1.51	2142	KGK951
2011	LUC237	28.11.50	2077	LYF15	25.1.51	2143	KGK952
2012	LUC238	28.11.50	2078	LYF16	25.1.51	2144	KGK953
2013	LUC239	28.11.50	2079	LYF17	26.1.51	2145	KGK954
2014	LUC240	29.11.50	2080	LYF18	25.1.51	2146	KGK955
2015	LUC241	29.11.50	2081	LYF19	31.1.51	2147	KGK956
2016	LUC242	1.12.50	2082	LYF20	26.1.51	2148	KGK957
2017	LUC243	6.12.50	2083	LYF21	30.1.51	2149	KGK958
2018	LUC244	30.11.50	2084	LYF22	30.1.51	2150	KGK959
2019	LUC245	1.12.50	2085	LYF23	29.1.51	2151	KGK960
2020	LUC246	1.12.50	2086	LYF24	31.1.51	2152	KGK961
2021	LUC247	6.12.50	2087	LYF25	1.2.51	2153	KGK962
2022	LUC248	1.12.50	2088	LYF26	5.2.51	2154	KGK963
2023	LUC249	4.12.50	2089	LYF27	1.2.51	2155	KGK964
2024	LUC266	12.12.50	2090	LYF28	2.2.51	2156	KGK965
2025	LUC267	12.12.50	2091	LYF29	5.2.51	2157	KGK966
2026	LUC268	13.12.50	2092	LYF30	2.2.51	2158	KGK967
2027	LUC269	13.12.50	2093	LYF31	2.2.51	2159	KGK968
2028	LUC270	13.12.50	2094	LYF32	5.2.51	2160	KGK969
2029	LUC271	14.12.50	2095	LYF33	8.2.51	2161	KGK970
2030	LUC272	15.12.50	2096	LYF72	1.3.51	2162	KGK971
2031	LUC273	14.12.50	2097	LYF73	27.2.51	2163	KGK972
2032	LUC274	18.12.50	2098	LYF74	2.3.51	2164	KGK973
2033	LUC275	18.12.50	2099	LYF75	2.3.51	2165	KGK974
2034	LUC276	15.12.50	2100	LYF76	2.3.51	2166	KGK975
2035	LUC277	18.12.50	2101	LYF77	2.3.51	2167	KGK976
2036	LUC278	18.12.50	2102	LYF78	2.3.51	2168	KGK977
2037	LUC279	19.12.50	2103	LYF79	2.3.51	2169	KGK978
2038	LUC280	20.12.50	2104	LYF80	5.3.51	2170	KGK979
2039	LUC281	20.12.50	2105	LYF81	5.3.51	2171	KGK980
2040	LUC288	22.12.50	2106	LYF82	6.3.51	2172	KGU101
2041	LUC289	28.12.50	2107	LYF83	6.3.51	2173	KGU102
2042	LUC290	22.12.50	2108	LYF84	9.3.51	2174	KGU103
2043	LUC291	29.12.50	2109	LYF85	8.3.51	2175	KGU104
2044	LUC292	29.12.50	2110	LYF86	7.3.51	2176	KGU105
2045	LUC293	29.12.50	2111	LYF87	9.3.51	2177	KGU106
2046	LUC294	29.12.50	2112	LYF88	9.3.51	2178	KGU107
2047	LUC295	29.12.50	2113	LYF168	7.5.51	2179	KGU108
2048	LUC296	1.1.51	2114	LYF169	4.5.51	2180	KGU109
2049	LUC297	2.1.51	2115	LYF170	7.5.51	2181	KGU110
2050	LUC298	2.1.51	2116	KLB981		2182	KGU111
2051	LUC299	3.1.51	2117	KLB982		2183	KGU112
2052	LUC300	3.1.51	2118	KLB983		2184	KGU113
2053	LUC301	3.1.51	2119	KLB984		2185	KGU114
2054	LUC302	4.1.51	2120	KLB985		2186	KGU115
2055	LUC303	4.1.51	2121	KLB986		2187	KGU116
2056	LUC304	4.1.51	2122	KGK931		2188	KGU117
2057	LUC320	12.1.51	2123	KGK932		2189	KGU118
2058	LUC321	15.1.51	2124	KGK933		2190	KGU119
2059	LUC322	15.1.51	2125	KGK934		2191	KGU120
2060	LUC323	16.1.51	2126	KGK935		2192	KGU121
2061	LUC324	16.1.51	2127	KGK936		2193	KGU122
2062	LUC325	18.1.51	2128	KGK937		2194	KGU123
2063	LYF1	17.1.51	2129	KGK938		2195	KGU124
2064	LYF2	18.1.51	2130	KGK939		2196	KGU125
2065	LYF3	17.1.51	2131	KGK940		2197	KGU126
2066	LYF4	19.1.51	2132	KGK941		2198	KGU127
2067	LYF5	19.1.51	2133	KGK942		2199	KGU128
2068	LYF6	19.1.51	2134	KGK943		2200	KGU129
2069	LYF7	19.1.51	2135	KGK944		2201	KGU130
2070	LYF8	22.1.51	2136	KGK945		2202	KGU131

RT

RT	Code	RT	Code	RT	Code	RT	Code	RT	Code	Date into stock
2203	KGU132	2269	KGU198	2335	KGU364	2401	KLB780	2467	KLB846	
2204	KGU133	2270	KGU199	2336	KGU365	2402	KLB781	2468	KLB847	3.1.50
2205	KGU134	2271	KGU200	2337	KGU366	2403	KLB782	2469	KLB848	4.1.50
2206	KGU135	2272	KGU301	2338	KGU367	2404	KLB783	2470	KLB849	4.1.50
2207	KGU136	2273	KGU302	2339	KGU368	2405	KLB784	2471	KLB850	5.1.50
2208	KGU137	2274	KGU303	2340	KGU369	2406	KLB785	2472	KXW101	5.1.50
2209	KGU138	2275	KGU304	2341	KGU370	2407	KLB786	2473	KXW102	6.1.50
2210	KGU139	2276	KGU305	2342	KGU371	2408	KLB787	2474	KXW103	6.1.50
2211	KGU140	2277	KGU306	2343	KGU372	2409	KLB788	2475	KXW104	9.1.50
2212	KGU141	2278	KGU307	2344	KGU373	2410	KLB789	2476	KXW105	9.1.50
2213	KGU142	2279	KGU308	2345	KGU374	2411	KLB790	2477	KXW106	10.1.50
2214	KGU143	2280	KGU309	2346	KGU375	2412	KLB791	2478	KXW107	10.1.50
2215	KGU144	2281	KGU310	2347	KGU376	2413	KLB792	2479	KXW108	11.1.50
2216	KGU145	2282	KGU311	2348	KGU377	2414	KLB793	2480	KXW109	11.1.50
2217	KGU146	2283	KGU312	2349	KGU378	2415	KLB794	2481	KXW110	12.1.50
2218	KGU147	2284	KGU313	2350	KGU379	2416	KLB795	2482	KXW111	12.1.50
2219	KGU148	2285	KGU314	2351	KGU380	2417	KLB796	2483	KXW112	13.1.50
2220	KGU149	2286	KGU315	2352	KGU381	2418	KLB797	2484	KXW113	13.1.50
2221	KGU150	2287	KGU316	2353	KGU382	2419	KLB798	2485	KXW114	16.1.50
2222	KGU151	2288	KGU317	2354	KGU383	2420	KLB799	2486	KXW115	17.1.50
2223	KGU152	2289	KGU318	2355	KGU384	2421	KLB800	2487	KXW116	17.1.50
2224	KGU153	2290	KGU319	2356	KGU385	2422	KLB801	2488	KXW117	18.1.50
2225	KGU154	2291	KGU320	2357	KGU386	2423	KLB802	2489	KXW118	18.1.50
2226	KGU155	2292	KGU321	2358	KGU387	2424	KLB803	2490	KXW119	18.1.50
2227	KGU156	2293	KGU322	2359	KGU388	2425	KLB804	2491	KXW120	19.1.50
2228	KGU157	2294	KGU323	2360	KGU389	2426	KLB805	2492	KXW121	19.1.50
2229	KGU158	2295	KGU324	2361	KGU390	2427	KLB806	2493	KXW122	20.1.50
2230	KGU159	2296	KGU325	2362	KGU391	2428	KLB807	2494	KXW123	20.1.50
2231	KGU160	2297	KGU326	2363	KGU392	2429	KLB808	2495	KXW124	23.1.50
2232	KGU161	2298	KGU327	2364	KGU393	2430	KLB809	2496	KXW125	24.1.50
2233	KGU162	2299	KGU328	2365	KGU394	2431	KLB810	2497	KXW126	24.1.50
2234	KGU163	2300	KGU329	2366	KGU395	2432	KLB811	2498	KXW127	25.1.50
2235	KGU164	2301	KGU330	2367	KGU396	2433	KLB812	2499	KXW128	25.1.50
2236	KGU165	2302	KGU331	2368	KGU397	2434	KLB813	2500	KXW129	26.1.50
2237	KGU166	2303	KGU332	2369	KGU398	2435	KLB814	2501	KXW130	26.1.50
2238	KGU167	2304	KGU333	2370	KGU399	2436	KLB815	2502	KXW131	27.1.50
2239	KGU168	2305	KGU334	2371	KGU400	2437	KLB816	2503	KXW132	27.1.50
2240	KGU169	2306	KGU335	2372	KLB751	2438	KLB817	2504	KXW133	30.1.50
2241	KGU170	2307	KGU336	2373	KLB752	2439	KLB818	2505	KXW134	30.1.50
2242	KGU171	2308	KGU337	2374	KLB753	2440	KLB819	2506	KXW135	31.1.50
2243	KGU172	2309	KGU338	2375	KLB754	2441	KLB820	2507	KXW136	31.1.50
2244	KGU173	2310	KGU339	2376	KLB755	2442	KLB821	2508	KXW137	1.2.50
2245	KGU174	2311	KGU340	2377	KLB756	2443	KLB822	2509	KXW138	2.2.50
2246	KGU175	2312	KGU341	2378	KLB757	2444	KLB823	2510	KXW139	2.2.50
2247	KGU176	2313	KGU342	2379	KLB758	2445	KLB824	2511	KXW140	3.2.50
2248	KGU177	2314	KGU343	2380	KLB759	2446	KLB825	2512	KXW141	3.2.50
2249	KGU178	2315	KGU344	2381	KLB760	2447	KLB826	2513	KXW142	6.2.50
2250	KGU179	2316	KGU345	2382	KLB761	2448	KLB827	2514	KXW143	6.2.50
2251	KGU180	2317	KGU346	2383	KLB762	2449	KLB828	2515	KXW144	7.2.50
2252	KGU181	2318	KGU347	2384	KLB763	2450	KLB829	2516	KXW145	8.2.50
2253	KGU182	2319	KGU348	2385	KLB764	2451	KLB830	2517	KXW146	8.2.50
2254	KGU183	2320	KGU349	2386	KLB765	2452	KLB831	2518	KXW147	9.2.50
2255	KGU184	2321	KGU350	2387	KLB766	2453	KLB832	2519	KXW148	9.2.50
2256	KGU185	2322	KGU351	2388	KLB767	2454	KLB833	2520	KXW149	14.2.50
2257	KGU186	2323	KGU352	2389	KLB768	2455	KLB834	2521	KXW150	14.2.50
2258	KGU187	2324	KGU353	2390	KLB769	2456	KLB835	2522	LYF171	8.5.51
2259	KGU188	2325	KGU354	2391	KLB770	2457	KLB836	2523	LYF172	9.5.51
2260	KGU189	2326	KGU355	2392	KLB771	2458	KLB837	2524	LYF173	8.5.51
2261	KGU190	2327	KGU356	2393	KLB772	2459	KLB838	2525	LYF174	9.5.51
2262	KGU191	2328	KGU357	2394	KLB773	2460	KLB839	2526	LYF175	10.5.51
2263	KGU192	2329	KGU358	2395	KLB774	2461	KLB840	2527	LYF176	11.5.51
2264	KGU193	2330	KGU359	2396	KLB775	2462	KLB841	2528	LYF177	10.5.51
2265	KGU194	2331	KGU360	2397	KLB776	2463	KLB842	2529	LYF178	10.5.51
2266	KGU195	2332	KGU361	2398	KLB777	2464	KLB843	2530	LYF179	15.5.51
2267	KGU196	2333	KGU362	2399	KLB778	2465	KLB844	2531	LYF180	15.5.51
2268	KGU197	2334	KGU363	2400	KLB779	2466	KLB845	2532	LYF181	15.5.51

RT		Date into stock	RT		Date into stock	RT		Date into stock
2533	LYF182	17.5.51	2600	LYF325	2.7.51	2667	LYR651	24.8.51
2534	LYF183	16.5.51	2601	LYF326	29.6.51	2668	LYR652	28.8.51
2535	LYF184	17.5.51	2602	LYF327	3.7.51	2669	LYR653	29.8.51
2536	LYF185	18.5.51	2603	LYF328	6.7.51	2670	LYR654	29.8.51
2537	LYF186	18.5.51	2604	LYF329	4.7.51	2671	LYR655	30.8.51
2538	LYF187	18.5.51	2605	LYF330	6.7.51	2672	LYR656	30.8.51
2539	LYF188	18.5.51	2606	LYF331	6.7.51	2673	LYR657	31.8.51
2540	LYF189	21.5.51	2607	LYF332	6.7.51	2674	LYR658	31.8.51
2541	LYF190	22.5.51	2608	LYF333	6.7.51	2675	LYR659	31.8.51
2542	LYF191	22.5.51	2609	LYF334	6.7.51	2676	LYR660	31.8.51
2543	LYF192	23.5.51	2610	LYF335	10.7.51	2677	LYR661	4.9.51
2544	LYF193	24.5.51	2611	LYF336	10.7.51	2678	LYR662	5.9.51
2545	LYF194	23.5.51	2612	LYF337	10.7.51	2679	LYR663	5.9.51
2546	LYF195	24.5.51	2613	LYF338	12.7.51	2680	LYR664	5.9.51
2547	LYF196	24.5.51	2614	LYF339	12.7.51	2681	LYR665	6.9.51
2548	LYF197	25.5.51	2615	LYF340	13.7.51	2682	LYR666	7.9.51
2549	LYF198	25.5.51	2616	LYF341	13.7.51	2683	LYR667	7.9.51
2550	LYF199	28.5.51	2617	LYF342	13.7.51	2684	LYR668	12.9.51
2551	LYF200	28.5.51	2618	LYF343	13.7.51	2685	LYR669	7.9.51
2552	LYF277	28.5.51	2619	LYF344	13.7.51	2686	LYR670	7.9.51
2553	LYF278	31.5.51	2620	LYF345	17.7.51	2687	LYR671	13.9.51
2554	LYF279	30.5.51	2621	LYF346	18.7.51	2688	LYR672	11.9.51
2555	LYF280	1.6.51	2622	LYF347	19.7.51	2689	LYR673	13.9.51
2556	LYF281	1.6.51	2623	LYF348	20.7.51	2690	LYR674	14.9.51
2557	LYF282	1.6.51	2624	LYF349	19.7.51	2691	LYR675	14.9.51
2558	LYF283	1.6.51	2625	LYF350	20.7.51	2692	LYR676	14.9.51
2559	LYF284	1.6.51	2626	LYF351	20.7.51	2693	LYR677	14.9.51
2560	LYF285	4.6.51	2627	LYF352	24.7.51	2694	LYR678	14.9.51
2561	LYF286	4.6.51	2628	LYF353	20.7.51	2695	LYR679	20.9.51
2562	LYF287	7.6.51	2629	LYF354	20.7.51	2696	LYR680	20.9.51
2563	LYF288	7.6.51	2630	LYF355	25.7.51	2697	LYR681	20.9.51
2564	LYF289	8.6.51	2631	LYF356	26.7.51	2698	LYR682	20.9.51
2565	LYF290	13.6.51	2632	LYF357	26.7.51	2699	LYR683	21.9.51
2566	LYF291	8.6.51	2633	LYF358	26.7.51	2700	LYR684	21.9.51
2567	LYF292	7.6.51	2634	LYF359	27.7.51	2701	LYR685	21.9.51
2568	LYF293	8.6.51	2635	LYF360	27.7.51	2702	LYR686	21.9.51
2569	LYF294	8.6.51	2636	LYF361	27.7.51	2703	LYR687	21.9.51
2570	LYF295	11.6.51	2637	LYF362	27.7.51	2704	LYR688	26.9.51
2571	LYF296	12.6.51	2638	LYF363	30.7.51	2705	LYR689	26.9.51
2572	LYF297	14.6.51	2639	LYF364	31.7.51	2706	LYR690	26.9.51
2573	LYF298	13.6.51	2640	LYF365	1.8.51	2707	LYR691	26.9.51
2574	LYF299	14.6.51	2641	LYF366	3.8.51	2708	LYR692	28.9.51
2575	LYF300	14.6.51	2642	LYF367	3.8.51	2709	LYR693	28.9.51
2576	LYF301	15.6.51	2643	LYF368	9.8.51	2710	LYR694	28.9.51
2577	LYF302	15.6.51	2644	LYF369	10.8.51	2711	LYR695	28.9.51
2578	LYF303	15.6.51	2645	LYF370	10.8.51	2712	LYR696	28.9.51
2579	LYF304	15.6.51	2646	LYF371	10.8.51	2713	LYR697	2.10.51
2580	LYF305	21.6.51	2647	LYF372	13.8.51	2714	LYR698	3.10.51
2581	LYF306	20.6.51	2648	LYF373	13.8.51	2715	LYR699	3.10.51
2582	LYF307	19.6.51	2649	LYF374	13.8.51	2716	LYR700	5.10.51
2583	LYF308	20.6.51	2650	LYF375	15.8.51	2717	LYR701	5.10.51
2584	LYF309	21.6.51	2651	LYF376	16.8.51	2718	LYR702	5.10.51
2585	LYF310	21.6.51	2652	LYR636	16.8.51	2719	LYR703	5.10.51
2586	LYF311	22.6.51	2653	LYR637	17.8.51	2720	LYR704	5.10.51
2587	LYF312	21.6.51	2654	LYR638	17.8.51	2721	LYR705	5.10.51
2588	LYF313	22.6.51	2655	LYR639	17.8.51	2722	LYR706	12.10.51
2589	LYF314	22.6.51	2656	LYR640	17.8.51	2723	LYR707	11.10.51
2590	LYF315	25.6.51	2657	LYR641	17.8.51	2724	LYR708	11.10.51
2591	LYF316	25.6.51	2658	LYR642	17.8.51	2725	LYR709	12.10.51
2592	LYF317	26.6.51	2659	LYR643	22.8.51	2726	LYR710	12.10.51
2593	LYF318	27.6.51	2660	LYR644	22.8.51	2727	LYR711	12.10.51
2594	LYF319	29.6.51	2661	LYR645	23.8.51	2728	LYR712	12.10.51
2595	LYF320	29.6.51	2662	LYR646	23.8.51	2729	LYR713	15.10.51
2596	LYF321	29.6.51	2663	LYR647	24.8.51	2730	LYR714	18.10.51
2597	LYF322	28.6.51	2664	LYR648	24.8.51	2731	LYR715	19.10.51
2598	LYF323	29.6.51	2665	LYR649	24.8.51	2732	LYR716	18.10.51
2599	LYF324	2.7.51	2666	LYR650	24.8.51	2733	LYR717	18.10.51

RT		Date into stock	RT		Date into stock	RT		Date into stock
2734	LYR718	19.10.51	2801	LYR971	9.2.52	2868	MLL615	31.3.52
2735	LYR719	19.10.51	2802	LYR972	9.2.52	2869	MLL616	2.4.52
2736	LYR720	24.10.51	2803	LYR973	12.2.52	2870	MLL617	4.4.52
2737	LYR721	23.10.51	2804	LYR974	13.2.52	2871	MLL618	3.4.52
2738	LYR722	24.10.51	2805	LYR975	13.2.52	2872	MLL619	4.4.52
2739	LYR723	24.10.51	2806	LYR976	14.2.52	2873	MLL620	4.4.52
2740	LYR724	25.10.51	2807	LYR977	14.2.52	2874	MLL621	9.4.52
2741	LYR725	25.10.51	2808	LYR978	14.2.52	2875	MLL622	9.4.52
2742	LYR726	25.10.51	2809	LYR979	14.2.52	2876	MLL623	10.4.52
2743	LYR727	25.10.51	2810	LYR980	15.2.52	2877	MLL624	9.4.52
2744	LYR728	29.10.51	2811	LYR981	15.2.52	2878	MLL625	10.4.52
2745	LYR729	29.10.51	2812	LYR982	15.2.52	2879	MLL626	10.4.52
2746	LYR730	29.10.51	2813	LYR983	19.2.52	2880	MLL627	10.4.52
2747	LYR731	26.10.51	2814	LYR984	20.2.52	2881	MLL628	10.4.52
2748	LYR732	30.10.51	2815	LYR985	20.2.52	2882	MLL629	10.4.52
2749	LYR733	31.10.51	2816	LYR986	21.2.52	2883	MLL630	17.4.52
2750	LYR734	31.10.51	2817	LYR987	21.2.52	2884	MLL631	17.4.52
2751	LYR735	31.10.51	2818	LYR988	22.2.52	2885	MLL632	17.4.52
2752	LYR736	31.10.51	2819	LYR989	26.2.52	2886	MLL633	18.4.52
2753	LYR737	2.11.51	2820	LYR990	22.2.52	2887	MLL634	18.4.52
2754	LYR738	31.10.51	2821	LYR991	28.2.52	2888	MLL635	18.4.52
2755	LYR739	2.11.51	2822	LYR992	22.2.52	2889	MLL636	22.4.52
2756	LYR740	2.11.51	2823	LYR993	28.2.52	2890	MLL637	22.4.52
2757	LYR741	5.11.51	2824	LYR994	28.2.52	2891	MLL638	23.4.52
2758	LYR742	8.11.51	2825	LYR995	28.2.52	2892	MLL639	24.4.52
2759	LYR743	7.11.51	2826	LYR996	29.2.52	2893	MLL640	24.4.52
2760	LYR744	7.11.51	2827	LYR997	5.3.52	2894	MLL641	25.4.52
2761	LYR745	8.11.51	2828	LYR998	29.2.52	2895	MLL642	25.4.52
2762	LYR746	9.11.51	2829	LYR999	29.2.52	2896	MLL643	25.4.52
2763	LYR747	9.11.51	2830	LYF477	4.3.52	2897	MLL644	29.4.52
2764	LYR748	9.11.51	2831	LYF478	4.3.52	2898	MLL645	29.4.52
2765	LYR749	9.11.51	2832	LYF479	5.3.52	2899	MLL646	29.4.52
2766	LYR750	9.11.51	2833	LYF480	6.3.52	2900	MLL647	30.4.52
2767	LYR751	9.11.51	2834	LYF481	6.3.52	2901	MLL648	30.4.52
2768	LYR752	9.11.51	2835	LYF482	7.3.52	2902	MLL649	30.4.52
2769	LYR753	13.11.51	2836	LYF483	7.3.52	2903	MLL650	30.4.52
2770	LYR754	13.11.51	2837	LYF484	7.3.52	2904	MLL651	2.5.52
2771	LYR755	14.11.51	2838	LYF485	7.3.52	2905	MLL652	5.5.52
2772	LYR756	16.11.51	2839	LYF486	10.3.52	2906	MLL653	8.5.52
2773	LYR757	14.11.51	2840	LYF487	7.3.52	2907	MLL654	6.5.52
2774	LYR758	16.11.51	2841	LYF488	12.3.52	2908	MLL655	8.5.52
2775	LYR826	8.1.52	2842	LYF489	13.3.52	2909	MLL656	6.5.52
2776	LYR827	26.2.52	2843	LYF490	12.3.52	2910	MLL657	27.3.53
2777	LYR941	16.1.52	2844	LYF491	14.3.52	2911	MLL658	8.5.52
2778	LYR942	15.1.52	2845	LYF492	14.3.52	2912	MLL659	9.5.52
2779	LYR943	17.1.52	2846	LYF493	14.3.52	2913	MLL660	12.5.52
2780	LYR944	16.1.52	2847	LYF494	14.3.52	2914	MLL661	12.5.52
2781	LYR945	17.1.52	2848	LYF495	14.3.52	2915	MLL662	13.5.52
2782	LYR946	18.1.52	2849	LYF496	14.3.52	2916	MLL663	13.5.52
2783	LYR947	18.1.52	2850	LYF497	19.3.52	2917	MLL664	14.5.52
2784	LYR948	18.1.52	2851	LYF498	19.3.52	2918	MLL665	15.5.52
2785	LYR949	18.1.52	2852	LYF499	19.3.52	2919	MLL666	16.5.52
2786	LYR950	18.1.52	2853	LYF500	20.3.52	2920	MLL667	19.5.52
2787	LYR951	22.1.52	2854	MLL501	21.3.52	2921	MLL668	19.5.52
2788	LYR952	22.1.52	2855	MLL502	21.3.52	2922	MLL669	20.5.52
2789	LYR953	23.1.52	2856	MLL503	25.3.52	2923	MLL670	22.5.52
2790	LYR954	23.1.52	2857	MLL504	21.3.52	2924	MLL671	21.5.52
2791	LYR955	24.1.52	2858	MLL505	21.3.52	2925	MLL672	22.5.52
2792	LYR962	1.2.52	2859	MLL506	21.3.52	2926	MLL673	23.5.52
2793	LYR963	1.2.52	2860	MLL507	26.3.52	2927	MLL674	26.5.52
2794	LYR964	1.2.52	2861	MLL508	26.3.52	2928	MLL675	27.5.52
2795	LYR965	1.2.52	2862	MLL509	28.3.52	2929	MLL688	12.6.52
2796	LYR966	9.2.52	2863	MLL510	28.3.52	2930	MLL689	13.6.52
2797	LYR967	7.2.52	2864	MLL511	28.3.52	2931	MLL690	13.6.52
2798	LYR968	8.2.52	2865	MLL512	28.3.52	2932	MLL691	13.6.52
2799	LYR969	8.2.52	2866	MLL613	28.3.52	2933	MLL692	18.6.52
2800	LYR970	9.2.52	2867	MLL614	31.3.52	2934	MLL693	19.6.52

RT		Date into stock	RT		Date into stock	RT		Date into stock
2935	MLL694	20.6.52	3002	NLE773	16.4.53	3069	KXW178	6.3.50
2936	MLL695	20.6.52	3003	NLE774	16.4.53	3070	KXW179	6.3.50
2937	MLL696	20.6.52	3004	NLE775	17.4.53	3071	KXW180	7.3.50
2938	MLL704	3.7.52	3005	NLE776	17.4.53	3072	KXW181	7.3.50
2939	MLL705	10.10.52	3006	NLE777	17.4.53	3073	KXW182	8.3.50
2940	MLL706	10.10.52	3007	NLE778	17.4.53	3074	KXW183	9.3.50
2941	MLL707	10.10.52	3008	NLE779	21.4.53	3075	KXW184	9.3.50
2942	MLL708	14.10.52	3009	NLE780	22.4.53	3076	KXW185	10.3.50
2943	MLL709	15.10.52	3010	NLE781	22.4.53	3077	KXW186	10.3.50
2944	MLL710	20.10.52	3011	NLE901	29.4.53	3078	KXW187	13.3.50
2945	MLL711	23.10.52	3012	NLE902	30.4.53	3079	KXW188	13.3.50
2946	MLL712	21.10.52	3013	NLE903	30.4.53	3080	KXW189	14.3.50
2947	MXX31	23.10.52	3014	NLE904	30.4.53	3081	KXW190	14.3.50
2948	MXX36	31.10.52	3015	NLE905	30.4.53	3082	KXW191	15.3.50
2949	MXX37	31.10.52	3016	NLE906	30.4.53	3083	KXW192	15.3.50
2950	MXX38	31.10.52	3017	NLE907	1.5.53	3084	KXW193	16.3.50
2951	MXX39	31.10.52	3018	NLE908	1.5.53	3085	KXW194	16.3.50
2952	MXX41	3.11.52	3019	NLE909	1.5.53	3086	KXW195	17.3.50
2953	MXX42	31.10.52	3020	NLE910	6.5.53	3087	KXW196	17.3.50
2954	MXX43	3.11.52	3021	NLE911	1.5.53	3088	KXW197	20.3.50
2955	MXX44	3.11.52	3022	NLE912	5.5.53	3089	KXW198	20.3.50
2956	MXX45	5.11.52	3023	NLE913	5.5.53	3090	KXW199	21.3.50
2957	MXX46	6.11.52	3024	NLE914	6.5.53	3091	KXW200	21.3.50
2958	MXX47	6.11.52	3025	NLE915	5.5.53	3092	KXW201	23.3.50
2959	MXX48	10.11.52	3026	NLE916	7.5.53	3093	KXW202	23.3.50
2960	MXX49	10.11.52	3027	NLE917	7.5.53	3094	KXW203	23.3.50
2961	MXX50	10.11.52	3028	NLE918	8.5.53	3095	KXW204	24.3.50
2962	MXX51	10.11.52	3029	NLE919	8.5.53	3096	KXW205	24.3.50
2963	MXX52	10.11.52	3030	NLE920	12.5.53	3097	KXW206	27.3.50
2964	MXX53	12.11.52	3031	NLE921	8.5.53	3098	KXW207	27.3.50
2965	MXX54	12.11.52	3032	NLE922	13.5.53	3099	KXW208	28.3.50
2966	MXX55	12.11.52	3033	NLE923	13.5.53	3100	KXW209	28.3.50
2967	MXX56	13.11.52	3034	NLE924	14.5.53	3101	KXW210	29.3.50
2968	MXX57	14.11.52	3035	NLE925	14.5.53	3102	KXW211	29.3.50
2969	MXX58	14.11.52	3036	NLE926	15.5.53	3103	KXW212	30.3.50
2970	MXX59	14.11.52	3037	NLE927	15.5.53	3104	KXW213	30.3.50
2971	MXX60	14.11.52	3038	NLE928	15.5.53	3105	KXW214	31.3.50
2972	NLE740	10.3.53	3039	NLE929	15.5.53	3106	KXW215	31.3.50
2973	NLE741	11.3.53	3040	NLE930	20.5.53	3107	KXW216	3.4.50
2974	NLE742	11.3.53	3041	NLE931	20.5.53	3108	KXW217	3.4.50
2975	NLE743	12.3.53	3042	KXW151	13.2.50	3109	KXW218	4.4.50
2976	NLE744	12.3.53	3043	KXW152	13.2.50	3110	KXW219	5.4.50
2977	NLE745	13.3.53	3044	KXW153	15.2.50	3111	KXW220	6.4.50
2978	NLE746	13.3.53	3045	KXW154	15.2.50	3112	KXW221	6.4.50
2979	NLE747	17.3.53	3046	KXW155	15.2.50	3113	KXW222	6.4.50
2980	NLE748	17.3.53	3047	KXW156	16.2.50	3114	KXW223	11.4.50
2981	NLE749	18.3.53	3048	KXW157	16.2.50	3115	KXW224	11.4.50
2982	NLE750	18.3.53	3049	KXW158	17.2.50	3116	KXW225	12.4.50
2983	NLE754	20.3.53	3050	KXW159	17.2.50	3117	KXW226	12.4.50
2984	NLE755	25.3.53	3051	KXW160	20.2.50	3118	KXW227	13.4.50
2985	NLE756	25.3.53	3052	KXW161	20.2.50	3119	KXW228	13.4.50
2986	NLE757	26.3.53	3053	KXW162	21.2.50	3120	KXW229	14.4.50
2987	NLE758	26.3.53	3054	KXW163	21.2.50	3121	KXW230	14.4.50
2988	NLE759	27.3.53	3055	KXW164	22.2.50	3122	KXW231	17.4.50
2989	NLE760	27.3.53	3056	KXW165	23.2.50	3123	KXW232	17.4.50
2990	NLE761	27.3.53	3057	KXW166	23.2.50	3124	KXW233	18.4.50
2991	NLE762	31.3.53	3058	KXW167	24.2.50	3125	KXW234	18.4.50
2992	NLE763	2.4.53	3059	KXW168	24.2.50	3126	KXW235	19.4.50
2993	NLE764	2.4.53	3060	KXW169	27.2.50	3127	KXW236	19.4.50
2994	NLE765	2.4.53	3061	KXW170	27.2.50	3128	KXW237	21.4.50
2995	NLE766	9.4.53	3062	KXW171	28.2.50	3129	KXW238	20.4.50
2996	NLE767	9.4.53	3063	KXW172	28.2.50	3130	KXW239	21.4.50
2997	NLE768	10.4.53	3064	KXW173	1.3.50	3131	KXW240	21.4.50
2998	NLE769	10.4.53	3065	KXW174	2.3.50	3132	KXW241	24.4.50
2999	NLE770	10.4.53	3066	KXW175	2.3.50	3133	KXW242	24.4.50
3000	NLE771	14.4.53	3067	KXW176	3.3.50	3134	KXW243	25.4.50
3001	NLE772	15.4.53	3068	KXW177	3.3.50	3135	KXW244	25.4.50

RT		Date into stock	RT		Date into stock	RT		Date into stock
3136	KXW245	25.4.50	3203	KYY932	16.6.50	3270	LLU629	15.8.50
3137	KXW246	27.4.50	3204	KYY933	16.6.50	3271	LLU630	15.8.50
3138	KXW247	27.4.50	3205	KYY934	19.6.50	3272	LLU631	16.8.50
3139	KXW248	28.4.50	3206	KYY935	19.6.50	3273	LLU632	17.8.50
3140	KXW249	28.4.50	3207	KYY936	20.6.50	3274	LLU633	17.8.50
3141	KXW250	1.5.50	3208	KYY937	20.6.50	3275	LLU634	18.8.50
3142	KYY871	1.5.50	3209	KYY938	21.6.50	3276	LLU635	18.8.50
3143	KYY872	2.5.50	3210	KYY939	21.6.50	3277	LLU636	21.8.50
3144	KYY873	2.5.50	3211	KYY940	22.6.50	3278	LLU637	22.8.50
3145	KYY874	5.5.50	3212	KYY941	22.6.50	3279	LLU638	22.8.50
3146	KYY875	8.5.50	3213	KYY942	23.6.50	3280	LLU639	24.8.50
3147	KYY876	5.5.50	3214	KYY943	23.6.50	3281	LLU640	24.8.50
3148	KYY877	5.5.50	3215	KYY944	26.6.50	3282	LYR501	9.8.51
3149	KYY878	5.5.50	3216	KYY945	26.6.50	3283	LYR502	10.8.51
3150	KYY879	8.5.50	3217	KYY946	27.6.50	3284	LYR503	13.8.51
3151	KYY880	8.5.50	3218	KYY947	27.6.50	3285	LYR504	14.8.51
3152	KYY881	9.5.50	3219	KYY948	28.6.50	3286	LYR505	14.8.51
3153	KYY882	9.5.50	3220	KYY949	29.6.50	3287	LYR506	15.8.51
3154	KYY883	10.5.50	3221	KYY950	29.6.50	3288	LYR507	16.8.51
3155	KYY884	10.5.50	3222	KYY951	30.6.50	3289	LYR508	16.8.51
3156	KYY885	11.5.50	3223	KYY952	30.6.50	3290	LYR509	17.8.51
3157	KYY886	11.5.50	3224	KYY953	3.7.50	3291	LYR510	20.8.51
3158	KYY887	12.5.50	3225	KYY954	4.7.50	3292	LYR511	21.8.51
3159	KYY888	12.5.50	3226	KYY955	4.7.50	3293	LYR512	22.8.51
3160	KYY889	15.5.50	3227	KYY956	4.7.50	3294	LYR513	23.8.51
3161	KYY890	15.5.50	3228	KYY957	5.7.50	3295	LYR514	24.8.51
3162	KYY891	16.5.50	3229	KYY958	5.7.50	3296	LYR515	27.8.51
3163	KYY892	16.5.50	3230	KYY959	6.7.50	3297	LYR516	28.8.51
3164	KYY893	17.5.50	3231	KYY960	6.7.50	3298	LYR517	28.8.51
3165	KYY894	18.5.50	3232	KYY961	7.7.50	3299	LYR518	29.8.51
3166	KYY895	18.5.50	3233	KYY962	7.7.50	3300	LYR519	30.8.51
3167	KYY896	19.5.50	3234	KYY963	10.7.50	3301	LYR520	31.8.51
3168	KYY897	19.5.50	3235	KYY964	10.7.50	3302	LYR521	31.8.51
3169	KYY898	22.5.50	3236	KYY965	11.7.50	3303	LYR522	4.9.51
3170	KYY899	22.5.50	3237	KYY966	11.7.50	3304	LYR523	4.9.51
3171	KYY900	23.5.50	3238	KYY967	12.7.50	3305	LYR524	4.9.51
3172	KYY901	23.5.50	3239	KYY968	13.7.50	3306	LYR525	5.9.51
3173	KYY902	24.5.50	3240	KYY969	13.7.50	3307	LYR526	6.9.51
3174	KYY903	24.5.50	3241	KYY970	14.7.50	3308	LYR527	7.9.51
3175	KYY904	25.5.50	3242	LLU601	14.7.50	3309	LYR528	7.9.51
3176	KYY905	25.5.50	3243	LLU602	17.7.50	3310	LYR529	10.9.51
3177	KYY906	26.5.50	3244	LLU603	19.7.50	3311	LYR530	11.9.51
3178	KYY907	26.5.50	3245	LLU604	18.7.50	3312	LYR531	11.9.51
3179	KYY908	30.5.50	3246	LLU605	18.7.50	3313	LYR532	12.9.51
3180	KYY909	30.5.50	3247	LLU606	19.7.50	3314	LYR533	13.9.51
3181	KYY910	21.5.50	3248	LLU607	20.7.50	3315	LYR534	14.9.51
3182	KYY911	31.5.50	3249	LLU608	20.7.50	3316	LYR535	14.9.51
3183	KYY912	1.6.50	3250	LLU609	20.7.50	3317	LYR536	17.9.51
3184	KYY913	2.6.50	3251	LLU610	21.7.50	3318	LYR537	18.9.51
3185	KYY914	2.6.50	3252	LLU611	21.7.50	3319	LYR538	18.9.51
3186	KYY915	5.6.50	3253	LLU612	24.7.50	3320	LYR539	19.9.51
3187	KYY916	5.6.50	3254	LLU613	24.7.50	3321	LYR540	20.9.51
3188	KYY917	6.6.50	3255	LLU614	25.7.50	3322	LYR541	21.9.51
3189	KYY918	6.6.50	3256	LLU615	25.7.50	3323	LYR542	21.9.51
3190	KYY919	7.6.50	3257	LLU616	26.7.50	3324	LYR543	24.9.51
3191	KYY920	7.6.50	3258	LLU617	27.7.50	3325	LYR544	25.9.51
3192	KYY921	8.6.50	3259	LLU618	27.7.50	3326	LYR545	25.9.51
3193	KYY922	8.6.50	3260	LLU619	28.7.50	3327	LYR546	26.9.51
3194	KYY923	9.6.50	3261	LLU620	28.7.50	3328	LYR547	27.9.51
3195	KYY924	9.6.50	3262	LLU621	31.7.50	3329	LYR548	28.9.51
3196	KYY925	12.6.50	3263	LLU622	31.7.50	3330	LYR549	28.9.51
3197	KYY926	12.6.50	3264	LLU623	10.8.50	3331	LYR550	1.10.51
3198	KYY927	13.6.50	3265	LLU624	10.8.50	3332	LYR551	2.10.51
3199	KYY928	13.6.50	3266	LLU625	11.8.50	3333	LYR552	2.10.51
3200	KYY929	14.6.50	3267	LLU626	11.8.50	3334	LYR553	3.10.51
3201	KYY930	28.6.50	3268	LLU627	14.8.50	3335	LYR554	4.10.51
3202	KYY931	15.6.50	3269	LLU628	14.8.50	3336	LYR555	5.10.51

RT		Date into stock	RT		Date into stock	RT		Date into stock
3337	LYR556	5.10.51	3404	LYR623	12.12.51	3471	LYR890	4.3.52
3338	LYR557	8.10.51	3405	LYR624	13.12.51	3472	LYR891	5.3.52
3339	LYR558	9.10.51	3406	LYR625	14.12.51	3473	LYR892	6.3.52
3340	LYR559	9.10.51	3407	LYR626	14.12.51	3474	LYR893	7.3.52
3341	LYR560	10.10.51	3408	LYR627	17.12.51	3475	LYR894	7.3.52
3342	LYR561	11.10.51	3409	LYR628	18.12.51	3476	LYR895	10.3.52
3343	LYR562	12.10.51	3410	LYR629	18.12.51	3477	LYR896	11.3.52
3344	LYR563	12.10.51	3411	LYR630	19.12.51	3478	LYR897	12.3.52
3345	LYR564	15.10.51	3412	LYR631	20.12.51	3479	LYR898	13.3.52
3346	LYR565	16.10.51	3413	LYR632	21.12.51	3480	LYR899	14.3.52
3347	LYR566	16.10.51	3414	LYR633	21.12.51	3481	LYR900	14.3.52
3348	LYR567	17.10.51	3415	LYR634	27.3.52	3482	LYR901	17.3.52
3349	LYR568	18.10.51	3416	LYR635	31.12.51	3483	LYR902	18.3.52
3350	LYR569	19.10.51	3417	LYR836	2.1.52	3484	LYR903	19.3.52
3351	LYR570	19.10.51	3418	LYR837	3.1.52	3485	LYR904	20.3.52
3352	LYR571	22.10.51	3419	LYR838	4.1.52	3486	LYR905	21.3.52
3353	LYR572	23.10.51	3420	LYR839	7.1.52	3487	LYR906	21.3.52
3354	LYR573	24.10.51	3421	LYR840	7.1.52	3488	LYR907	24.3.52
3355	LYR574	24.10.51	3422	LYR841	7.1.52	3489	LYR908	25.3.52
3356	LYR575	25.10.51	3423	LYR842	8.1.52	3490	LYR909	26.3.52
3357	LYR576	26.10.51	3424	LYR843	9.1.52	3491	LYR910	28.3.52
3358	LYR577	26.10.51	3425	LYR844	10.1.52	3492	LYR911	28.3.52
3359	LYR578	29.10.51	3426	LYR845	11.1.52	3493	LYR912	31.3.52
3360	LYR579	30.10.51	3427	LYR846	14.1.52	3494	LYR913	1.4.52
3361	LYR580	31.10.51	3428	LYR847	14.1.52	3495	LYR914	2.4.52
3362	LYR581	1.11.51	3429	LYR848	15.1.52	3496	LYR915	3.4.52
3363	LYR582	1.11.51	3430	LYR849	16.1.52	3497	LYR916	4.4.52
3364	LYR583	2.11.51	3431	LYR850	17.1.52	3498	LYR917	4.4.52
3365	LYR584	2.11.51	3432	LYR851	18.1.52	3499	LYR918	7.4.52
3366	LYR585	5.11.51	3433	LYR852	18.1.52	3500	LYR919	8.4.52
3367	LYR586	6.11.51	3434	LYR853	21.1.52	3501	LYR920	9.4.52
3368	LYR587	6.11.51	3435	LYR854	22.1.52	3502	LYR921	10.4.52
3369	LYR588	7.11.51	3436	LYR855	23.1.52	3503	LYR922	16.4.52
3370	LYR589	8.11.51	3437	LYR856	24.1.52	3504	LYR923	15.4.52
3371	LYR590	9.11.51	3438	LYR857	25.1.52	3505	LYR924	17.4.52
3372	LYR591	9.11.51	3439	LYR858	25.1.52	3506	LYR925	18.4.52
3373	LYR592	12.11.51	3440	LYR859	28.1.52	3507	LYR926	21.4.52
3374	LYR593	13.11.51	3441	LYR860	29.1.52	3508	LYR927	22.4.52
3375	LYR594	14.11.51	3442	LYR861	30.1.52	3509	LYR928	23.4.52
3376	LYR595	15.11.51	3443	LYR862	31.1.52	3510	LYR929	24.4.52
3377	LYR596	16.11.51	3444	LYR863	1.2.52	3511	LYR930	25.4.52
3378	LYR597	16.11.51	3445	LYR864	1.2.52	3512	LYR931	28.4.52
3379	LYR598	19.11.51	3446	LYR865	4.2.52	3513	LYR932	29.4.52
3380	LYR599	20.11.51	3447	LYR866	5.2.52	3514	LYR933	30.4.52
3381	LYR600	13.11.51	3448	LYR867	6.2.52	3515	LYR934	1.5.52
3382	LYR601	20.11.51	3449	LYR868	7.2.52	3516	MLL826	2.5.52
3383	LYR602	21.11.51	3450	LYR869	8.2.52	3517	MLL827	5.5.52
3384	LYR603	22.11.51	3451	LYR870	9.2.52	3518	MLL828	6.5.52
3385	LYR604	23.11.51	3452	LYR871	11.2.52	3519	MLL829	7.5.52
3386	LYR605	23.11.51	3453	LYR872	12.2.52	3520	MLL830	8.5.52
3387	LYR606	26.11.51	3454	LYR873	13.2.52	3521	MLL831	9.5.52
3388	LYR607	27.11.51	3455	LYR874	14.2.52	3522	MLL832	12.5.52
3389	LYR608	27.11.51	3456	LYR875	15.2.52	3523	MLL833	13.5.52
3390	LYR609	28.11.51	3457	LYR876	15.2.52	3524	MLL834	14.5.52
3391	LYR610	29.11.51	3458	LYR877	18.2.52	3525	MLL835	15.5.52
3392	LYR611	30.11.51	3459	LYR878	19.2.52	3526	MLL836	16.5.52
3393	LYR612	30.11.51	3460	LYR879	20.2.52	3527	MLL837	19.5.52
3394	LYR613	3.12.51	3461	LYR880	21.2.52	3528	MLL838	20.5.52
3395	LYR614	4.12.51	3462	LYR881	22.2.52	3529	MLL839	21.5.52
3396	LYR615	4.12.51	3463	LYR882	22.2.52	3530	MLL840	22.5.52
3397	LYR616	5.12.51	3464	LYR883	25.2.52	3531	MLL841	23.5.52
3398	LYR617	6.12.51	3465	LYR884	26.2.52	3532	MLL842	26.5.52
3399	LYR618	7.12.51	3466	LYR885	27.2.52	3533	MLL843	27.5.52
3400	LYR619	7.12.51	3467	LYR886	28.2.52	3534	MLL844	28.5.52
3401	LYR620	10.12.51	3468	LYR887	29.2.52	3535	MLL845	29.5.52
3402	LYR621	11.12.51	3469	LYR888	29.2.52	3536	MLL846	3.6.52
3403	LYR622	11.12.51	3470	LYR889	3.3.52	3537	MLL847	5.6.52

RT		Date into stock	RT		Date into stock	RT		Date into stock
3538	MLL848	5.6.52	3605	MLL915	14.10.52	3672	MXX187	2.3.53
3539	MLL849	9.6.52	3606	MLL916	15.10.52	3673	MXX188	3.3.53
3540	MLL850	10.6.52	3607	MLL917	16.10.52	3674	MXX189	4.3.53
3541	MLL851	11.6.52	3608	MLL918	20.10.52	3675	MXX190	5.3.53
3542	MLL852	12.6.52	3609	MLL919	21.10.52	3676	MXX191	9.3.53
3543	MLL853	16.6.52	3610	MLL920	22.10.52	3677	MXX192	10.3.53
3544	MLL854	17.6.52	3611	MLL921	23.10.52	3678	MXX193	11.3.53
3545	MLL855	18.6.52	3612	MLL922	27.10.52	3679	MXX194	12.3.53
3546	MLL856	19.6.52	3613	MLL923	28.10.52	3680	MXX195	16.3.53
3547	MLL857	23.6.52	3614	MLL924	29.10.52	3681	MXX196	17.3.53
3548	MLL858	24.6.52	3615	MLL925	30.10.52	3682	MXX197	18.3.53
3549	MLL859	25.6.52	3616	MXX131	3.11.52	3683	MXX198	19.3.53
3550	MLL860	26.6.52	3617	MXX132	4.11.52	3684	MXX199	31.3.53
3551	MLL861	30.6.52	3618	MXX133	5.11.52	3685	MXX200	24.3.53
3552	MLL862	1.7.52	3619	MXX134	6.11.52	3686	MXX201	25.3.53
3553	MLL863	2.7.52	3620	MXX135	10.11.52	3687	MXX202	26.3.53
3554	MLL864	3.7.52	3621	MXX136	11.11.52	3688	MXX203	30.3.53
3555	MLL865	7.7.52	3622	MXX137	12.11.52	3689	MXX204	31.3.53
3556	MLL866	8.7.52	3623	MXX138	13.11.52	3690	MXX205	1.4.53
3557	MLL867	9.7.52	3624	MXX139	17.11.52	3691	MXX206	2.4.53
3558	MLL868	10.7.52	3625	MXX140	19.11.52	3692	MXX207	7.4.53
3559	MLL869	14.7.52	3626	MXX141	20.11.52	3693	MXX208	8.4.53
3560	MLL870	15.7.52	3627	MXX142	24.11.52	3694	NLE801	9.4.53
3561	MLL871	16.7.52	3628	MXX143	26.11.52	3695	NLE802	10.4.53
3562	MLL872	17.7.52	3629	MXX144	27.11.52	3696	NLE803	13.4.53
3563	MLL873	21.7.52	3630	MXX145	1.12.52	3697	NLE804	14.4.53
3564	MLL874	22.7.52	3631	MXX146	3.12.52	3698	NLE805	15.4.53
3565	MLL875	23.7.52	3632	MXX147	4.12.52	3699	NLE806	16.4.53
3566	MLL876	24.7.52	3633	MXX148	8.12.52	3700	NLE807	17.4.53
3567	MLL877	28.7.52	3634	MXX149	10.12.52	3701	NLE808	20.4.53
3568	MLL878	13.8.52	3635	MXX150	11.12.52	3702	NLE809	22.4.53
3569	MLL879	13.8.52	3636	MXX151	15.12.52	3703	NLE810	22.4.53
3570	MLL880	14.8.52	3637	MXX152	18.12.52	3704	NLE811	23.4.53
3571	MLL881	18.8.52	3638	MXX153	22.12.52	3705	NLE812	24.4.53
3572	MLL882	19.8.52	3639	MXX154	24.12.52	3706	NLE813	28.4.53
3573	MLL883	21.8.52	3640	MXX155	30.12.52	3707	NLE814	29.4.53
3574	MLL884	21.8.52	3641	MXX156	31.12.52	3708	NLE815	30.4.53
3575	MLL885	25.8.52	3642	MXX157	1.1.53	3709	NLE816	1.5.53
3576	MLL886	26.8.52	3643	MXX158	5.1.53	3710	NLE817	1.5.53
3577	MLL887	27.8.52	3644	MXX159	7.1.53	3711	NLE818	5.5.53
3578	MLL888	28.8.52	3645	MXX160	9.1.53	3712	NLE819	6.5.53
3579	MLL889	29.8.52	3646	MXX161	17.12.52	3713	NLE820	7.5.53
3580	MLL890	1.9.52	3647	MXX162	12.1.53	3714	NLE821	8.5.53
3581	MLL891	2.9.52	3648	MXX163	14.1.53	3715	NLE822	11.5.53
3582	MLL892	3.9.52	3649	MXX164	15.1.53	3716	NLE823	12.5.53
3583	MLL893	4.9.52	3650	MXX165	19.1.53	3717	NLE824	13.5.53
3584	MLL894	5.9.52	3651	MXX166	21.1.53	3718	NLE825	14.5.53
3585	MLL895	8.9.52	3652	MXX167	22.1.53	3719	NLE826	15.5.53
3586	MLL896	10.9.52	3653	MXX168	26.1.53	3720	NLE827	18.5.53
3587	MLL897	11.9.52	3654	MXX169	28.1.53	3721	NLE828	18.5.53
3588	MLL898	15.9.52	3655	MXX170	29.1.53	3722	NLE829	20.5.53
3589	MLL899	16.9.52	3656	MXX171	2.2.53	3723	NLE830	21.5.53
3590	MLL900	17.9.52	3657	MXX172	3.2.53	3724	NLE831	22.5.53
3591	MLL901	18.9.52	3658	MXX173	4.2.53	3725	NLE832	26.5.53
3592	MLL902	22.9.52	3659	MXX174	5.2.53	3726	NLE833	27.5.53
3593	MLL903	23.9.52	3660	MXX175	9.2.53	3727	NLE834	29.5.53
3594	MLL904	25.9.52	3661	MXX176	10.2.53	3728	NLE835	29.5.53
3595	MLL905	26.9.52	3662	MXX177	11.2.53	3729	NLE836	1.6.53
3596	MLL906	29.9.52	3663	MXX178	12.2.53	3730	NLE837	3.6.53
3597	MLL907	30.9.52	3664	MXX179	16.2.53	3731	NLE838	5.6.53
3598	MLL908	2.10.52	3665	MXX180	17.2.53	3732	NLE839	5.6.53
3599	MLL909	3.10.52	3666	MXX181	18.2.53	3733	NLE840	8.6.53
3600	MLL910	6.10.52	3667	MXX182	20.2.53	3734	NLE841	9.6.53
3601	MLL911	7.10.52	3668	MXX183	23.2.53	3735	NLE842	10.6.53
3602	MLL912	9.10.52	3669	MXX184	24.2.53	3736	NLE843	11.6.53
3603	MLL913	10.10.52	3670	MXX185	25.2.53	3737	NLE844	12.6.53
3604	MLL914	13.10.52	3671	MXX186	27.2.53	3738	NLE845	15.6.53

RT		Date into stock	RT		Date into stock	RT		Date into stock
3739	NLE846	18.6.53	3806	NXP813	2.10.53	3873	LLU672	15.9.50
3740	NLE847	17.6.53	3807	NXP814	6.10.53	3874	LLU673	18.9.50
3741	NLE848	18.6.53	3808	NXP815	7.10.53	3875	LLU674	18.9.50
3742	NLE849	22.6.53	3809	NXP816	7.10.53	3876	LLU675	20.9.50
3743	NLE850	23.6.53	3810	NXP817	8.10.53	3877	LLU676	20.9.50
3744	NLE851	24.6.53	3811	NXP818	9.10.53	3878	LLU677	20.9.50
3745	NLE852	25.6.53	3812	NXP819	12.10.53	3879	LLU678	22.9.50
3746	NLE853	26.6.53	3813	NXP820	13.10.53	3880	LLU679	21.9.50
3747	NLE854	29.6.53	3814	NXP821	14.10.53	3881	LLU680	25.9.50
3748	NLE855	30.6.53	3815	NXP822	15.10.53	3882	LLU681	22.9.50
3749	NLE856	1.7.53	3816	NXP823	16.10.53	3883	LLU682	25.9.50
3750	NLE857	2.7.53	3817	NXP824	19.10.53	3884	LLU683	25.9.50
3751	NLE858	3.7.53	3818	NXP825	20.10.53	3885	LLU684	26.9.50
3752	NLE859	6.7.53	3819	NXP826	21.10.53	3886	LLU685	27.9.50
3753	NLE860	7.7.53	3820	NXP827	22.10.53	3887	LLU686	27.9.50
3754	NLE861	8.7.53	3821	NXP828	26.10.53	3888	LLU687	27.9.50
3755	NLE862	9.7.53	3822	NXP829	27.10.53	3889	LLU688	28.9.50
3756	NLE863	10.7.53	3823	NXP830	28.10.53	3890	LLU689	28.9.50
3757	NLE864	13.7.53	3824	NXP831	4.11.53	3891	LLU690	29.9.50
3758	NLE865	14.7.53	3825	NXP832	30.10.53	3892	LLU691	29.9.50
3759	NLE866	15.7.53	3826	NXP833	2.11.53	3893	LLU692	2.10.50
3760	NLE867	16.7.53	3827	NXP834	3.11.53	3894	LLU693	2.10.50
3761	NLE868	17.7.53	3828	NXP835	4.11.53	3895	LLU694	3.10.50
3762	NLE869	20.7.53	3829	NXP836	5.11.53	3896	LLU695	3.10.50
3763	NLE870	21.7.53	3830	NXP837	9.11.53	3897	LLU696	4.10.50
3764	NLE871	22.7.53	3831	NXP838	9.11.53	3898	LLU697	4.10.50
3765	NLE872	23.7.53	3832	NXP839	12.11.53	3899	LLU698	4.10.50
3766	NLE873	24.7.53	3833	NXP840	13.11.53	3900	LLU699	4.10.50
3767	NLE874	27.7.53	3834	NXP841	16.11.53	3901	LLU700	6.10.50
3768	NLE875	11.8.53	3835	NXP842	17.11.53	3902	LLU701	6.10.50
3769	NLE876	12.8.53	3836	NXP843	18.11.53	3903	LLU702	9.10.50
3770	NLE877	13.8.53	3837	NXP844	19.11.53	3904	LLU703	9.10.50
3771	NLE878	14.8.53	3838	NXP845	23.11.53	3905	LLU704	10.10.50
3772	NLE879	17.8.53	3839	NXP846	24.11.53	3906	LLU705	10.10.50
3773	NLE880	18.8.53	3840	NXP847	25.11.53	3907	LLU706	11.10.50
3774	NLE881	19.8.53	3841	NXP848	26.11.53	3908	LLU707	12.10.50
3775	NLE882	20.8.53	3842	LLU641	24.8.50	3909	LLU708	12.10.50
3776	NLE883	21.8.53	3843	LLU642	25.8.50	3910	LLU709	13.10.50
3777	NLE884	24.8.53	3844	LLU643	25.8.50	3911	LLU710	13.10.50
3778	NLE885	25.8.53	3845	LLU644	28.8.50	3912	LLU711	16.10.50
3779	NLE886	26.8.53	3846	LLU645	29.8.50	3913	LLU712	16.10.50
3780	NLE887	27.8.53	3847	LLU646	30.8.50	3914	LLU713	17.10.50
3781	NLE888	2.9.53	3848	LLU647	30.8.50	3915	LLU714	17.10.50
3782	NLE889	31.8.53	3849	LLU648	30.8.50	3916	LLU715	18.10.50
3783	NLE890	1.9.53	3850	LLU649	31.8.50	3917	LLU716	18.10.50
3784	NLE891	2.9.53	3851	LLU650	1.9.50	3918	LLU717	20.10.50
3785	NLE892	3.9.53	3852	LLU651	1.9.50	3919	LLU718	20.10.50
3786	NLE893	4.9.53	3853	LLU652	1.9.50	3920	LLU719	18.10.50
3787	NLE894	7.9.53	3854	LLU653	4.9.50	3921	LLU720	18.10.50
3788	NLE895	8.9.53	3855	LLU654	4.9.50	3922	LLU721	23.10.50
3789	NLE896	9.9.53	3856	LLU655	5.9.50	3923	LLU722	23.10.50
3790	NLE897	10.9.53	3857	LLU656	6.9.50	3924	LLU723	24.10.50
3791	NLE898	11.9.53	3858	LLU657	6.9.50	3925	LLU724	24.10.50
3792	NLE899	14.9.53	3859	LLU658	6.9.50	3926	LLU725	25.10.50
3793	NLE900	15.9.53	3860	LLU659	7.9.50	3927	LLU726	26.10.50
3794	NXP801	16.9.53	3861	LLU660	7.9.50	3928	LLU727	27.10.50
3795	NXP802	17.9.53	3862	LLU661	8.9.50	3929	LLU728	27.10.50
3796	NXP803	18.9.53	3863	LLU662	11.9.50	3930	LLU729	27.10.50
3797	NXP804	21.9.53	3864	LLU663	11.9.50	3931	LLU730	30.10.50
3798	NXP805	22.9.53	3865	LLU664	11.9.50	3932	LLU731	31.10.50
3799	NXP806	23.9.53	3866	LLU665	12.9.50	3933	LLU732	1.11.50
3800	NXP807	24.9.53	3867	LLU666	12.9.50	3934	LLU733	1.11.50
3801	NXP808	25.9.53	3868	LLU667	13.9.50	3935	LLU734	1.11.50
3802	NXP809	28.9.53	3869	LLU668	13.9.50	3936	LLU735	2.11.50
3803	NXP810	29.9.53	3870	LLU669	14.9.50	3937	LLU736	2.11.50
3804	NXP811	1.10.53	3871	LLU670	14.9.50	3938	LLU737	3.11.50
3805	NXP812	2.10.53	3872	LLU671	19.9.50	3939	LLU738	3.11.50

RT		Date into stock	RT		Date into stock	RT		Date into stock
3940	LLU739	3.11.50	4007	LUC166	27.12.50	4074	LUC423	6.3.51
3941	LLU740	6.11.50	4008	LUC167	28.12.50	4075	LUC424	7.3.51
3942	LUC101	6.11.50	4009	LUC168	29.12.50	4076	LUC425	8.3.51
3943	LUC102	7.11.50	4010	LUC169	29.12.50	4077	LUC426	8.3.51
3944	LUC103	7.11.50	4011	LUC170	2.1.51	4078	LUC427	9.3.51
3945	LUC104	8.11.50	4012	LUC171	2.1.51	4079	LUC428	12.3.51
3946	LUC105	9.11.50	4013	LUC172	3.1.51	4080	LUC429	12.3.51
3947	LUC106	9.11.50	4014	LUC173	4.1.51	4081	LUC430	13.3.51
3948	LUC107	10.11.50	4015	LUC174	4.1.51	4082	LUC431	14.3.51
3949	LUC108	10.11.50	4016	LUC175	5.1.51	4083	LUC432	15.3.51
3950	LUC109	13.11.50	4017	LUC176	6.1.51	4084	LUC433	15.3.51
3951	LUC110	13.11.50	4018	LUC177	7.1.51	4085	LUC434	16.3.51
3952	LUC111	14.11.50	4019	LUC178	10.1.51	4086	LUC435	19.3.51
3953	LUC112	14.11.50	4020	LUC179	11.1.51	4087	LUC436	19.3.51
3954	LUC113	15.11.50	4021	LUC180	11.1.51	4088	LUC437	20.3.51
3955	LUC114	15.11.50	4022	LUC181	12.1.51	4089	LUC438	21.3.51
3956	LUC115	16.11.50	4023	LUC182	15.1.51	4090	LUC439	22.3.51
3957	LUC116	16.11.50	4024	LUC183	15.1.51	4091	LUC440	22.3.51
3958	LUC117	17.11.50	4025	LUC184	16.1.51	4092	LUC441	22.3.51
3959	LUC118	17.11.50	4026	LUC185	17.1.51	4093	LUC442	28.3.51
3960	LUC119	20.11.50	4027	LUC186	18.1.51	4094	LUC443	28.3.51
3961	LUC120	20.11.50	4028	LUC187	18.1.51	4095	LUC444	29.3.51
3962	LUC121	21.11.50	4029	LUC188	19.1.51	4096	LUC445	30.3.51
3963	LUC122	21.11.50	4030	LUC189	30.1.51	4097	LUC446	2.4.51
3964	LUC123	22.11.50	4031	LUC190	22.1.51	4098	LUC447	2.4.51
3965	LUC124	23.11.50	4032	LUC191	23.1.51	4099	LUC448	3.4.51
3966	LUC125	23.11.50	4033	LUC192	24.1.51	4100	LUC449	4.4.51
3967	LUC126	24.11.50	4034	LUC193	29.1.51	4101	LUC450	5.4.51
3968	LUC127	24.11.50	4035	LUC194	29.1.51	4102	LUC451	5.4.51
3969	LUC128	27.11.50	4036	LUC195	29.1.51	4103	LUC452	6.4.51
3970	LUC129	27.11.50	4037	LUC196	30.1.51	4104	LUC453	9.4.51
3971	LUC130	28.11.50	4038	LUC197	30.1.51	4105	LUC454	9.4.51
3972	LUC131	28.11.50	4039	LUC198	31.1.51	4106	LUC455	10.4.51
3973	LUC132	29.11.50	4040	LUC199	1.2.51	4107	LUC456	11.4.51
3974	LUC133	29.11.50	4041	LUC200	1.2.51	4108	LUC457	12.4.51
3975	LUC134	30.11.50	4042	LUC391	2.2.51	4109	LUC458	13.4.51
3976	LUC135	30.11.50	4043	LUC392	2.2.51	4110	LUC459	13.4.51
3977	LUC136	1.12.50	4044	LUC393	5.2.51	4111	LUC460	16.4.51
3978	LUC137	1.12.50	4045	LUC394	6.2.51	4112	LUC461	16.4.51
3979	LUC138	4.12.50	4046	LUC395	6.2.51	4113	LUC462	17.4.51
3980	LUC139	4.12.50	4047	LUC396	7.2.51	4114	LUC463	18.4.51
3981	LUC140	5.12.50	4048	LUC397	8.2.51	4115	LUC464	20.4.51
3982	LUC141	5.12.50	4049	LUC398	8.2.51	4116	LUC465	19.4.51
3983	LUC142	6.12.50	4050	LUC399	9.2.51	4117	LUC466	20.4.51
3984	LUC143	8.12.50	4051	LUC400	12.2.51	4118	LUC467	24.4.51
3985	LUC144	7.12.50	4052	LUC401	12.2.51	4119	LUC468	23.4.51
3986	LUC145	8.12.50	4053	LUC402	13.2.51	4120	LUC469	24.4.51
3987	LUC146	8.12.50	4054	LUC403	14.2.51	4121	LUC470	25.4.51
3988	LUC147	11.12.50	4055	LUC404	15.2.51	4122	LUC471	26.4.51
3989	LUC148	11.12.50	4056	LUC405	15.2.51	4123	LUC472	26.4.51
3990	LUC149	12.12.50	4057	LUC406	16.2.51	4124	LUC473	27.4.51
3991	LUC150	12.12.50	4058	LUC407	19.2.51	4125	LUC474	30.4.51
3992	LUC151	13.12.50	4059	LUC408	19.2.51	4126	LUC475	1.5.51
3993	LUC152	13.12.50	4060	LUC409	20.2.51	4127	LUC476	1.5.51
3994	LUC153	14.12.50	4061	LUC410	21.2.51	4128	LUC477	2.5.51
3995	LUC154	14.12.50	4062	LUC411	22.2.51	4129	LUC478	3.5.51
3996	LUC155	15.12.50	4063	LUC412	22.2.51	4130	LUC479	3.5.51
3997	LUC156	15.12.50	4064	LUC413	23.2.51	4131	LUC480	4.5.51
3998	LUC157	18.12.50	4065	LUC414	26.2.51	4132	LUC481	7.5.51
3999	LUC158	18.12.50	4066	LUC415	26.2.51	4133	LUC482	7.5.51
4000	LUC159	19.12.50	4067	LUC416	27.2.51	4134	LUC483	8.5.51
4001	LUC160	19.12.50	4068	LUC417	28.2.51	4135	LUC484	9.5.51
4002	LUC161	20.12.50	4069	LUC418	1.3.51	4136	LUC485	10.5.51
4003	LUC162	21.12.50	4070	LUC419	1.3.51	4137	LUC486	10.5.51
4004	LUC163	21.12.50	4071	LUC420	2.3.51	4138	LUC487	11.5.51
4005	LUC164	22.12.50	4072	LUC421	5.3.51	4139	LUC488	15.5.51
4006	LUC165	27.12.50	4073	LUC422	5.3.51	4140	LUC489	16.5.51

RT		Date into stock	RT		Date into stock	RT		Date into stock
4141	LUC490	16.5.51	4208	LYF267	23.7.51	4275	NLE939	27.5.53
4142	LYF201	17.5.51	4209	LYF268	24.7.51	4276	NLE940	27.5.53
4143	LYF202	18.5.51	4210	LYF269	24.7.51	4277	NLE941	29.5.53
4144	LYF203	21.5.51	4211	LYF270	25.7.51	4278	NLE942	29.5.53
4145	LYF204	21.5.51	4212	LYF271	26.7.51	4279	NLE943	29.5.53
4146	LYF205	22.5.51	4213	LYF272	27.7.51	4280	NLE944	29.5.53
4147	LYF206	23.5.51	4214	LYF273	27.7.51	4281	NLE945	5.6.53
4148	LYF207	23.5.51	4215	LYF274	30.7.51	4282	NLE946	5.6.53
4149	LYF208	24.5.51	4216	LYF275	8.8.51	4283	NLE947	5.6.53
4150	LYF209	25.5.51	4217	LYF276	8.8.51	4284	NLE948	8.6.53
4151	LYF210	28.5.51	4218	KYY821	1.9.50	4285	NLE949	10.6.53
4152	LYF211	28.5.51	4219	KYY822	1.9.50	4286	NLE950	10.6.53
4153	LYF212	31.5.51	4220	KYY823	1.9.50	4287	NLE951	12.6.53
4154	LYF213	30.5.51	4221	KYY824	1.9.50	4288	NLE952	11.6.53
4155	LYF214	30.5.51	4222	KYY825	1.9.50	4289	NLE953	12.6.53
4156	LYF215	31.5.51	4223	KYY826	1.9.50	4290	NLE954	11.6.53
4157	LYF216	1.6.51	4224	KYY827	8.9.50	4291	NLE955	12.6.53
4158	LYF217	1.6.51	4225	KYY828	8.9.50	4292	NLE956	12.6.53
4159	LYF218	4.6.51	4226	KYY829	8.9.50	4293	NLE957	17.6.53
4160	LYF219	5.6.51	4227	KYY830	15.9.50	4294	NLE958	17.6.53
4161	LYF220	5.6.51	4228	KYY831	15.9.50	4295	NLE959	17.6.53
4162	LYF221	6.6.51	4229	KYY832	15.9.50	4296	NLE960	19.6.53
4163	LYF222	7.6.51	4230	KYY833	22.9.50	4297	NLE961	19.6.53
4164	LYF223	8.6.51	4231	KYY834	22.9.50	4298	NLE962	19.6.53
4165	LYF224	8.6.51	4232	KYY835	22.9.50	4299	NLE963	22.6.53
4166	LYF225	11.6.51	4233	KYY836	22.9.50	4300	NLE964	22.6.53
4167	LYF226	12.6.51	4234	KYY837	29.9.50	4301	NLE965	23.6.53
4168	LYF227	12.6.51	4235	KYY838	29.9.50	4302	NLE966	24.6.53
4169	LYF228	13.6.51	4236	KYY839	29.9.50	4303	NLE967	25.6.53
4170	LYF229	14.6.51	4237	KYY840	6.10.50	4304	NLE968	25.6.53
4171	LYF230	15.6.51	4238	KYY841	6.10.50	4305	NLE969	26.6.53
4172	LYF231	15.6.51	4239	KYY842	6.10.50	4306	NLE970	26.6.53
4173	LYF232	18.6.51	4240	KYY843	13.10.50	4307	NLE971	26.6.53
4174	LYF233	19.6.51	4241	KYY844	13.10.50	4308	NLE972	26.6.53
4175	LYF234	19.6.51	4242	KYY845	13.10.50	4309	NLE973	30.6.53
4176	LYF235	20.6.51	4243	KYY846	13.10.50	4310	NLE974	30.6.53
4177	LYF236	21.6.51	4244	KYY847	20.10.50	4311	NLE975	30.6.53
4178	LYF237	22.6.51	4245	KYY848	20.10.50	4312	NLE976	3.7.53
4179	LYF238	22.6.51	4246	KYY849	20.10.50	4313	NLE977	3.7.53
4180	LYF239	25.6.51	4247	KYY850	27.10.50	4314	NLE978	3.7.53
4181	LYF240	26.6.51	4248	KYY851	27.10.50	4315	NLE979	3.7.53
4182	LYF241	26.6.51	4249	KYY852	27.10.50	4316	NLE980	3.7.53
4183	LYF242	27.6.51	4250	KYY853	3.11.50	4317	NLE981	8.7.53
4184	LYF243	28.6.51	4251	KYY854	3.11.50	4318	NLE982	8.7.53
4185	LYF244	29.6.51	4252	KYY855	3.11.50	4319	NLE983	9.7.53
4186	LYF245	29.6.51	4253	KYY856	3.11.50	4320	NLE984	9.7.53
4187	LYF246	2.7.51	4254	KYY857	10.11.50	4321	NLE985	10.7.53
4188	LYF247	3.7.51	4255	KYY858	10.11.50	4322	NLE986	10.7.53
4189	LYF248	3.7.51	4256	KYY859	10.11.50	4323	NLE987	10.7.53
4190	LYF249	4.7.51	4257	KYY860	17.11.50	4324	NLE988	10.7.53
4191	LYF250	5.7.51	4258	KYY861	17.11.50	4325	NLE989	15.7.53
4192	LYF251	6.7.51	4259	KYY862	17.11.50	4326	NLE990	15.7.53
4193	LYF252	6.7.51	4260	KYY863	24.11.50	4327	NLE991	16.7.53
4194	LYF253	9.7.51	4261	KYY864	24.11.50	4328	NLE992	16.7.53
4195	LYF254	10.7.51	4262	KYY865	24.11.50	4329	NLE993	17.7.53
4196	LYF255	10.7.51	4263	KYY866	1.12.50	4330	NLE994	17.7.53
4197	LYF256	11.7.51	4264	KYY867	1.12.50	4331	NLE995	17.7.53
4198	LYF257	12.7.51	4265	KYY868	4.1.51	4332	NLE996	17.7.53
4199	LYF258	13.7.51	4266	KYY869	4.1.51	4333	NLE997	21.7.53
4200	LYF259	13.7.51	4267	KYY870	2.2.51	4334	NLE998	22.7.53
4201	LYF260	16.7.51	4268	NLE932	21.5.53	4335	NLE999	22.7.53
4202	LYF261	17.7.51	4269	NLE933	22.5.53	4336	NLP501	23.7.53
4203	LYF262	17.7.51	4270	NLE934	22.5.53	4337	NLP502	23.7.53
4204	LYF263	18.7.51	4271	NLE935	22.5.53	4338	NLP503	24.7.53
4205	LYF264	19.7.51	4272	NLE936	27.5.53	4339	NLP504	24.7.53
4206	LYF265	20.7.51	4273	NLE937	22.5.53	4340	NLP505	24.7.53
4207	LYF266	20.7.51	4274	NLE938	27.5.53	4341	NLP506	28.7.53

RT		Date into stock	RT		Date into stock	RT		Date into stock
4342	NLP507	29.7.53	4361	NLP526	25.8.53	4380	NLP545	11.9.53
4343	NLP508	31.7.53	4362	NLP527	26.8.53	4381	NLP546	10.9.53
4344	NLP509	31.7.53	4363	NLP528	26.8.53	4382	NLP547	11.9.53
4345	NLP510	6.8.53	4364	NLP529	27.8.53	4383	NLP548	11.9.53
4346	NLP511	7.8.53	4365	NLP530	27.8.53	4384	NLP549	15.9.53
4347	NLP512	7.8.53	4366	NLP531	28.8.53	4385	NLP550	16.9.53
4348	NLP513	12.8.53	4367	NLP532	28.8.53	4386	NLP551	16.9.53
4349	NLP514	14.8.53	4368	NLP533	3.9.53	4387	NLP552	17.9.53
4350	NLP515	14.8.53	4369	NLP534	2.9.53	4388	NLP553	18.9.53
4351	NLP516	18.8.53	4370	NLP535	2.9.53	4389	NLP554	17.9.53
4352	NLP517	19.8.53	4371	NLP536	4.9.53	4390	NLP555	18.9.53
4353	NLP518	19.8.53	4372	NLP537	3.9.53	4391	NLP556	18.9.53
4354	NLP519	20.8.53	4373	NLP538	3.9.53	4392	NLP557	22.9.53
4355	NLP520	20.8.53	4374	NLP539	4.9.53	4393	NLP558	22.9.53
4356	NLP521	21.8.53	4375	NLP540	4.9.53	4394	NLP559	23.9.53
4357	NLP522	21.8.53	4376	NLP541	10.9.53	4395	NLP560	23.9.53
4358	NLP523	21.8.53	4377	NLP542	7.9.53	4396	NLP561	24.9.53
4359	NLP524	21.8.53	4378	NLP543	9.9.53			
4360	NLP525	25.8.53	4379	NLP544	10.9.53			

The following RTs were new chassis fitted with second hand bodies from scrapped SRT chassis.

RT		Body mounted	From SRT	RT		Body mounted	From SRT	RT		Body mounted	From SRT
4397	NXP751	31.7.53	68	4441	NXP795	16.12.53	9	4485	OLD705	17.3.54	88
4398	NXP752	31.7.53	16	4442	NXP796	23.12.53	24	4486	OLD706	19.3.54	89
4399	NXP753	10.8.53	42	4443	NXP797	30.12.53	31	4487	OLD707	23.3.54	70
4400	NXP754	18.8.53	43	4444	NXP798	6.1.54	18	4488	OLD708	24.3.54	90
4401	NXP755	20.8.53	47	4445	NXP799	14.1.54	12	4489	OLD709	26.3.54	91
4402	NXP756	7.9.53	53	4446	NXP800	20.1.54	26	4490	OLD710	30.3.54	67
4403	NXP757	9.9.53	48	4447	OLD667	27.1.54	37	4491	OLD711	31.3.54	94
4404	NXP758	16.9.53	50	4448	OLD668	3.2.54	28	4492	OLD712	2.4.54	93
4405	NXP759	23.9.53	51	4449	OLD669	10.2.54	22	4493	OLD713	6.4.54	73
4406	NXP760	30.9.53	55	4450	OLD670	17.2.54	29	4494	OLD714	7.4.54	92
4407	NXP761	7.10.53	56	4451	OLD671	24.2.54	38	4495	OLD715	9.4.54	95
4408	NXP762	14.10.53	57	4452	OLD672	3.3.54	41	4496	OLD716	13.4.54	74
4409	NXP763	21.10.53	58	4453	OLD673	10.3.54	39	4497	OLD717	14.4.54	96
4410	NXP764	28.10.53	59	4454	OLD674	17.3.54	40	4498	OLD718	15.4.54	98
4411	NXP765	4.11.53	60	4455	OLD675	24.3.54	45	4499	OLD719	20.4.54	75
4412	NXP766	11.11.53	61	4456	OLD676	31.3.54	44	4500	OLD720	21.4.54	99
4413	NXP767	2.12.53	126	4457	OLD677	7.4.54	62	4501	OLD721	23.4.54	76
4414	NXP768	9.12.53	127	4458	OLD678	21.4.54	54	4502	OLD722	27.4.54	77
4415	NXP769	16.12.53	128	4459	OLD679	23.4.54	17	4503	OLD723	28.4.54	78
4416	NXP770	23.12.53	131	4460	OLD680	28.4.54	35	4504	OLD724	30.4.54	100
4417	NXP771	30.12.53	107	4461	OLD681	5.5.54	87	4505	OLD725	4.5.54	79
4418	NXP772	6.1.54	116	4462	OLD682	12.5.54	34	4506	OLD726	5.5.54	80
4419	NXP773	11.1.54	117	4463	OLD683	19.5.54	52	4507	OLD727	7.5.54	81
4420	NXP774	13.1.54	118	4464	OLD684	26.5.54	14	4508	OLD728	11.5.54	101
4421	NXP775	18.1.54	119	4465	OLD685	2.6.54	32	4509	OLD729	12.5.54	103
4422	NXP776	20.1.54	120	4466	OLD686	9.6.54	36	4510	OLD730	14.5.54	104
4423	NXP777	31.7.53	11	4467	OLD687	7.7.54	49	4511	OLD731	18.5.54	106
4424	NXP778	17.8.53	1	4468	OLD688	21.7.54	33	4512	OLD732	19.5.54	142
4425	NXP779	24.8.53	8	4469	OLD689	28.7.54	27	4513	OLD733	21.5.54	129
4426	NXP780	1.9.53	30	4470	OLD690	22.9.54	46	4514	OLD734	25.5.54	132
4427	NXP781	8.9.53	15	4471	OLD691	25.1.54	121	4515	OLD735	26.5.54	134
4428	NXP782	15.9.53	3	4472	OLD692	27.1.54	122	4516	OLD736	28.5.54	108
4429	NXP783	22.9.53	10	4473	OLD693	1.2.54	97	4517	OLD737	1.6.54	109
4430	NXP784	29.9.53	13	4474	OLD694	3.2.54	105	4518	OLD738	2.6.54	135
4431	NXP785	7.10.53	25	4475	OLD695	8.2.54	123	4519	OLD739	4.6.54	136
4432	NXP786	14.10.53	20	4476	OLD696	10.2.54	71	4520	OLD740	8.6.54	137
4433	NXP787	21.10.53	19	4477	OLD697	15.2.54	64	4521	OLD741	9.6.54	111
4434	NXP788	28.10.53	21	4478	OLD698	17.2.54	69	4522	OLD742	11.6.54	112
4435	NXP789	4.11.53	23	4479	OLD699	24.2.54	65	4523	OLD743	15.6.54	113
4436	NXP790	9.11.53	4	4480	OLD700	1.3.54	66	4524	OLD744	16.6.54	138
4437	NXP791	18.11.53	6	4481	OLD701	3.3.54	102	4525	OLD745	5.7.54	155
4438	NXP792	25.11.53	5	4482	OLD702	8.3.54	63	4526	OLD746	5.7.54	139
4439	NXP793	1.12.53	7	4483	OLD703	10.3.54	72	4527	OLD747	7.7.54	133
4440	NXP794	9.12.53	2	4484	OLD704	15.3.54	110	4528	OLD748	9.7.54	140

RT	Body mounted	From SRT	RT	Body mounted	From SRT	RT	Body mounted	From SRT
4529	OLD749	13.7.54	146	4539	OLD759	12.8.54	83	4549	OLD769	14.9.54	151
4530	OLD750	14.7.54	141	4540	OLD760	17.8.54	115	4550	OLD770	14.9.54	150
4531	OLD751	16.7.54	114	4541	OLD761	23.8.54	152	4551	OLD771	8.9.54	153
4532	OLD752	20.7.54	143	4542	OLD762	24.8.54	130	4552	OLD772	9.9.54	156
4533	OLD753	21.7.54	125	4543	OLD763	23.8.54	157	4553	OLD773	15.9.54	154
4534	OLD754	23.7.54	82	4544	OLD764	25.8.54	160	4554	OLD774	16.9.54	144
4535	OLD755	27.7.54	85	4545	OLD765	1.9.54	145	4555	OLD775	16.9.54	158
4536	OLD756	29.7.54	84	4546	OLD766	6.9.54	147	4556	OLD776	20.9.54	159
4537	OLD757	5.8.54	86	4547	OLD767	6.9.54	148				
4538	OLD758	5.8.54	124	4548	OLD768	7.9.54	149				

RT		Date into stock	RT		Date into stock	RT		Date into stock
4557	NXP849	30.11.53	4611	NXP864	9.11.53	4665	NXP918	13.1.54
4558	NXP850	1.12.53	4612	NXP865	10.11.53	4666	NXP919	15.1.54
4559	NXP851	2.12.53	4613	NXP866	11.11.53	4667	NXP920	18.1.54
4560	NXP852	3.12.53	4614	NXP867	11.11.53	4668	MXX 40	25.9.53
4561	NXP853	7.12.53	4615	NXP868	12.11.53	4669	NXP921	18.1.54
4562	NXP854	8.12.53	4616	NXP869	17.11.53	4670	NXP922	19.1.54
4563	NXP855	9.12.53	4617	NXP870	16.11.53	4671	NXP923	20.1.54
4564	NXP856	10.12.53	4618	NXP871	17.11.53	4672	NXP924	21.1.54
4565	NXP857	15.12.53	4619	NXP872	18.11.53	4673	NXP925	22.1.54
4566	NXP858	16.12.53	4620	NXP873	19.11.53	4674	NXP926	25.1.54
4567	NXP859	16.12.53	4621	NXP874	19.11.53	4675	NXP927	25.1.54
4568	NXP860	17.12.53	4622	NXP875	23.11.53	4676	NXP928	26.1.54
4569	NLP562	24.9.53	4623	NXP876	23.11.53	4677	NXP929	27.1.54
4570	NLP563	25.9.53	4624	NXP877	24.11.53	4678	NXP930	29.1.54
4571	NLP564	25.9.53	4625	NXP878	24.11.53	4679	NXP931	29.1.54
4572	NLP565	1.10.53	4626	NXP879	26.11.53	4680	NXP932	1.2.54
4573	NLP566	1.10.53	4627	NXP880	26.11.53	4681	NXP933	1.2.54
4574	NLP567	1.10.53	4628	NXP881	1.12.53	4682	NXP934	2.2.54
4575	NLP568	2.10.53	4629	NXP882	1.12.53	4683	NXP935	3.2.54
4576	NLP569	2.10.53	4630	NXP883	1.12.53	4684	NXP936	4.2.54
4577	NLP570	2.10.53	4631	NXP884	2.12.53	4685	NXP970	21.12.53
4578	NLP571	2.10.53	4632	NXP885	2.12.53	4686	NXP971	23.12.53
4579	NLP572	2.10.53	4633	NXP886	3.12.53	4687	NXP972	23.12.53
4580	NLP573	7.10.53	4634	NXP887	7.12.53	4688	NXP973	1.1.54
4581	NLP574	7.10.53	4635	NXP888	7.12.53	4689	NXP974	5.1.54
4582	NLP575	8.10.53	4636	NXP889	8.12.53	4690	NXP975	4.1.54
4583	NLP576	9.10.53	4637	NXP890	9.12.53	4691	NXP976	6.1.54
4584	NLP577	8.10.53	4638	NXP891	10.12.53	4692	NXP977	7.1.54
4585	NLP578	8.10.53	4639	NXP892	10.12.53	4693	NXP978	11.1.54
4586	NLP579	12.10.53	4640	NXP893	14.12.53	4694	NXP979	8.1.54
4587	NLP580	13.10.53	4641	NXP894	14.12.53	4695	NXP980	12.1.54
4588	NLP581	14.10.53	4642	NXP895	16.12.53	4696	NXP981	13.1.54
4589	NLP582	13.10.53	4643	NXP896	16.12.53	4697	NXP982	14.1.54
4590	NLP583	15.10.53	4644	NXP897	18.12.53	4698	NXP983	18.1.54
4591	NLP584	15.10.53	4645	NXP898	18.12.53	4699	NXP984	19.1.54
4592	NLP585	19.10.53	4646	NXP899	21.12.53	4700	NXP985	20.1.54
4593	NLP586	19.10.53	4647	NXP900	21.12.53	4701	NXP986	22.1.54
4594	NLP587	20.10.53	4648	NXP901	22.12.53	4702	NXP987	25.1.54
4595	NLP588	21.10.53	4649	NXP902	23.12.53	4703	NXP988	26.1.54
4596	NLP589	21.10.53	4650	NXP903	29.12.53	4704	NXP989	27.1.54
4597	NLP590	22.10.53	4651	NXP904	29.12.53	4705	NXP990	28.1.54
4598	NLP591	26.10.53	4652	NXP905	31.12.53	4706	NXP991	3.2.54
4599	NLP592	26.10.53	4653	NXP906	1.1.54	4707	NXP992	3.2.54
4600	NLP593	28.10.53	4654	NXP907	1.1.54	4708	NXP993	3.2.54
4601	NLP594	28.10.53	4655	NXP908	4.1.54	4709	NXP994	8.2.54
4602	NLP595	2.11.53	4656	NXP909	4.1.54	4710	NXP995	8.2.54
4603	NLP596	2.11.53	4657	NXP910	5.1.54	4711	NXP996	12.2.54
4604	NLP597	2.11.53	4658	NXP911	7.1.54	4712	NXP997	12.2.54
4605	NLP598	2.11.53	4659	NXP912	8.1.54	4713	NXP998	15.2.54
4606	NLP599	3.11.53	4660	NXP913	8.1.54	4714	NXP999	17.2.54
4607	NLP600	3.11.53	4661	NXP914	11.1.54	4715	OLD501	19.2.54
4608	NXP861	5.11.53	4662	NXP915	11.1.54	4716	OLD502	22.2.54
4609	NXP862	5.11.53	4663	NXP916	12.1.54	4717	OLD503	24.2.54
4610	NXP863	9.11.53	4664	NXP917	13.1.54	4718	OLD504	26.2.54

RT		Date into stock	RT		Date into stock	RT		Date into stock
4719	OLD505	1.3.54	4755	OLD542	28.5.54	4791	OLD828	25.8.54
4720	OLD506	2.3.54	4756	OLD543	31.5.54	4792	OLD829	26.8.54
4721	OLD507	4.3.54	4757	OLD544	31.5.54	4793	OLD830	27.8.54
4722	OLD508	8.3.54	4758	OLD545	1.6.54	*4794	OLD861	11.11.54
4723	OLD509	10.3.54	4759	OLD546	2.6.54	4795	NXP937	8.2.54
4724	OLD510	12.3.54	4760	OLD547	22.5.54	4796	NXP938	10.2.54
4725	OLD511	15.3.54	4761	OLD548	3.6.54	4797	NXP939	9.2.54
4726	OLD512	16.3.54	4762	OLD549	8.6.54	4798	NXP940	12.2.54
4727	OLD513	18.3.54	4763	OLD550	9.6.54	4799	NXP941	11.2.54
4728	OLD514	22.3.54	4764	OLD551	10.6.54	4800	NXP942	12.2.54
4729	OLD515	22.3.54	4765	OLD552	11.6.54	4801	NXP943	15.2.54
4730	OLD516	25.3.54	4766	OLD553	15.6.54	4802	NXP944	16.2.54
4731	OLD517	29.3.54	4767	OLD554	16.6.54	4803	NXP945	17.2.54
4732	OLD518	29.3.54	4768	OLD555	19.6.54	4804	NXP946	18.2.54
4733	OLD519	31.3.54	4769	OLD556	18.6.54	4805	NXP947	22.2.54
4734	OLD520	1.4.54	4770	OLD557	23.6.54	4806	NXP948	23.2.54
4735	OLD521	6.4.54	4771	OLD558	25.6.54	4807	NXP949	24.2.54
4736	OLD522	9.4.54	4772	OLD559	28.6.54	4808	NXP950	24.2.54
4737	OLD523	8.4.54	4773	OLD560	1.7.54	4809	NXP951	25.2.54
4738	OLD524	12.4.54	4774	OLD561	2.7.54	4810	NXP952	26.2.54
4739	OLD525	13.4.54	4775	OLD562	5.7.54	4811	NXP953	26.2.54
4740	OLD526	15.4.54	4776	OLD563	7.7.54	4812	NXP954	26.2.54
4741	OLD527	20.4.54	4777	OLD564	9.7.54	4813	OLD577	15.3.54
4742	OLD528	22.4.54	4778	OLD565	13.7.54	4814	OLD578	16.3.54
4743	OLD529	22.4.54	4779	OLD566	15.7.54	4815	OLD579	17.3.54
4744	OLD530	22.4.54	4780	OLD567	16.7.54	4816	OLD580	18.3.54
4745	OLD531	23.4.54	4781	OLD568	23.7.54	4817	OLD581	19.3.54
4746	OLD532	26.4.54	4782	OLD569	22.7.54	4818	OLD582	19.3.54
4747	OLD533	28.4.54	4783	OLD570	11.8.54	4819	OLD583	24.3.54
4748	OLD534	3.5.54	4784	OLD821	12.8.54	4820	OLD584	22.3.54
4749	OLD535	3.5.54	4785	OLD822	16.8.54	4821	OLD585	24.3.54
4750	OLD537	6.5.54	4786	OLD823	17.8.54	4822	OLD586	25.3.54
4751	OLD538	7.5.54	4787	OLD824	19.8.54	4823	OLD587	26.3.54
4752	OLD539	10.5.54	4788	OLD825	20.8.54	4824	OLD588	26.3.54
4753	OLD540	11.5.54	4789	OLD826	23.8.54	4825	OLD589	29.3.54
4754	OLD541	27.5.54	4790	OLD827	24.8.54			

* Last RT into stock

RTC

RTC 1 was intended as a prototype for the large fleet of double-deck Green Line coaches which was planned as part of the post-war vehicle replacement programme. It was not a new bus but a heavily modified 2RT2. RT 97 was one of the first production batch of RTs and was built in April 1940. It suffered bomb damage during the war and was one of the buses chosen for Pay-As-You-Enter experiments in 1946. On completion of these experiments, it was taken into the experimental shop at Chiswick Works and extensively rebuilt. The modified vehicle had a low full width downward sloping bonnet incorporating the nearside wing and there was an oblong chromium finished grille, although the radiator itself was transferred to a position under the stairs. Opening windows were of the single piece type but could be opened only half way. Interior decor was predominantly green with cream window cappings and ceiling panels and the experimental seats were to 'airline standards' with 'Dunlopillo' filled squabs loosely covered in a new design of moquette. Fluorescent saloon and indicator lighting was fitted to a London bus for the first time. RTC 1 operated experimentally from 6th April 1949 on routes 715, 711, 708 and 704 but was relegated to bus work at Leatherhead garage in December. It was withdrawn from service in March 1953 and used for a time in heating development trials at Chiswick.

Experimental Green Line double-deck coach RTC 1 in service as a bus at Leatherhead, where it operated between December 1949 and March 1953, usually on route 416 but also on the 468. The nearside rear view shows its origin as an RT in the distinctive rear dome, and also its special coach features, including the unusual bonnet arrangement, the single piece opening windows and the recess where the door had been. The unusual platform step arrangement was a relic of its days as a Pay As You Enter bus, when it was still RT 97. F.G. Reynolds

Chassis: AEC Regent 0661
Engine: AEC A185B 6-cylinder 9.6 litre direct injection 125 bhp (derated to 115 bhp)
Transmission: AEC D140 four speed air operated preselective with fluid flywheel
Bodywork: LPTB rebuilt by LTE
Capacity: H26/20RD
L.T. code: 5RT5
Built: 1940 (as RT 97) rebuilt 1949
Number built: 1
Number in stock: 1.1.50: 1
                              31.12.54: 1

RTC

1   FXT272

The only clues to the peculiar nature of SRT 157, seen when new at Staines, are its registration inherited from STL 2155 and the flatter profile of its front wheel hubs; otherwise it could pass for an RT. Its body was later used for RT 4543. J. H. Aston

SRT

Deliveries of standard RT family buses to London Transport in the early post-war years were slow and the availability of bodies and chassis frequently did not match. To overcome a temporary excess of body building over chassis building capacity, London Transport decided to modify the chassis frames of the 300 best pre-war STLs to enable them to be mounted with standard RT family bodywork. They were also fitted with RT-type steering column mounted gear change levers but their mechanical specification was unchanged. The first SRTs went into service in April 1949 but proved to be unsatisfactory in service because the extra weight made them sluggish and, most crucially, caused the brakes to be inadequate. The sixty-one so far built were taken out of service in June 1949 for modifications to be made to the braking system after which the buses were relegated to second line duties wherever possible. Production was halted after the first 160 and all were withdrawn in 1954. Their bodies were then transferred to new RT chassis.

Chassis: AEC Regent 0661 rebuilt by London Transport
Engine: AEC A173 6-cylinder 7.7 litre direct injection 95bhp oil
Transmission: AEC D132 direct selection preselective with fluid flywheel
Bodywork: Park Royal
Capacity: H30/26R
L.T. code: 8RT9 (1-125) or 1/8RT9
Built: 1949
Number built: 160
Number in stock: 1.1.50: 146   31.12.54: 16 (chassis only)

SRT		Date out of stock	SRT		Date out of stock	SRT		Date into stock	Date out of stock
1	FJJ746	21.10.53	55	FXT76	11.11.53	109	FJJ693		6.7.54
2	FJJ680	16.12.53	56	FJJ683	11.11.53	110	FJJ742		6.4.54
3	FJJ690	21.10.53	57	FXT93	25.11.53	111	FJJ710		31.8.54
4	FXT53	2.12.53	58	FXT92	2.12.53	112	FJJ740		31.8.54
5	FJJ756	9.12.53	59	FJJ695	2.12.53	113	FJJ749		24.8.54
6	FJJ700	9.12.53	60	FXT71	25.11.53	114	FJJ714		
7	FJJ676	9.12.53	61	FXT85	9.12.53	115	FJJ724		
8	FXT56	4.11.53	62	FXT74	13.4.54	116	FJJ701		13.1.54
9	FXT60	22.12.53	63	FJJ723	13.4.54	117	FJJ741		27.1.54
10	FJJ721	14.10.53	64	FXT84	2.3.54	118	FJJ702		27.1.54
11	FJJ717	7.10.53	65	FXT55	10.3.54	119	FJJ694		27.1.54
12	FJJ725	20.1.54	66	FJJ697	10.3.54	120	FXT82		27.1.54
13	FJJ754	18.11.53	67	FXT94	20.4.54	121	FJJ743		4.2.54
14	FJJ686	15.6.54	68	FJJ687	14.10.53	122	FJJ745		4.2.54
15	FJJ707	7.10.53	69	FJJ733	2.3.54	123	FJJ728		24.2.54
16	FJJ750	7.10.53	70	FJJ732	27.4.54	124	FJJ689		8.12.54
17	FXT63	4.5.54	71	FJJ712	24.2.54	125	FXT91		
18	FJJ716	13.1.54	72	FJJ730	13.4.54	126	DLU126		9.12.53
19	FXT62	25.11.53	73	FXT81	27.4.54	127	DLU56		16.12.53
20	FXT64	2.12.53	74	FJJ678	27.4.54	128	DLU103		22.12.53
21	FXT68	25.11.53	75	FJJ699	18.5.54	129	DYL819		6.7.54
22	FJJ737	17.2.54	76	FJJ735	18.5.54	130	DLU86		26.10.54
23	FJJ679	2.12.53	77	FJJ718	1.6.54	131	DGX352		6.1.54
24	FXT61	30.12.53	78	FJJ734	25.5.54	132	DLU93		6.7.54
25	FJJ691	11.11.53	79	FXT66	25.5.54	133	DLU102		24.8.54
26	FXT67	27.1.54	80	FJJ748	1.6.54	134	DLU67		6.7.54
27	FJJ692	9.8.54	81	FXT52	15.6.54	135	EGO395		24.8.54
28	FXT75	10.2.54	82	FXT90	26.10.54	136	EGO342		10.8.54
29	FJJ736	24.2.54	83	FXT95		137	DYL812		10.8.54
30	FXT83	21.10.53	84	FJJ682		138	EGO463		
31	FXT87	6.1.54	85	FXT50	19.10.54	139	DLU100		
32	FXT57	6.7.54	86	FJJ757	2.11.54	140	EGO466		
33	FXT70	10.8.54	87	FJJ709	18.5.54	141	EGO488		
34	FJJ696	1.6.54	88	FXT79	13.4.54	142	DLU101		15.6.54
35	FJJ684	18.5.54	89	FXT51	13.4.54	143	ELP171		
36	FJJ688	31.8.54	90	FJJ727	27.4.54	144	DLU60		
37	FXT72	4.2.54	91	FJJ681	11.5.54	145	DLU118		19.10.54
38	FXT73	2.3.54	92	FXT59	20.4.54	146	DLU84	3.1.50	
39	FJJ759	23.3.54	93	FJJ726	27.4.54	147	DLU24	3.1.50	2.11.54
40	FJJ747	20.4.54	94	FJJ720	4.5.54	148	ELP126	4.1.50	
41	FXT88	10.3.54	95	FXT78	27.4.54	149	DLU129	4.1.50	19.10.54
42	FXT49	14.10.53	96	FJJ698	4.5.54	150	EGO407	9.1.50	2.11.54
43	FXT80	21.10.53	97	FJJ738	10.2.54	151	EGO459	4.1.50	19.10.54
44	FJJ752	13.4.54	98	FJJ729	11.5.54	152	DLU25	6.1.50	2.11.54
45	FJJ711	5.10.54†	99	FJJ719	11.5.54	153	DLU96	5.1.50	2.11.54
46	FJJ731	26.10.54	100	FJJ739	25.5.54	154	DLU54	5.1.50	
47	FXT77	14.10.53	101	FJJ677	8.6.54	155	DLU74	6.1.50	17.8.54
48	FJJ705	7.10.53	102	FJJ713	17.3.54	156	DYL857	6.1.50	26.10.54
49	FJJ751		103	FJJ758	8.6.54	157	DYL807	6.1.50	5.10.54
50	FXT65	4.11.53	104	FJJ715	15.6.54	158	DLU110	6.1.50	
51	FXT89	21.10.53	105	FJJ708	17.2.54	159	EGO453	6.1.50	5.10.54
52	FXT58	15.6.54	106	FXT86	15.6.54	160	EGO482	11.1.50	26.10.54
53	FXT54	7.10.53	107	FJJ706	6.1.54				
54	FJJ753	4.5.54	108	FJJ704	15.6.54				

† To Service Vehicle 1019J with body of RT 1 - mobile instruction unit.

Prototype RTL 501 was the only Leyland built with an RT3 body and therefore the only RTL with a pillar route number plate. Being the odd man out, it did not normally carry a route number in that position even when most London buses were dressed immaculately. Alan B. Cross

RTL

To meet the unprecedented requirements for new vehicles immediately after the Second World War, London Transport decided to purchase part of its new fleet from Leyland Motors Ltd. An initial order for 1,000 7ft 6in wide chassis was placed in 1947 and this was supplemented by further orders until a total of 1,631 was reached. The RTL chassis was based on the standard Titan PD2/1 model modified to make it as comparable as possible to the AEC RT. The chassis frame had the same outline as the RT and the specification included the AEC preselective gearbox and fluid flywheel, which were not offered on the standard Titan. The engine was the new Leyland 9.8 litre model which developed 125 bhp at 1,800 rpm, derated by LT to 115 bhp for fuel economy and improved engine life. The original intention had been that the first 1,000 chassis would be bodied by Metro-Cammell to the standard RT3 specification but this was later altered to a modified version of the company's standard product. This had a different method of body mounting and was not interchangeable with other RTs and RTLs. London Transport therefore reduced the order to 450 and in compensation placed the entire order for the RF class with Metro-Cammell. Most of the remaining RTL bodies were supplied by Park Royal but RTL 1307 and the last thirty-one had Weymann bodywork.

The majority of the bodies for production RTLs was supplied by Park Royal to the standard RT8 design, a total of 1,148 being turned out between 1948 and 1954. RTL 1139 is seen on a tram replacement route at Tooting. Alan B. Cross

The other main supplier of RTLs was Metropolitan-Cammell Carriage & Wagon Co. Ltd of Elmdon, Birmingham, which built 450 using its own metal-framed structure. The body design, coded RT7, was a copy of the RT8 but had a number of minor internal differences and could be distinguished externally by the inverted scroll above the central cream band. They made a significant contribution to the replacement of south London's trams, RTL 954 being one of forty-seven licensed at Clapham in January 1951. It is seen at Raynes Park on new route 189A. F.G. Reynolds

The prototype was numbered RTL 501, as the first five hundred numbers were originally reserved for the eight-foot wide version (RTW). It took the body and registration number intended for RT 657 and was therefore the only RTL built with an RT3 body. RTL 501 entered service at Turnham Green garage on 16th June 1948 and delivery of the production buses from Park Royal began on 24th November 1948. The first Metro-Cammell bus (RTL 551) was received on 11th August 1949. RTL 1307 was specially fitted with a Weymann body when new in 1952 so that both manufacturers could be represented on the tour of north America, when it was fitted out as an information office. The first of the main Weymann batch of RT8/2s (RTL 1601) was taken into stock on 5th May 1954 and the rest were delivered between August and November 1954. Another RTL to go overseas was RTL 1459 which went to Zurich and Malmô with RT 3710 in 1953.

Following extensive trials at the Motor Industry Research Association's establishment at Nuneaton of a prototype modification to RTL 1337, from RTL 1469 onwards the front end of the chassis frame was strengthened and the steering geometry modified. These were later classified 2/7RT. These modifications were never made on the remainder of the class. On its return from MIRA, RTL 1337 was given a new body and was re-registered OLD813 when it belatedly entered service in October 1954. Its original body and registration were transferred to RT 4668. The last RTLs were delivered from Park Royal on 29th September and Weymann on 10th November 1954. Sixty-three were not required for service and were placed in store, mainly at Garston garage (RTLs 1568-1600 and 1602-1631). The first RTL to be withdrawn was RTL 1222, burnt out at Walworth garage in January 1953.

RTL 1307 was specially fitted with a Weymann body for its participation as an information office in the north American tour of 1952 and remained unique for two years. The canopy route number blind shines brightly in this gloomy winter view on the short-lived Woolwich to Shooters Hill local route 256. Alan B. Cross

At the very end of RTL production, Weymann unexpectedly supplied thirty-one more bodies on 7RT chassis but only one had been licensed by the end of 1954. RTL 1601, looking no different from the Park Royal version, is at the Vauxhall Bridge Road terminus of route 36A, within days of first being licensed in May 1954. W.R. Legg

Chassis: Leyland Titan 7RT: Engine: Leyland O600 6-cylinder 9.8 litre oil 125 bhp (derated to 115 bhp)
Transmission: AEC D140 4-speed air operated preselective with fluid flywheel
Bodywork: Park Royal (1-550, 1001-1306, 1308-1600); Metro-Cammell (551-1000); Weymann (1307, 1601-1631)   Capacity: H30/26R
L.T. chassis codes: 7RT (551-1000: 1/7RT; 1337, 1469-1631: 2/7RT)
Body codes: RT3 (501); RT3/1 (1-118); RT7 (551-1000); RT8 (119-500, 502-550, 1001-1312); RT8/2 (1313-1631)
Built: 1948-1954
Number built: 1631
Number in stock: 1. 1.50: 550
                31.12.54: 1631

RTL		RTL		RTL		RTL		RTL		RTL	
1	JXN313	67	JXN390	133	KGK797	199	KGK863	265	KGU211	331	KGU289
2	JXN314	68	JXN391	134	KGK798	200	KGK864	266	KGU212	332	KGU401
3	JXN315	69	JXN392	135	KGK799	201	KGK865	267	KGU213	333	KGU402
4	JXN316	70	JXN393	136	KGK800	202	KGK866	268	KGU214	334	KGU403
5	JXN317	71	JXN394	137	KGK801	203	KGK867	269	KGU215	335	KGU404
6	JXN318	72	JXN395	138	KGK802	204	KGK868	270	KGU216	336	KGU405
7	JXN319	73	JXN396	139	KGK803	205	KGK869	271	KGU217	337	KGU406
8	JXN320	74	JXN397	140	KGK804	206	KGK870	272	KGU218	338	KGU407
9	JXN321	75	JXN398	141	KGK805	207	KGK871	273	KGU219	339	KGU408
10	JXN322	76	JXN399	142	KGK806	208	KGK872	274	KGU220	340	KGU409
11	JXN323	77	JXN400	143	KGK807	209	KGK873	275	KGU221	341	KGU417
12	JXN324	78	JXN401	144	KGK808	210	KGK874	276	KGU222	342	KGU418
13	JXN333	79	JXN402	145	KGK809	211	KGK875	277	KGU223	343	KGU419
14	JXN334	80	JXN403	146	KGK810	212	KGK876	278	KGU224	344	KGU420
15	JXN335	81	JXN404	147	KGK811	213	KGK877	279	KGU225	345	KGU421
16	JXN336	82	JXN405	148	KGK812	214	KGK878	280	KGU226	346	KGU422
17	JXN337	83	JXN406	149	KGK813	215	KGK879	281	KGU227	347	KGU423
18	JXN338	84	JXN407	150	KGK814	216	KGK880	282	KGU228	348	KGU424
19	JXN339	85	JXN408	151	KGK815	217	KGK881	283	KGU229	349	KGU425
20	JXN340	86	JXN409	152	KGK816	218	KGK882	284	KGU230	350	KGU426
21	JXN341	87	JXN410	153	KGK817	219	KGK883	285	KGU231	351	KGU427
22	JXN342	88	JXN411	154	KGK818	220	KGK884	286	KGU244	352	KGU428
23	JXN344	89	JXN412	155	KGK819	221	KGK885	287	KGU245	353	KGU429
24	JXN347	90	JXN413	156	KGK820	222	KGK886	288	KGU246	354	KGU430
25	JXN348	91	JXN414	157	KGK821	223	KGK887	289	KGU247	355	KGU431
26	JXN349	92	JXN415	158	KGK822	224	KGK888	290	KGU248	356	KGU432
27	JXN350	93	JXN416	159	KGK823	225	KGK889	291	KGU249	357	KGU433
28	JXN351	94	JXN417	160	KGK824	226	KGK890	292	KGU250	358	KGU434
29	JXN352	95	JXN418	161	KGK825	227	KGK891	293	KGU251	359	KGU435
30	JXN353	96	JXN419	162	KGK826	228	KGK892	294	KGU252	360	KGU436
31	JXN354	97	JXN420	163	KGK827	229	KGK893	295	KGU253	361	KGU437
32	JXN355	98	JXN421	164	KGK828	230	KGK894	296	KGU254	362	KGU438
33	JXN356	99	JXN422	165	KGK829	231	KGK895	297	KGU255	363	KGU439
34	JXN357	100	JXN423	166	KGK830	232	KGK896	298	KGU256	364	KGU451
35	JXN358	101	JXN424	167	KGK831	233	KGK897	299	KGU257	365	KGU452
36	JXN359	102	JXN425	168	KGK832	234	KGK898	300	KGU258	366	KGU453
37	JXN360	103	JXN426	169	KGK833	235	KGK899	301	KGU259	367	KGU454
38	JXN361	104	JXN427	170	KGK834	236	KGK900	302	KGU260	368	KGU455
39	JXN362	105	JXN428	171	KGK835	237	KGK901	303	KGU261	369	KGU456
40	JXN363	106	JXN429	172	KGK836	238	KGK902	304	KGU262	370	KGU457
41	JXN364	107	JXN430	173	KGK837	239	KGK903	305	KGU263	371	KGU458
42	JXN365	108	JXN431	174	KGK838	240	KGK904	306	KGU264	372	KGU459
43	JXN366	109	JXN432	175	KGK839	241	KGK905	307	KGU265	373	KGU460
44	JXN367	110	JXN433	176	KGK840	242	KGK906	308	KGU266	374	KGU461
45	JXN368	111	JXN434	177	KGK841	243	KGK907	309	KGU267	375	KGU462
46	JXN369	112	JXN435	178	KGK842	244	KGK908	310	KGU268	376	KGU463
47	JXN370	113	JXN436	179	KGK843	245	KGK909	311	KGU269	377	KGU464
48	JXN371	114	JXN437	180	KGK844	246	KGK910	312	KGU270	378	KGU465
49	JXN372	115	JXN438	181	KGK845	247	KGK911	313	KGU271	379	KGU466
50	JXN373	116	JXN439	182	KGK846	248	KGK912	314	KGU272	380	KGU467
51	JXN374	117	KGK781	183	KGK847	249	KGK913	315	KGU273	381	KGU468
52	JXN375	118	KGK782	184	KGK848	250	KGK914	316	KGU274	382	KGU469
53	JXN376	119	KGK783	185	KGK849	251	KGK915	317	KGU275	383	KGU470
54	JXN377	120	KGK784	186	KGK850	252	KGK916	318	KGU276	384	KGU471
55	JXN378	121	KGK785	187	KGK851	253	KGK929	319	KGU277	385	KGU472
56	JXN379	122	KGK786	188	KGK852	254	KGK930	320	KGU278	386	KGU473
57	JXN380	123	KGK787	189	KGK853	255	KGU201	321	KGU279	387	KGU474
58	JXN381	124	KGK788	190	KGK854	256	KGU202	322	KGU280	388	KGU475
59	JXN382	125	KGK789	191	KGK855	257	KGU203	323	KGU281	389	KGU476
60	JXN383	126	KGK790	192	KGK856	258	KGU204	324	KGU282	390	KGU477
61	JXN384	127	KGK791	193	KGK857	259	KGU205	325	KGU283	391	KGU478
62	JXN385	128	KGK792	194	KGK858	260	KGU206	326	KGU284	392	KGU479
63	JXN386	129	KGK793	195	KGK859	261	KGU207	327	KGU285	393	KGU480
64	JXN387	130	KGK794	196	KGK860	262	KGU208	328	KGU286	394	KGU481
65	JXN388	131	KGK795	197	KGK861	263	KGU209	329	KGU287	395	KGU482
66	JXN389	132	KGK796	198	KGK862	264	KGU210	330	KGU288	396	KGU483

RTL		Date into stock	RTL		Date into stock	RTL		Date into stock
397	KGU484		463	KLB682	12.1.50	529	KYY558	5.5.50
398	KGU485		464	KLB683	12.1.50	530	KYY559	5.5.50
399	KGU486		465	KLB684	12.1.50	531	KYY560	5.5.50
400	KGU487		466	KLB685	13.1.50	532	KYY561	5.5.50
401	KGU488		467	KLB686	13.1.50	533	KYY562	5.5.50
402	KGU489		468	KLB687	13.1.50	534	KYY563	5.5.50
403	KGU490		469	KLB688	13.1.50	535	KYY564	10.5.50
404	KGU491		470	KLB689	13.1.50	536	KYY565	10.5.50
405	KGU492		471	KLB690	16.1.50	537	KYY566	10.5.50
406	KGU493		472	KLB691	16.1.50	538	KYY567	10.5.50
407	KGU494		473	KLB692	17.1.50	539	KYY568	10.5.50
408	KGU495		474	KLB693	17.1.50	540	KYY633	15.6.50
409	KGU496		475	KLB694	18.1.50	541	KYY634	16.6.50
410	KGU497		476	KLB695	19.1.50	542	KYY635	16.6.50
411	KGU498		477	KLB696	19.1.50	543	KYY636	16.6.50
412	KGU499		478	KLB697	19.1.50	544	KYY637	16.6.50
413	KGU500		479	KLB698	20.1.50	545	KYY638	16.6.50
414	KLB601		480	KLB699	19.1.50	546	KYY639	21.6.50
415	KLB602		481	KLB700	20.1.50	547	KYY640	20.6.50
416	KLB603		482	KLB701	20.1.50	548	KYY641	22.6.50
417	KLB604		483	KLB702	23.1.50	549	KYY642	22.6.50
418	KLB605		484	KLB703	20.1.50	550	KYY643	22.6.50
419	KLB606		485	KLB704	25.1.50	551	KGU1	
420	KLB607		486	KLB705	25.1.50	552	KGU2	
421	KLB608		487	KLB706	23.1.50	553	KGU3	
422	KLB609		488	KLB707	27.1.50	554	KGU4	
423	KLB610		489	KLB708	24.1.50	555	KGU5	
424	KLB611		490	KLB709	25.1.50	556	KGU6	
425	KLB612		491	KLB710	25.1.50	557	KGU7	
426	KLB613		492	KLB711	25.1.50	558	KGU8	
427	KLB614		493	KXW277	1.3.50	559	KGU9	
428	KLB615		494	KXW278	3.3.50	560	KGU10	
429	KLB616		495	KXW279	3.3.50	561	KGU11	
430	KLB617		496	KXW280	6.3.50	562	KGU12	
431	KLB618		497	KXW281	8.3.50	563	KGU13	
432	KLB619		498	KXW282	3.3.50	564	KGU14	
433	KLB620		499	KXW283	7.3.50	565	KGU15	
434	KLB621		500	KXW284	7.3.50	566	KGU16	
435	KLB622		501	JXC20		567	KGU17	
436	KLB623		502	KXW285	7.3.50	568	KGU18	
437	KLB624		503	KXW286	9.3.50	569	KGU19	
438	KLB625		504	KXW287	8.3.50	570	KGU20	
439	KLB626		505	KXW288	10.3.50	571	KGU21	
440	KLB627		506	KXW289	10.3.30	572	KGU22	
441	KLB628		507	KXW290	10.3.50	573	KGU23	
442	KLB629		508	KXW291	10.3.50	574	KGU24	
443	KLB630		509	KXW292	14.3.50	575	KGU25	
444	KLB639		510	KXW293	10.3.50	576	KGU26	
445	KLB640		511	KXW294	10.3.50	577	KGU27	
446	KLB641		512	KXW295	13.3.50	578	KGU28	
447	KLB642		513	KXW296	13.3.50	579	KGU29	
448	KLB643		514	KXW297	13.3.50	580	KGU30	
449	KLB644		515	KXW298	14.3.50	581	KGU31	
450	KLB645		516	KXW299	15.3.50	582	KGU32	
451	KLB646		517	KXW300	16.3.50	583	KGU33	
452	KLB647		518	KXW344	6.4.50	584	KGU34	
453	KLB648		519	KXW345	14.4.50	585	KGU35	
454	KLB649		520	KXW346	13.4.50	586	KGU36	
455	KLB650		521	KXW347	14.4.50	587	KGU37	
456	KLB651		522	KXW348	13.4.50	588	KGU38	
457	KLB652		523	KXW349	14.4.50	589	KGU39	
458	KLB653		524	KXW350	14.4.50	590	KGU40	
459	KLB654		525	KYY521	14.4.50	591	KGU41	
460	KLB679	11.1.50	526	KYY522	14.4.50	592	KGU42	
461	KLB680	11.1.50	527	KYY523	14.4.50	593	KGU43	
462	KLB681	12.1.50	528	KYY524	14.4.50	594	KGU44	

RTL		Date into stock	RTL		Date into stock	RTL		Date into stock
595	KGU45		661	KXW11	3.2.50	727	KXW77	17.4.50
596	KGU46		662	KXW12	7.2.50	728	KXW78	20.4.50
597	KGU47		663	KXW13	9.2.50	729	KXW79	14.4.50
598	KGU48		664	KXW14	10.2.50	730	KXW80	20.4.50
599	KGU49		665	KXW15	8.2.50	731	KXW81	13.4.50
600	KGU50		666	KXW16	8.2.50	732	KXW82	17.4.50
601	KGU51		667	KXW17	10.2.50	733	KXW83	21.4.50
602	KGU52		668	KXW18	9.2.50	734	KXW84	24.4.50
603	KGU53		669	KXW19	9.2.50	735	KXW85	21.4.50
604	KGU54		670	KXW20	10.2.50	736	KXW86	21.4.50
605	KGU55		671	KXW21	10.2.50	737	KXW87	27.4.50
606	KGU56		672	KXW22	16.2.50	738	KXW88	24.4.50
607	KGU57		673	KXW23	17.2.50	739	KXW89	27.4.50
608	KGU58		674	KXW24	13.2.50	740	KXW90	27.4.50
609	KGU59		675	KXW25	17.2.50	741	KXW91	2.5.50
610	KGU60		676	KXW26	13.2.50	742	KXW92	28.4.50
611	KGU61		677	KXW27	16.2.50	743	KXW93	27.4.50
612	KGU62		678	KXW28	17.2.50	744	KXW94	28.4.50
613	KGU63		679	KXW29	17.2.50	745	KXW95	2.5.50
614	KGU64		680	KXW30	20.2.50	746	KXW96	28.4.50
615	KGU65		681	KXW31	16.2.50	747	KXW97	10.5.50
616	KGU66		682	KXW32	24.2.50	748	KXW98	10.5.50
617	KGU67		683	KXW33	24.2.50	749	KXW99	5.5.50
618	KGU68		684	KXW34	20.2.50	750	KXW100	5.5.50
619	KGU69		685	KXW35	27.2.50	751	KYY721	10.5.50
620	KGU70		686	KXW36	24.2.50	752	KYY722	12.5.50
621	KGU71		687	KXW37	24.2.50	753	KYY723	11.5.50
622	KGU72		688	KXW38	1.3.50	754	KYY724	7.5.50
623	KGU73		689	KXW39	27.2.50	755	KYY725	11.5.50
624	KGU74		690	KXW40	3.3.50	756	KYY726	12.5.50
625	KGU75		691	KXW41	28.2.50	757	KYY727	17.5.50
626	KGU76		692	KXW42	1.3.50	758	KYY728	12.5.50
627	KGU77		693	KXW43	10.3.50	759	KYY729	17.5.50
628	KGU78		694	KXW44	9.3.50	760	KYY730	18.5.50
629	KGU79		695	KXW45	10.3.50	761	KYY731	19.5.50
630	KGU80		696	KXW46	9.3.50	762	KYY732	18.5.50
631	KGU81		697	KXW47	10.3.50	763	KYY733	19.5.50
632	KGU82		698	KXW48	9.3.50	764	KYY734	18.5.50
633	KGU83		699	KXW49	10.3.50	765	KYY735	22.5.50
634	KGU84		700	KXW50	15.3.50	766	KYY736	25.5.50
635	KGU85		701	KXW51	15.3.50	767	KYY737	22.5.50
636	KGU86		702	KXW52	15.3.50	768	KYY738	25.5.50
637	KGU87		703	KXW53	15.3.50	769	KYY739	26.5.50
638	KGU88		704	KXW54	17.3.50	770	KYY740	25.5.50
639	KGU89		705	KXW55	22.3.50	771	KYY741	25.5.50
640	KGU90		706	KXW56	24.3.50	772	KYY742	9.6.50
641	KGU91	4.1.50	707	KXW57	17.3.50	773	KYY743	26.5.50
642	KGU92	6.1.50	708	KXW58	24.3.50	774	KYY744	2.6.50
643	KGU93	4.1.50	709	KXW59	17.3.50	775	KYY745	2.6.50
644	KGU94	9.1.50	710	KXW60	24.3.50	776	KYY746	2.6.50
645	KGU95	9.1.50	711	KXW61	22.3.50	777	KYY747	9.6.50
646	KGU96	13.1.50	712	KXW62	30.3.50	778	KYY748	26.5.50
647	KGU97	13.1.50	713	KXW63	24.3.50	779	KYY749	9.6.50
648	KGU98	6.1.50	714	KXW64	28.3.50	780	KYY750	9.6.50
649	KGU99	13.1.50	715	KXW65	28.3.50	781	KYY751	15.6.50
650	KGU100	13.1.50	716	KXW66	30.3.50	782	KYY752	9.6.50
651	KXW1	18.1.50	717	KXW67	30.3.50	783	KYY753	15.6.50
652	KXW2	18.1.50	718	KXW68	30.3.50	784	KYY754	9.6.50
653	KXW3	20.1.50	719	KXW69	31.3.50	785	KYY755	9.6.50
654	KXW4	25.1.50	720	KXW70	31.3.50	786	KYY756	9.6.50
655	KXW5	25.1.50	721	KXW71	6.4.50	787	KYY757	16.6.50
656	KXW6	27.1.50	722	KXW72	6.4.50	788	KYY758	15.6.50
657	KXW7	7.2.50	723	KXW73	31.3.50	789	KYY759	15.6.50
658	KXW8	30.1.50	724	KXW74	14.4.50	790	KYY760	16.6.50
659	KXW9	3.2.50	725	KXW75	20.4.50	791	KYY761	16.6.50
660	KXW10	8.2.50	726	KXW76	13.4.50	792	KYY762	16.6.50

RTL		Date into stock	RTL		Date into stock	RTL		Date into stock
793	KYY763	23.6.50	859	LLU849	23.8.50	925	LLU915	12.10.50
794	KYY764	23.6.50	860	LLU850	23.8.50	926	LLU916	13.10.50
795	KYY765	23.6.50	861	LLU851	21.8.50	927	LLU917	13.10.50
796	KYY766	23.6.50	862	LLU852	23.8.50	928	LLU918	17.10.50
797	KYY767	23.6.50	863	LLU853	21.8.50	929	LLU919	17.10.50
798	KYY768	23.6.50	864	LLU854	25.8.50	930	LLU920	20.10.50
799	KYY769	29.6.50	865	LLU855	23.8.50	931	LLU921	3.11.50
800	KYY770	23.6.50	866	LLU856	25.8.50	932	LLU922	20.10.50
801	KYY771	29.6.50	867	LLU857	25.8.50	933	LLU923	20.10.50
802	KYY772	23.6.50	868	LLU858	25.8.50	934	LLU924	23.10.50
803	KYY773	29.6.50	869	LLU859	25.8.50	935	LLU925	2.11.50
804	KYY774	29.6.50	870	LLU860	30.8.50	936	LLU926	23.10.50
805	KYY775	3.7.50	871	LLU861	25.8.50	937	LLU927	23.10.50
806	KYY776	29.6.50	872	LLU862	30.8.50	938	LLU928	26.10.50
807	KYY777	3.7.50	873	LLU863	30.8.50	939	LLU929	26.10.50
808	KYY778	29.6.50	874	LLU864	30.8.50	940	LLU930	2.11.50
809	KYY779	3.7.50	875	LLU865	1.9.50	941	LLU931	13.11.50
810	KYY780	3.7.50	876	LLU866	30.8.50	942	LLU932	26.10.50
811	KYY781	3.7.50	877	LLU867	1.9.50	943	LLU933	3.11.50
812	KYY782	3.7.50	878	LLU868	8.9.50	944	LLU934	13.11.50
813	KYY783	3.7.50	879	LLU869	1.9.50	945	LLU935	3.11.50
814	KYY784	4.7.50	880	LLU870	6.9.50	946	LLU936	6.11.50
815	KYY785	4.7.50	881	LLU871	4.9.50	947	LLU937	3.11.50
816	KYY786	4.7.50	882	LLU872	13.9.50	948	LLU938	6.11.50
817	KYY787	13.7.50	883	LLU873	1.9.50	949	LLU939	2.11.50
818	KYY788	17.7.50	884	LLU874	5.9.50	950	LLU940	13.11.50
819	KYY789	13.7.50	885	LLU875	13.9.50	951	LUC326	13.11.50
820	KYY790	21.7.50	886	LLU876	8.9.50	952	LUC327	13.11.50
821	KYY791	13.7.50	887	LLU877	18.9.50	953	LUC328	16.11.50
822	KYY792	13.7.50	888	LLU878	13.9.50	954	LUC329	16.11.50
823	KYY793	17.7.50	889	LLU879	18.9.50	955	LUC330	16.11.50
824	KYY794	21.7.50	890	LLU880	18.9.50	956	LUC331	16.11.50
825	KYY795	17.7.50	891	LLU881	20.9.50	957	LUC332	17.11.50
826	KYY796	21.7.50	892	LLU882	13.9.50	958	LUC333	17.11.50
827	KYY797	1.8.50	893	LLU883	18.9.50	959	LUC334	17.11.50
828	KYY798	24.7.50	894	LLU884	25.9.50	960	LUC335	17.11.50
829	KYY799	27.7.50	895	LLU885	20.9.50	961	LUC336	21.11.50
830	KYY800	27.7.50	896	LLU886	22.9.50	962	LUC337	21.11.50
831	KYY801	21.7.50	897	LLU887	22.9.50	963	LUC338	21.11.50
832	KYY802	24.7.50	898	LLU888	25.9.50	964	LUC339	24.11.50
833	KYY803	24.7.50	899	LLU889	28.9.50	965	LUC340	24.11.50
834	KYY804	28.7.50	900	LLU890	22.9.50	966	LUC341	24.11.50
835	KYY805	24.7.50	901	LLU891	28.9.50	967	LUC342	1.12.50
836	KYY806	28.7.50	902	LLU892	29.9.50	968	LUC343	4.12.50
837	KYY807	28.7.50	903	LLU893	25.9.50	969	LUC344	4.12.50
838	KYY808	28.7.50	904	LLU894	28.9.50	970	LUC345	8.12.50
839	KYY809	28.7.50	905	LLU895	28.9.50	971	LUC346	1.12.50
840	KYY810	31.7.50	906	LLU896	28.9.50	972	LUC347	7.12.50
841	KYY811	31.7.50	907	LLU897	29.9.50	973	LUC348	7.12.50
842	KYY812	28.7.50	908	LLU898	28.9.50	974	LUC349	4.12.50
843	KYY813	31.7.50	909	LLU899	29.9.50	975	LUC350	1.12.50
844	KYY814	11.8.50	910	LLU900	29.9.50	976	LUC351	12.12.50
845	KYY815	11.8.50	911	LLU901	2.10.50	977	LUC352	8.12.50
846	KYY816	11.8.50	912	LLU902	29.9.50	978	LUC353	14.12.50
847	KYY817	11.8.50	913	LLU903	2.10.50	979	LUC354	12.12.50
848	KYY818	11.8.50	914	LLU904	6.10.50	980	LUC355	15.12.50
849	KYY819	16.8.50	915	LLU905	2.10.50	981	LUC356	14.12.50
850	KYY820	17.8.50	916	LLU906	2.10.50	982	LUC357	15.12.50
851	LLU841	16.8.50	917	LLU907	12.10.50	983	LUC358	22.12.50
852	LLU842	16.8.50	918	LLU908	6.10.50	984	LUC359	22.12.50
853	LLU843	11.8.50	919	LLU909	6.10.50	985	LUC360	22.12.50
854	LLU844	11.8.50	920	LLU910	12.10.50	986	LUC361	29.12.50
855	LLU845	21.8.50	921	LLU911	17.10.50	987	LUC362	1.1.51
856	LLU846	17.8.50	922	LLU912	12.10.50	988	LUC363	1.1.51
857	LLU847	17.8.50	923	LLU913	13.10.50	989	LUC364	29.12.50
858	LLU848	21.8.50	924	LLU914	13.10.50	990	LUC365	1.1.51

RTL		Date into stock	RTL		Date into stock	RTL		Date into stock
991	LUC366	1.1.51	1057	LUC28	19.10.50	1123	LYF47	14.2.51
992	LUC367	9.1.51	1058	LUC41	20.10.50	1124	LYF48	13.2.51
993	LUC368	9.1.51	1059	LUC42	20.10.50	1125	LYF49	14.2.51
994	LUC369	17.1.51	1060	LUC43	26.10.50	1126	LYF50	14.2.51
995	LUC370	16.1.51	1061	LUC68	7.11.50	1127	LYF51	15.2.51
996	LUC371	2.2.51	1062	LUC69	7.11.50	1128	LYF52	15.2.51
997	LUC372	2.2.51	1063	LUC70	7.11.50	1129	LYF53	15.2.51
998	LUC373	2.2.51	1064	LUC71	8.11.50	1130	LYF54	16.2.51
999	LUC374	2.2.51	1065	LUC72	8.11.50	1131	LYF55	16.2.51
1000	LUC375	15.3.51	1066	LUC73	8.11.50	1132	LYF56	19.2.51
1001	KYY644	22.6.50	1067	LUC74	9.11.50	1133	LYF57	19.2.51
1002	KYY645	22.6.50	1068	LUC75	10.11.50	1134	LYF58	19.2.51
1003	KYY646	23.6.50	1069	LUC76	8.11.50	1135	LYF59	20.2.51
1004	KYY647	23.6.50	1070	LUC77	13.11.50	1136	LYF60	21.2.51
1005	KYY648	23.6.50	1071	LUC78	10.11.50	1137	LYF61	20.2.51
1006	KYY649	23.6.50	1072	LUC79	10.11.50	1138	LYF62	23.2.51
1007	KYY705	26.7.50	1073	LUC250	5.12.50	1139	LYF63	20.2.51
1008	KYY706	27.7.50	1074	LUC251	5.12.50	1140	LYF64	22.2.51
1009	KYY707	27.7.50	1075	LUC252	4.12.50	1141	LYF65	23.2.51
1010	KYY708	27.7.50	1076	LUC253	6.12.50	1142	LYF66	26.2.51
1011	KYY709	27.7.50	1077	LUC254	6.12.50	1143	LYF67	23.2.51
1012	KYY710	28.7.50	1078	LUC255	7.12.50	1144	LYF68	23.2.51
1013	KYY711	28.7.50	1079	LUC256	7.12.50	1145	LYF69	28.2.51
1014	KYY712	28.7.50	1080	LUC257	7.12.50	1146	LYF70	27.2.51
1015	KYY713	28.7.50	1081	LUC258	8.12.50	1147	LYF71	28.2.51
1016	KYY714	28.7.50	1082	LUC259	8.12.50	1148	LYF89	9.3.51
1017	KYY715	28.7.50	1083	LUC260	8.12.50	1149	LYF90	12.3.51
1018	LLU772	23.8.50	1084	LUC261	8.12.50	1150	LYF91	9.3.51
1019	LLU773	25.8.50	1085	LUC262	8.12.50	1151	LYF92	13.3.51
1020	LLU774	25.8.50	1086	LUC263	8.12.50	1152	LYF93	12.3.51
1021	LLU775	25.8.50	1087	LUC264	11.12.50	1153	LYF94	13.3.51
1022	LLU776	31.8.50	1088	LUC265	11.12.50	1154	LYF95	14.3.51
1023	LLU777	25.8.50	1089	LUC282	20.12.50	1155	LYF96	14.3.51
1024	LLU778	1.9.50	1090	LUC283	20.12.50	1156	LYF97	15.3.51
1025	LLU779	31.8.50	1091	LUC284	21.12.50	1157	LYF98	16.3.51
1026	LLU780	28.8.50	1092	LUC285	21.12.50	1158	LYF99	16.3.51
1027	LLU781	1.9.50	1093	LUC286	21.12.50	1159	LYF100	21.3.51
1028	LLU782	28.8.50	1094	LUC287	23.12.50	1160	LYF101	19.3.51
1029	LLU783	31.8.50	1095	LUC305	5.1.51	1161	LYF102	19.3.51
1030	LLU784	1.9.50	1096	LUC306	5.1.51	1162	LYF103	19.3.51
1031	LLU785	31.8.50	1097	LUC307	5.1.51	1163	LYF104	21.3.51
1032	LLU786	31.9.50	1098	LUC308	8.1.51	1164	LYF105	20.3.51
1033	LLU787	1.9.50	1099	LUC309	5.1.51	1165	LYF106	21.3.51
1034	LLU788	1.9.50	1100	LUC310	8.1.51	1166	LYF107	22.3.51
1035	LLU789	5.9.50	1101	LUC311	9.1.51	1167	LYF108	22.3.51
1036	LLU790	1.9.50	1102	LUC312	9.1.51	1168	LYF109	22.3.51
1037	LLU791	4.9.50	1103	LUC313	10.1.51	1169	LYF110	27.3.51
1038	LLU792	6.9.50	1104	LUC314	11.1.51	1170	LYF111	28.3.51
1039	LLU793	6.9.50	1105	LUC315	11.1.51	1171	LYF112	29.3.51
1040	LLU819	15.9.50	1106	LUC316	10.1.51	1172	LYF113	29.3.51
1041	LLU820	22.9.50	1107	LUC317	11.1.51	1173	LYF114	29.3.51
1042	LLU821	22.9.50	1108	LUC318	12.1.51	1174	LYF115	30.3.51
1043	LLU822	29.9.50	1109	LUC319	12.1.51	1175	LYF116	30.3.51
1044	LLU823	22.9.50	1110	LYF34	5.2.51	1176	LYF117	2.4.51
1045	LLU824	25.9.50	1111	LYF35	8.2.51	1177	LYF118	30.3.51
1046	LLU825	22.9.50	1112	LYF36	9.2.51	1178	LYF119	3.4.51
1047	LLU826	27.9.50	1113	LYF37	8.2.51	1179	LYF120	30.3.51
1048	LLU827	25.9.50	1114	LYF38	8.2.51	1180	LYF121	4.4.51
1049	LLU828	29.9.50	1115	LYF39	9.2.51	1181	LYF122	4.4.51
1050	LLU829	27.9.50	1116	LYF40	8.2.51	1182	LYF123	5.4.51
1051	LLU830	28.9.50	1117	LYF41	9.2.51	1183	LYF124	5.4.51
1052	LUC23	13.10.50	1118	LYF42	9.2.51	1184	LYF125	6.4.51
1053	LUC24	31.10.50	1119	LYF43	9.2.51	1185	LYF126	6.4.51
1054	LUC25	13.10.50	1120	LYF44	13.2.51	1186	LYF127	6.4.51
1055	LUC26	18.10.50	1121	LYF45	13.2.51	1187	LYF128	6.4.51
1056	LUC27	18.10.50	1122	LYF46	12.2.51	1188	LYF129	9.4.51

RTL		Date into stock	**RTL**		Date into stock	**RTL**		Date into stock
1189	LYF130	10.4.51	1255	LYR787	3.12.51	1321	MLL683	5.6.52
1190	LYF131	12.4.51	1256	LYR788	5.12.51	1322	MLL684	6.6.52
1191	LYF132	12.4.51	1257	LYR789	4.12.51	1323	MLL685	9.6.52
1192	LYF133	11.4.51	1258	LYR790	5.12.51	1324	MLL686	9.6.52
1193	LYF134	12.4.51	1259	LYR791	5.12.51	1325	MLL687	11.6.52
1194	LYF135	13.4.51	1260	LYR792	6.12.51	1326	MLL697	24.6.52
1195	LYF136	13.4.51	1261	LYR793	6.12.51	1327	MLL698	26.6.52
1196	LYF137	13.4.51	1262	LYR794	6.12.51	1328	MLL699	26.6.52
1197	LYF138	13.4.51	1263	LYR795	6.12.51	1329	MLL700	26.6.52
1198	LYF139	16.4.51	1264	LYR796	7.12.51	1330	MLL701	27.6.52
1199	LYF140	18.4.51	1265	LYR797	7.12.51	1331	MLL702	27.6.52
1200	LYF141	17.4.51	1266	LYR798	7.12.51	1332	MLL703	2.7.52
1201	LYF142	18.4.51	1267	LYR799	11.12.51	1333	MXX32	23.10.52
1202	LYF143	18.4.51	1268	LYR800	14.12.51	1334	MXX33	24.10.52
1203	LYF144	19.4.51	1269	LYR801	14.12.51	1335	MXX34	24.10.52
1204	LYF145	20.4.51	1270	LYR802	17.12.51	1336	MXX35	27.10.52
1205	LYF146	20.4.51	1271	LYR803	21.12.51	1337	OLD813	20.9.54
1206	LYF147	20.4.51	1272	LYR804	21.12.51	1338	MXX61	19.11.52
1207	LYF148	20.4.51	1273	LYR805	21.12.51	1339	MXX62	19.11.52
1208	LYF149	24.4.51	1274	LYR806	28.12.51	1340	MXX63	19.11.52
1209	LYF150	23.4.51	1275	LYR807	31.12.51	1341	MXX64	20.11.52
1210	LYF151	24.4.51	1276	LYR808	28.12.51	1342	MXX65	21.11.52
1211	LYF152	25.4.51	1277	LYR809	31.12.51	1343	MXX66	21.11.52
1212	LYF153	25.4.51	1278	LYR810	31.12.51	1344	MXX67	21.11.52
1213	LYF154	26.4.51	1279	LYR811	31.12.51	1345	MXX68	21.11.52
1214	LYF155	26.4.51	1280	LYR812	31.12.51	1346	MXX69	21.11.52
1215	LYF156	27.4.51	1281	LYR813	31.12.51	1347	MXX70	25.11.52
1216	LYF157	27.4.51	1282	LYR814	2.1.52	1348	MXX71	26.11.52
1217	LYF158	30.4.51	1283	LYR815	2.1.52	1349	MXX72	26.11.52
1218	LYF159	30.4.51	1284	LYR816	2.1.52	1350	MXX73	27.11.52
1219	LYF160	30.4.51	1285	LYR817	3.1.52	1351	MXX74	27.11.52
1220	LYF161	2.5.51	1286	LYR818	3.1.52	1352	MXX75	27.11.52
1221	LYF162	1.5.51	1287	LYR819	3.1.52	1353	MXX76	28.11.52
1222	LYF163	2.5.51	1288	LYR820	4.1.52	1354	MXX77	28.11.52
1223	LYF164	3.5.51	1289	LYR821	4.1.52	1355	MXX78	28.11.52
1224	LYF165	3.5.51	1290	LYR822	4.1.52	1356	MXX79	2.12.52
1225	LYF166	4.5.51	1291	LYR823	4.1.52	1357	MXX80	2.12.52
1226	LYF167	4.5.51	1292	LYR824	4.1.52	1358	MXX81	3.12.52
1227	LYR759	16.11.51	1293	LYR825	8.1.52	1359	MXX82	3.12.52
1228	LYR760	16.11.51	1294	LYR828	8.1.52	1360	MXX83	4.12.52
1229	LYR761	16.11.51	1295	LYR829	8.1.52	1361	MXX84	4.12.52
1230	LYR762	16.11.51	1296	LYR830	9.1.52	1362	MXX85	5.12.52
1231	LYR763	16.11.51	1297	LYR831	10.1.52	1363	MXX86	5.12.52
1232	LYR764	20.11.51	1298	LYR832	9.1.52	1364	MXX87	5.12.52
1233	LYR765	21.11.51	1299	LYR833	10.1.52	1365	MXX88	9.12.52
1234	LYR766	22.11.51	1300	LYR834	11.1.52	1366	MXX89	9.12.52
1235	LYR767	22.11.51	1301	LYR835	11.1.52	1367	MXX90	10.12.52
1236	LYR768	22.11.51	1302	LYR936	11.1.52	1368	MXX91	10.12.52
1237	LYR769	22.11.51	1303	LYR937	11.1.52	1369	MXX92	11.12.52
1238	LYR770	26.11.51	1304	LYR938	11.1.52	1370	MXX93	12.12.52
1239	LYR771	26.11.51	1305	LYR939	16.1.52	1371	MXX94	12.12.52
1240	LYR772	26.11.51	1306	LYR940	15.1.52	1372	MXX95	12.12.52
1241	LYR773	26.11.51	1307	LYR935	22.2.52	1373	MXX96	12.12.52
1242	LYR774	26.11.51	1308	LYR956	25.1.52	1374	MXX97	16.12.52
1243	LYR775	26.11.51	1309	LYR957	28.1.52	1375	MXX98	16.12.52
1244	LYR776	28.11.51	1310	LYR958	1.2.52	1376	MXX99	17.12.52
1245	LYR777	28.11.51	1311	LYR959	31.1.52	1377	MXX100	17.12.52
1246	LYR778	29.11.51	1312	LYR960	31.1.52	1378	MXX101	18.12.52
1247	LYR779	29.11.51	1313	LYR961	1.2.52	1379	MXX102	18.12.52
1248	LYR780	29.11.51	1314	MLL676	29.5.52	1380	MXX103	19.12.52
1249	LYR781	30.11.51	1315	MLL677	28.5.52	1381	MXX104	19.12.52
1250	LYR782	30.11.51	1316	MLL678	30.5.52	1382	MXX105	19.12.52
1251	LYR783	30.11.51	1317	MLL679	30.5.52	1383	MXX106	23.12.52
1252	LYR784	30.11.51	1318	MLL680	30.5.52	1384	MXX107	23.12.52
1253	LYR785	30.11.51	1319	MLL681	3.6.52	1385	MXX108	24.12.52
1254	LYR786	30.11.51	1320	MLL682	4.6.52	1386	MXX109	24.12.52

RTL		Date into stock	RTL		Date into stock	RTL		Date into stock
1387	MXX110	24.12.52	1453	NLE727	27.2.53	1519	OLD628	19.5.54
1388	MXX111	30.12.52	1454	NLE728	27.2.53	1520	OLD629	20.5.54
1389	MXX112	30.12.52	1455	NLE729	27.2.53	1521	OLD630	21.5.54
1390	MXX113	31.12.52	1456	NLE730	3.3.53	1522	OLD631	21.5.54
1391	MXX114	1.1.53	1457	NLE731	4.3.53	1523	OLD632	21.5.54
1392	MXX115	8.1.53	1458	NLE732	4.3.53	1524	OLD633	26.5.54
1393	MXX116	8.1.53	1459	NLE733	1.4.53	1525	OLD634	26.5.54
1394	MXX117	8.1.53	1460	NLE734	4.3.53	1526	OLD635	27.5.54
1395	MXX118	9.1.53	1461	NLE735	5.3.53	1527	OLD636	28.5.54
1396	MXX119	9.1.53	1462	NLE736	6.3.53	1528	OLD637	28.5.54
1397	MXX120	9.1.53	1463	NLE737	6.3.53	1529	OLD638	1.6.54
1398	MXX121	9.1.53	1464	NLE738	6.3.53	1530	OLD639	2.6.54
1399	MXX122	9.1.53	1465	NLE739	10.3.53	1531	OLD640	3.6.54
1400	MXX123	9.1.53	1466	NLE751	20.3.53	1532	OLD641	4.6.54
1401	MXX124	13.1.53	1467	NLE752	19.3.53	1533	OLD642	4.6.54
1402	MXX125	14.1.53	1468	NLE753	20.3.53	1534	OLD643	9.6.54
1403	MXX126	15.1.53	1469	NXP955	1.3.54	1535	OLD644	11.6.54
1404	MXX127	15.1.53	1470	NXP956	3.3.54	1536	OLD645	11.6.54
1405	MXX128	15.1.53	1471	NXP957	3.3.54	1537	OLD646	11.6.54
1406	MXX129	16.1.53	1472	NXP958	4.3.54	1538	OLD647	11.6.54
1407	MXX130	16.1.53	1473	NXP959	5.3.54	1539	OLD648	16.6.54
1408	MXX215	16.1.53	1474	NXP960	9.3.54	1540	OLD649	16.6.54
1409	MXX216	16.1.53	1475	OLD571	5.3.54	1541	OLD650	17.6.54
1410	MXX217	20.1.53	1476	OLD572	9.3.54	1542	OLD651	18.6.54
1411	MXX218	21.1.53	1477	OLD573	10.3.54	1543	OLD652	18.6.54
1412	MXX219	21.1.53	1478	OLD574	11.3.54	1544	OLD653	22.6.54
1413	MXX220	22.1.53	1479	OLD575	12.3.54	1545	OLD654	23.6.54
1414	NLE501	23.1.53	1480	OLD576	12.3.54	1546	OLD655	23.6.54
1415	NLE502	23.1.53	1481	OLD590	30.3.54	1547	OLD656	24.6.54
1416	NLE503	27.1.53	1482	OLD591	31.3.54	1548	OLD657	25.6.54
1417	NLE504	28.1.53	1483	OLD592	1.4.54	1549	OLD658	28.6.54
1418	NLE505	29.1.53	1484	OLD593	2.4.54	1550	OLD659	1.7.54
1419	NLE506	29.1.53	1485	OLD594	5.4.54	1551	OLD660	1.7.54
1420	NLE507	29.1.53	1486	OLD595	5.4.54	1552	OLD661	1.7.54
1421	NLE508	29.1.53	1487	OLD596	7.4.54	1553	OLD662	2.7.54
1422	NLE509	30.1.53	1488	OLD597	7.4.54	1554	OLD663	5.7.54
1423	NLE510	30.1.53	1489	OLD598	9.4.54	1555	OLD664	6.7.54
1424	NLE511	30.1.53	1490	OLD599	9.4.54	1556	OLD665	7.7.54
1425	NLE512	3.2.53	1491	OLD600	12.4.54	1557	OLD666	8.7.54
1426	NLE513	4.2.53	1492	OLD601	13.4.54	1558	OLD777	9.7.54
1427	NLE701	4.2.53	1493	OLD602	14.4.54	1559	OLD778	13.7.54
1428	NLE702	5.2.53	1494	OLD603	15.4.54	1560	OLD779	14.7.54
1429	NLE703	6.2.53	1495	OLD604	20.4.54	1561	OLD780	15.7.54
1430	NLE704	10.2.53	1496	OLD605	22.4.54	1562	OLD781	16.7.54
1431	NLE705	10.2.53	1497	OLD606	22.4.54	1563	OLD782	16.7.54
1432	NLE706	6.2.53	1498	OLD607	23.4.54	1564	OLD783	20.7.54
1433	NLE707	11.2.53	1499	OLD608	23.4.54	1565	OLD784	21.7.54
1434	NLE708	11.2.53	1500	OLD609	23.4.54	1566	OLD785	23.7.54
1435	NLE709	12.2.53	1501	OLD610	27.4.54	1567	OLD786	30.7.54
1436	NLE710	16.2.53	1502	OLD611	28.4.54	1568	OLD787	5.8.54
1437	NLE711	16.2.53	1503	OLD612	29.4.54	1569	OLD788	6.8.54
1438	NLE712	16.2.53	1504	OLD613	30.4.54	1570	OLD789	13.8.54
1439	NLE713	18.2.53	1505	OLD614	30.4.54	1571	OLD790	19.8.54
1440	NLE714	18.2.53	1506	OLD615	30.4.54	1572	OLD791	20.8.54
1441	NLE715	18.2.53	1507	OLD616	5.5.54	1573	OLD792	20.8.54
1442	NLE716	18.2.53	1508	OLD617	5.5.54	1574	OLD793	20.8.54
1443	NLE717	20.2.53	1509	OLD618	6.5.54	1575	OLD794	26.8.54
1444	NLE718	20.2.53	1510	OLD619	7.5.54	1576	OLD795	26.8.54
1445	NLE719	20.2.53	1511	OLD620	7.5.54	1577	OLD796	27.8.54
1446	NLE720	20.2.53	1512	OLD621	11.5.54	1578	OLD797	27.8.54
1447	NLE721	20.2.53	1513	OLD622	11.5.54	1579	OLD798	27.8.54
1448	NLE722	24.2.53	1514	OLD623	12.5.54	1580	OLD799	1.9.54
1449	NLE723	24.2.53	1515	OLD624	13.5.54	1581	OLD800	1.9.54
1450	NLE724	25.2.53	1516	OLD625	14.5.54	1582	OLD801	2.9.54
1451	NLE725	26.2.53	1517	OLD626	14.5.54	1583	OLD802	3.9.54
1452	NLE726	27.2.53	1518	OLD627	18.5.54	1584	OLD803	3.9.54

RTL		Date into stock	RTL		Date into stock	RTL		Date into stock
1585	OLD804	8.9.54	1601	OLD536	5.5.54	1617	OLD846	23.9.54
1586	OLD805	8.9.54	1602	OLD831	30.8.54	1618	OLD847	24.9.54
1587	OLD806	9.9.54	1603	OLD832	1.9.54	1619	OLD848	24.9.54
1588	OLD807	9.9.54	1604	OLD833	2.9.54	1620	OLD849	1.10.54
1589	OLD808	10.9.54	1605	OLD834	6.9.54	1621	OLD850	4.10.54
1590	OLD809	13.9.54	1606	OLD835	7.9.54	1622	OLD851	5.10.54
1591	OLD810	16.9.54	1607	OLD836	8.9.54	1623	OLD852	6.10.54
1592	OLD811	16.9.54	1608	OLD837	10.9.54	1624	OLD853	19.10.54
1593	OLD812	17.9.54	1609	OLD838	13.9.54	1625	OLD854	20.10.54
1594	OLD814	22.9.54	1610	OLD839	14.9.54	1626	OLD855	25.10.54
1595	OLD815	23.9.54	1611	OLD840	15.9.54	1627	OLD856	26.10.54
1596	OLD816	23.9.54	1612	OLD841	16.9.54	1628	OLD857	27.10.54
1597	OLD817	24.9.54	1613	OLD842	20.9.54	1629	OLD858	27.10.54
1598	OLD818	27.9.54	1614	OLD843	17.9.54	1630	OLD859	2.11.54
1599	OLD819	29.9.54	1615	OLD844	29.9.54	1631	OLD860	10.11.54
1600	OLD820	29.9.54	1616	OLD845	21.9.54			

RTL 1582 at Aldenham Works on 6th September 1954, four days after delivery and when RT family production was drawing to its close. Just over two months later, the last RTL was taken into stock one day before the last RT. Alan B. Cross

The bodies built by Leyland for the 6RT6s were another good copy of the basic RT8 design but, apart from their obvious extra width, had a number of idiosyncrasies. The rubber mounting of the destination and route indicators was more obvious when they still had restricted blinds, as in this view of RTW 260 at Dagenham on one of the suburban routes to which they were confined until the end of 1950. The other difference visible here is the metal 'scroll' above the cantrail relief band, while at the back the rain gutter had a reverse upward curve, a peculiarly Leyland feature. F.W. Ivey

RTW

The manufacturing agreement with Leyland in 1947 included five hundred eight-foot wide Titans, modified in the same way as the RTLs. The bodywork was supplied by Leyland, using their standard metal framed construction but modified to resemble the standard RT3/1 design. RTW 1 went into service at Tottenham garage in May 1949 and the whole class was in service by December 1950. These were London's first 8ft wide motor buses and were at first restricted to specifically approved suburban routes. Following a series of tests in 1950 during which all routes serving Notting Hill Gate, then Shaftesbury Avenue and finally Threadneedle Street were converted temporarily to RTW, agreement was secured for them to operate in central London, although still subject to specific route approval. Transfers onto central area routes took place from May 1951 and eventually the majority were so allocated. Only two of the class have been overseas. RTWs 421 and 422 visited Berlin for the British Industries Fair in September/October 1950, making a journey through communist East Germany.

The first central London route to receive eight footers as a normal allocation was the 74, on which RTW 420 is passing Brompton Cemetery when less than two months old in October 1950. G.H.F. Atkins

Chassis: Leyland Titan 6RT
Engine: Leyland O600 six-cylinder 9.8 litre oil 125 bhp (derated to 115bhp)
Transmission: AEC D140 4-speed air operated preselective with fluid flywheel
Bodywork: Leyland
Capacity: H30/26R
L.T.code: 6RT6
Built: 1949-50
Number built: 500
Number in stock: 1.1.50: 213
                31.12.54: 500

RTW

1	KGK501
2	KGK502
3	KGK503
4	KGK504
5	KGK505
6	KGK506
7	KGK507
8	KGK508
9	KGK509
10	KGK510
11	KGK511
12	KGK512
13	KGK513
14	KGK514
15	KGK515
16	KGK516
17	KGK517
18	KGK518
19	KGK519
20	KGK520
21	KGK521
22	KGK522
23	KGK523
24	KGK524
25	KGK525
26	KGK526
27	KGK527
28	KGK528
29	KGK529
30	KGK530
31	KGK531
32	KGK532
33	KGK533
34	KGK534
35	KGK535
36	KGK536
37	KGK537
38	KGK538
39	KGK539
40	KGK540
41	KGK541
42	KGK542
43	KGK543
44	KGK544
45	KGK545
46	KGK546
47	KGK547
48	KGK548
49	KGK549
50	KGK550
51	KGK551
52	KGK552
53	KGK553
54	KGK554
55	KGK555
56	KGK556
57	KGK557
58	KGK558
59	KGK559
60	KGK560
61	KGK561
62	KGK562
63	KGK563
64	KGK564
65	KGK565
66	KGK566
67	KGK567
68	KGK568
69	KGK569
70	KGK570
71	KGK571

RTW

72	KGK572
73	KGK573
74	KGK574
75	KGK575
76	KGK576
77	KGK577
78	KGK578
79	KGK579
80	KGK580
81	KGK581
82	KGK582
83	KGK583
84	KGK584
85	KGK585
86	KGK586
87	KGK587
88	KGK588
89	KGK589
90	KGK590
91	KGK591
92	KGK592
93	KGK593
94	KGK594
95	KGK595
96	KGK596
97	KGK597
98	KGK598
99	KGK599
100	KGK600
101	KGK601
102	KGK602
103	KGK603
104	KGK604
105	KGK605
106	KGK606
107	KGK607
108	KGK608
109	KGK609
110	KGK610
111	KGK611
112	KGK612
113	KGK613
114	KGK614
115	KGK615
116	KGK616
117	KGK617
118	KGK618
119	KGK619
120	KGK620
121	KGK621
122	KGK622
123	KGK623
124	KGK624
125	KGK625
126	KGK626
127	KGK627
128	KGK628
129	KGK629
130	KGK630
131	KGK631
132	KGK632
133	KGK633
134	KGK634
135	KGK635
136	KGK636
137	KGK637
138	KGK638
139	KGK639
140	KGK640
141	KGK641
142	KGK642

RTW

143	KGK643
144	KGK644
145	KGK645
146	KGK646
147	KGK647
148	KGK648
149	KGK649
150	KGK650
151	KLB881
152	KLB882
153	KLB883
154	KLB884
155	KLB885
156	KLB886
157	KLB887
158	KLB888
159	KLB889
160	KLB890
161	KLB891
162	KLB892
163	KLB893
164	KLB894
165	KLB895
166	KLB896
167	KLB897
168	KLB898
169	KLB899
170	KLB900
171	KLB901
172	KLB902
173	KLB903
174	KLB904
175	KLB905
176	KLB906
177	KLB907
178	KLB908
179	KLB909
180	KLB910
181	KLB911
182	KLB912
183	KLB913
184	KLB914
185	KLB915
186	KLB916
187	KLB917
188	KLB918
189	KLB919
190	KLB920
191	KLB921
192	KLB922
193	KLB923
194	KLB924
195	KLB925
196	KLB926
197	KLB927
198	KLB928
199	KLB929
200	KLB930
201	KLB931
202	KLB932
203	KLB933
204	KLB934
205	KLB935
206	KLB936
207	KLB937
208	KLB938
209	KLB939
210	KLB940
211	KLB941
212	KLB942
213	KLB943

RTW

		Date into stock
214	KLB944	6.1.50
215	KLB945	6.1.50
216	KLB946	10.1.50
217	KLB947	11.1.50
218	KLB948	10.1.50
219	KLB949	13.1.50
220	KLB950	12.1.50
221	KLB951	13.1.50
222	KLB952	13.1.50
223	KLB953	17.1.50
224	KLB954	13.1.50
225	KLB955	17.1.50
226	KLB956	20.1.50
227	KLB957	19.1.50
228	KLB958	23.1.50
229	KLB959	20.1.50
230	KLB960	26.1.50
231	KLB961	25.1.50
232	KLB962	25.1.50
233	KLB963	27.1.50
234	KLB964	27.1.50
235	KLB965	27.1.50
236	KLB966	27.1.50
237	KLB967	1.2.50
238	KLB968	2.2.50
239	KLB969	1.2.50
240	KLB970	27.1.50
241	KLB971	3.2.50
242	KLB972	3.2.50
243	KLB973	3.2.50
244	KLB974	8.2.50
245	KLB975	7.2.50
246	KLB976	9.2.50
247	KLB977	9.2.50
248	KLB978	13.2.50
249	KLB979	13.2.50
250	KLB980	15.2.50
251	KXW351	17.2.50
252	KXW352	15.2.50
253	KXW353	17.2.50
254	KXW354	17.2.50
255	KXW355	17.2.50
256	KXW356	22.2.50
257	KXW357	22.2.50
258	KXW358	24.2.50
259	KXW359	24.2.50
260	KXW360	24.2.50
261	KXW361	24.2.50
262	KXW362	3.3.50
263	KXW363	24.2.50
264	KXW364	2.3.50
265	KXW365	1.3.50
266	KXW366	3.3.50
267	KXW367	3.3.50
268	KXW368	10.3.50
269	KXW369	3.3.50
270	KXW370	10.3.50
271	KXW371	10.3.50
272	KXW372	10.3.50
273	KXW373	10.3.50
274	KXW374	17.3.50
275	KXW375	10.3.50
276	KXW376	17.3.50
277	KXW377	17.3.50
278	KXW378	22.3.50
279	KXW379	22.3.50
280	KXW380	22.3.50
281	KXW381	23.3.50
282	KXW382	23.3.50
283	KXW383	24.3.50
284	KXW384	24.3.50

RTW		Date into stock	RTW		Date into stock	RTW		Date into stock
285	KXW385	24.3.50	357	LLU507	26.6.50	429	LLU579	19.9.50
286	KXW386	30.3.50	358	LLU508	21.6.50	430	LLU580	20.9.50
287	KXW387	30.3.50	359	LLU509	22.6.50	431	LLU581	19.9.50
288	KXW388	4.4.50	360	LLU510	3.7.50	432	LLU582	21.9.50
289	KXW389	5.4.50	361	LLU511	22.6.50	433	LLU583	22.9.50
290	KXW390	31.3.50	362	LLU512	26.6.50	434	LLU584	22.9.50
291	KXW391	6.4.50	363	LLU513	28.6.50	435	LLU585	26.9.50
292	KXW392	4.4.50	364	LLU514	28.6.50	436	LLU586	29.9.50
293	KXW393	6.4.50	365	LLU515	29.6.50	437	LLU587	29.9.50
294	KXW394	6.4.50	366	LLU516	30.6.50	438	LLU588	29.9.50
295	KXW395	6.4.50	367	LLU517	5.7.50	439	LLU589	29.9.50
296	KXW396	14.4.50	368	LLU518	30.6.50	440	LLU590	29.9.50
297	KXW397	14.4.50	369	LLU519	3.7.50	441	LLU591	29.9.50
298	KXW398	14.4.50	370	LLU520	30.6.50	442	LLU592	4.10.50
299	KXW399	14.4.50	371	LLU521	6.7.50	443	LLU593	4.10.50
300	KXW400	14.4.50	372	LLU522	7.7.50	444	LLU594	4.10.50
301	KXW401	14.4.50	373	LLU523	5.7.50	445	LLU595	10.10.50
302	KXW402	24.4.50	374	LLU524	10.7.50	446	LLU596	5.10.50
303	KXW403	24.4.50	375	LLU525	10.7.50	447	LLU597	6.10.50
304	KXW404	27.4.50	376	LLU526	11.7.50	448	LLU598	13.10.50
305	KXW405	24.4.50	377	LLU527	10.7.50	449	LLU599	13.10.50
306	KXW406	27.4.50	378	LLU528	12.7.50	450	LLU600	9.10.50
307	KXW407	27.4.50	379	LLU529	12.7.50	451	LLU941	12.10.50
308	KXW408	28.4.50	380	LLU530	13.7.50	452	LLU942	12.10.50
309	KXW409	28.4.50	381	LLU531	13.7.50	453	LLU943	11.10.50
310	KXW410	28.4.50	382	LLU532	14.7.50	454	LLU944	23.10.50
311	KXW411	28.4.50	383	LLU533	25.7.50	455	LLU945	19.10.50
312	KXW412	2.5.50	384	LLU534	26.7.50	456	LLU946	19.10.50
313	KXW413	5.5.50	385	LLU535	27.7.50	457	LLU947	19.10.50
314	KXW414	5.5.50	386	LLU536	3.8.50	458	LLU948	20.10.50
315	KXW415	5.5.50	387	LLU537	28.7.50	459	LLU949	20.10.50
316	KXW416	8.5.50	388	LLU538	31.7.50	460	LLU950	28.11.50
317	KXW417	8.5.50	389	LLU539	28.7.50	461	LLU951	16.10.50
318	KXW418	5.5.50	390	LLU540	1.8.50	462	LLU952	25.10.50
319	KXW419	9.5.50	391	LLU541	3.8.50	463	LLU953	25.10.50
320	KXW420	12.5.50	392	LLU542	4.8.50	464	LLU954	26.10.50
321	KXW421	12.5.50	393	LLU543	4.8.50	465	LLU955	30.10.50
322	KXW422	12.5.50	394	LLU544	4.8.50	466	LLU956	27.10.50
323	KXW423	17.5.50	395	LLU545	9.8.50	467	LLU957	30.10.50
324	KXW424	15.5.50	396	LLU546	10.8.50	468	LLU958	30.10.50
325	KXW425	15.5.50	397	LLU547	14.8.50	469	LLU959	1.11.50
326	KXW426	22.5.50	398	LLU548	14.8.50	470	LLU960	1.11.50
327	KXW427	19.5.50	399	LLU549	15.8.50	471	LLU961	7.11.50
328	KXW428	19.5.50	400	LLU550	17.8.50	472	LLU962	1.11.50
329	KXW429	23.5.50	401	LLU551	17.8.50	473	LLU963	2.11.50
330	KXW430	22.5.50	402	LLU552	21.8.50	474	LLU964	3.11.50
331	KXW431	19.5.50	403	LLU553	21.8.50	475	LLU965	13.11.50
332	KXW432	2.6.50	404	LLU554	18.8.50	476	LLU966	7.11.50
333	KXW433	26.5.50	405	LLU555	23.8.50	477	LLU967	13.11.50
334	KXW434	2.6.50	406	LLU556	22.8.50	478	LLU968	14.11.50
335	KXW435	5.6.50	407	LLU557	23.8.50	479	LLU969	14.11.50
336	KXW436	5.6.50	408	LLU558	25.8.50	480	LLU970	13.11.50
337	KXW437	6.6.50	409	LLU559	24.8.50	481	LLU971	28.11.50
338	KXW438	6.6.50	410	LLU560	28.8.50	482	LLU972	13.11.50
339	KXW439	7.6.50	411	LLU561	29.8.50	483	LLU973	14.11.50
340	KXW440	7.6.50	412	LLU562	28.8.50	484	LLU974	29.11.50
341	KXW441	8.6.50	413	LLU563	30.8.50	485	LLU975	16.11.50
342	KXW442	9.6.50	414	LLU564	31.8.50	486	LLU976	16.11.50
343	KXW443	13.6.50	415	LLU565	1.9.50	487	LLU977	17.11.50
344	KXW444	13.6.50	416	LLU566	4.9.50	488	LLU978	24.11.50
345	KXW445	14.6.50	417	LLU567	4.9.50	489	LLU979	23.11.50
346	KXW446	14.6.50	418	LLU568	4.9.50	490	LLU980	23.11.50
347	KXW447	15.6.50	419	LLU569	6.9.50	491	LLU981	20.11.50
348	KXW448	16.6.50	420	LLU570	7.9.50	492	LLU982	1.12.50
349	KXW449	16.6.50	421	LLU571	7.9.50	493	LLU983	1.12.50
350	KXW450	20.6.50	422	LLU572	8.9.50	494	LLU984	7.12.50
351	LLU501	19.6.50	423	LLU573	12.9.50	495	LLU985	4.12.50
352	LLU502	29.6.50	424	LLU574	13.9.50	496	LLU986	13.12.50
353	LLU503	19.6.50	425	LLU575	14.9.50	497	LLU987	29.11.50
354	LLU504	19.6.50	426	LLU576	15.9.50	498	LLU988	12.12.50
355	LLU505	3.7.50	427	LLU577	18.9.50	499	LLU989	8.12.50
356	LLU506	23.6.50	428	LLU578	18.9.50	500	LLU990	20.12.50

The first twenty RLHs were an order diverted from the Midland General Omnibus Company and marked a break from the rigid standardisation of the period. The AEC Regent III 9612E chassis was a standard provincial model from Southall and the lowbridge bodywork was a standard Weymann product, owing no allegiance to London Transport practice. RLH 12 was one of eight allocated to Addlestone garage in the summer of 1950. G.A. Rixon

Facing Page **A repeat order for fifty-six RLHs differed from the first twenty in having the new 9613E chassis but were otherwise identical, except for having a polished aluminium instead of chromium plated radiator shell. Twenty-three were painted red for routes 127 and 230 and RLH 64, seen at Kenton, was one of these.** C. Carter

RLH

London Transport's fleet of lowbridge buses was always small but LT had intended designing a post-war replacement which would also have been suitable to operate through Blackwall Tunnel. This plan was abandoned when the Road Transport Executive of the British Transport Commission offered London Transport twenty lowbridge AEC Regents which were surplus to the requirements of the newly acquired Midland General Omnibus Company. These were standard 'provincial' versions of the Regent III very similar in specification to the RT but differing in a number of details. The differences included a higher bonnet line and deeper chromium plated radiator shell. The dynamo was driven by the engine, rather than the propeller shaft and this caused a bulge in the bonnet side. The fifty-three seat body was also a standard Weymann product, similar in basic design to the 18STL20s. All twenty buses were painted green and were used to replace STs in regular service and to expand services in the Country Area.

The remaining pre-war and wartime lowbridge buses were replaced by a further batch of fifty-six almost identical RLHs in 1952. The chassis of these were the later 9613E model designed for 27 foot long bodywork but those for the RLHs were built to the old standard of 26 feet. RLH 21-53 were painted green for Country Bus use; the remainder were red. Some Country Area RLHs replaced highbridge buses on several routes to create a pool of spares.

Chassis: AEC Regent III 9612E (1-20); 9613E (21-76)
Engine: AEC A208 6-cylinder 9.6 litre 125 bhp (derated to 115 bhp)
Transmission: AEC D140 4-speed air operated preselective with fluid flywheel
Bodywork: Weymann   Capacity: L27/26R   L.T. code: 1RLH1 (1-20); 2RLH1/1 (21-76)
Built: 1950 (1-20); 1952 (21-76)   Number built: 76
Number in stock: 1. 1.50: Nil   31.12.54: 76

RLH		Date into stock	RLH		Date into stock	RLH		Date into stock
1	KYY501	12. 5.50	27	MXX227	10.10.52	53	MXX253	14.11.52
2	KYY502	18. 5.50	28	MXX228	10.10.52	54	MXX254	17.11.52
3	KYY503	18. 5.50	29	MXX229	13.10.52	55	MXX255	17.11.52
4	KYY504	18. 5.50	30	MXX230	13.10.52	56	MXX256	18.11.52
5	KYY505	22. 5.50	31	MXX231	13.10.52	57	MXX257	19.11.52
6	KYY506	1. 6.50	32	MXX232	14.10.52	58	MXX258	20.11.52
7	KYY507	2. 6.50	33	MXX233	15.10.52	59	MXX259	21.11.52
8	KYY508	5. 6.50	34	MXX234	15.10.52	60	MXX260	25.11.52
9	KYY509	6. 6.50	35	MXX235	16.10.52	61	MXX261	25.11.52
10	KYY510	7. 6.50	36	MXX236	16.10.52	62	MXX262	27.11.52
11	KYY511	15. 6.50	37	MXX237	17.10.52	63	MXX263	27.11.52
12	KYY512	15. 6.50	38	MXX238	17.10.52	64	MXX264	28.11.52
13	KYY513	16. 6.50	39	MXX239	20.10.52	65	MXX265	1.12.52
14	KYY514	19. 6.50	40	MXX240	20.10.52	66	MXX266	2.12.52
15	KYY515	20. 6.50	41	MXX241	21.10.52	67	MXX267	4.12.52
16	KYY516	29. 6.50	42	MXX242	21.10.52	68	MXX268	5.12.52
17	KYY517	30. 6.50	43	MXX243	22.10.52	69	MXX269	5.12.52
18	KYY518	3. 7.50	44	MXX244	22.10.52	70	MXX270	8.12.52
19	KYY519	4. 7.50	45	MXX245	23.10.52	71	MXX271	9.12.52
20	KYY520	5. 7.50	46	MXX246	23.10.52	72	MXX272	9.12.52
21	MXX221	8.10.52	47	MXX247	27.10.52	73	MXX273	11.12.52
22	MXX222	8.10.52	48	MXX248	27.10.52	74	MXX274	11.12.52
23	MXX223	9.10.52	49	MXX249	7.11.52	75	MXX275	12.12.52
24	MXX224	9.10.52	50	MXX250	10.11.52	76	MXX276	22.12.52
25	MXX225	9.10.52	51	MXX251	11.11.52			
26	MXX226	10.10.52	52	MXX252	12.11.52			

These views of RM 1 when new show the sleek and neat appearance of its original condition, without the bulbous radiator grille which was to disfigure the production model. The first ideas on destination indicators are also apparent in the small single front screen and the strip aperture above the platform. The photo opposite was taken at the 1954 Commercial Motor Show at Earls Court. L.T. Museum

RM

The Routemaster was the last new model to be inspired by the London Passenger Transport Board who authorised design work to start in 1947. This was carried out jointly by London Transport, AEC Ltd and Park Royal Vehicles Ltd and the prototype (RM 1) was completed in 1954. The Routemaster is a fully chassisless vehicle in which all running units (engine, gearbox, axles, suspension and brakes) are attached to an aluminium alloy body built as a rigid box. It was built to the maximum box dimensions permitted at the time: 27ft long and 8ft wide; but the radiator and fan were installed under the floor to enable the front bulkhead to be moved forward. This, combined with a more upright front to the body, enabled the capacity to be increased to a total of sixty-four (36 up; 28 down). Other new features in the RM were: independent front suspension; coil springs; power hydraulic brakes; and a hydraulically operated direct acting epicyclic gearbox. The 9.6 litre A204 engine was the same as the RT.

RM 1 was shown at the Commercial Motor Show in September 1954. At this stage it had very restricted indicator displays as part of the drive towards weight saving. Only one small box was provided at the front and rear and a single strip destination display on the side over the platform.

Chassis units: AEC Routemaster R2RH
Engine: AEC A204 9.6 litre 125 bhp, derated to 115 bhp.
Transmission: SCG RV35 Wilson type 4-speed electro-hydraulic direct acting semi-
  automatic epicyclic, with fluid flywheel.
Bodywork: LTE   Capacity: H36/28R   L.T. code: 1RM1
Built: 1954

RM		Date into stock	
1	SLT56*	27. 9.54	* Originally allocated OLD862 but this was never carried.

LT

There were originally 201 single-deck LTs, 199 delivered to the LGOC during 1931 and two to London General Country Services Ltd in 1932, all to the same basic specification. Sixty were rebuilt during 1948 and 1949 by Marshalls of Cambridge and these could be distinguished from others by the absence of the deep mouldings on the original body sides and by being in the post-war red and cream livery. These and those unrebuilt examples which had not been replaced by TDs between 1948 and 1950 (ninety-eight in total) were fitted with oil engines recovered from scrapped STLs in 1950. All were replaced in 1952 and 1953 by the RF class.

Chassis: AEC Renown 664
Engine: AEC A171 direct injection 6-cylinder 7.7 litre 95 bhp oil
Transmission: AEC D124 4 speed crash
Bodywork: LGOC (Chiswick)
Capacity: B35F
L.T. chassis code: 1LTL
L.T. Body codes: LTL1, 1/1, 1/2, 1/3
Built: 1931-1932   Number built: 201   Number in stock: 1.1.50: 120; 31.12.54: Nil

LT		Date out of stock	LT		Date out of stock	LT		Date out of stock
1002	GN4775	21.2.50	1083	GO7119	21.7.53	1148	GP3448	27.1.53
1005	GO601	21.2.50	1085	GO7125	14.8.53	1149	GP3457	11.2.53
1006	GN4784	9.4.53	1087	GO7120	23.1.53	1150	GP3455	30.4.53
1007	GO606	24.8.50	1089	GO7118	18.12.52	1152	GT5005	21.7.53
1008	GN4763	24.2.53	1090	GO7128	30.4.53	1153	GT5002	10.8.53
1009	GN4783	9.2.53	1093	GO7149	8.5.53	1156	GT5014	8.11.50
1010	GO637	15.8.50	1094	GO7145	5.12.52	1157	GT5003	11.5.53
1011	GN4777	13.2.53	1096	GO7152	17.2.53	1158	GT5006	17.2.53
1012	GO625	18.2.53	1098	GO7144	19.8.53	1160	GT5007	16.2.53
1015	GO648	15.4.53	1099	GO7146	11.5.53	1161	GT5013	8.5.53
1016	GN4785	10.4.53	1100	GO7147	18.12.52	1162	GT5016	23.1.53
1018	GO688	16.2.53	1101	GO7150	18.10.50	1163	GT5022	12.2.53
1019	GO626	4.6.53	1102	GO7161	28.2.50	1164	GT5030	18.6.53
1022	GO641	19.10.50	1103	GO7165	10.8.53	1167	GT5027	5.12.52
1023	GO631	7.11.50	1104	GO7159	5.12.52	1168	GT5033	19.2.53
1024	GO630	15.4.53	1105	GO7163	26.5.53	1172	GT5046	12.5.53
1025	GO650	12.8.53	1106	GO7167	27.7.53	1173	GT5052	13.2.53
1026	GO689	12.12.52	1107	GO7171	17.4.53	1174	GT5047	27.2.50
1027	GO649	9.5.50	1108	GO7166	25.9.50c	1175	GT5044	21.7.53
1028	GO629	18.6.53	1109	GO7158	11.2.53	1176	GT5045	8.5.53
1029	GO644	9.2.53	1112	GO7172	7.8.53	1177	GT5054	13.5.53
1031	GO638	15.4.53	1113	GO7173	13.5.53	1178	GT5053	23.2.53
1033	GO627	12.12.52	1114	GO7186	10.4.53	1179	GT5059	12.6.53
1041	GO684	9.2.53	1115	GO7181	25.10.50	1180	GT5060	11.5.53
1045	GO651	15.4.53	1116	GO7179	17.4.53	1181	GT5061	18.2.53
1047	GO673	10.8.50	1117	GO7184	12.6.53	1182	GT5079	4.7.50
1048	GO670	17.2.53	1118	GO7180	14.8.53	1185	GT5072	22.12.52
1049	GO665	22.12.52	1120	GO7178	22.4.50	1186	GT5080	13.2.53
1057	GO5162	27.1.53	1121	GO7185	7.8.53	1187	GT5075	12.5.53
1058	GO5165	10.2.53	1123	GP3402	17.2.53	1188	GT5076	10.2.53
1060	GO5166	19.8.53	1127	GP3406	22.7.53	1189	GT5077	4.7.50
1062	GO5178	19.1.50	1128	GP3405	26.1.53	1190	GT5078	19.2.53
1063	GO5173	28.1.53	1129	GP3404	30.4.53	1191	GT5098	17.2.53
1066	GO5175	3.8.50	1131	GP3407	9.2.53	1193	GT5083	14.8.53
1069	GO5177	7.5.53	1135	GP3435	20.2.53	1195	GT5094	12.5.53
1074	GO5197	23.1.53	1136	GP3420	12.12.52	1197	GT5100	14.8.53
1076	GO5198	27.6.50	1140	GP3422	6.7.53	1199	GT5102	7.5.53
1078	GO7141	13.5.53	1143	GP3438	20.2.53	1201	GT5120	12.2.53
1080	GO7151	13.2.53	1144	GP3434	c 25.4.50	1427	GX5337	26.1.53
1082	GO7116	21.5.53	1145	GP3437	c 25.9.50	1428	GX5338	13.2.53

c   Chassis only, body scrapped earlier

The original lines of the 1931 Chiswick-built bodies were not altered when Marshalls of Cambridge rebuilt eighteen Ts and sixty LTs in 1948/49, but they were made to look substantially tidier by eliminating the side mouldings. They were also painted in the post-war single-deck red and cream livery, an honour not accorded any of the vehicles that were not rebuilt. LT 1128, shown laying over in Bridge Street, Staines, had one of the original type of body without a rear destination indicator and was therefore reclassified 1LTL1/2. Alan B. Cross

LT 1049 was one of the single-deck Renowns not rebuilt by Marshalls but it survived in service until almost the end of operation of the class, ending its life at Dalston garage in November 1952 when route 208A received RFs. Although showing its age, it was looking smart when photographed at Clapton Pond during its last summer, on 25th June 1952. It carried one of the seventy-six bodies which were built with rear route indicator boxes and was therefore a 1LTL1/1. Alan B. Cross

T 37 was one of eighteen of the original fifty LGOC Regals to be renovated by Marshalls of Cambridge during 1949 and, as part of a programme covering all survivors, had its petrol engine replaced by an oiler recovered from a scrapped STL in March 1950. The twenty-six 1T1s that remained stayed at Kingston to work on routes 218 and 264 until 1953. G.F. Ashwell

T

The T class was first introduced as a bus by the London General Omnibus Company in 1929, when fifty 30-seaters (T 1-37, 39-50, 156) were put into service. As required by contemporary regulations, they originally had doorless rear entrances but these were later replaced on all but five by front entrances. T 38 was a prototype coach for the newly developing coach services (later Green Line) and this was followed by a further 250 (T 51-149, 155, 157-206 with rear entrances; 207-306, front entrances) but only eleven remained in stock with their original bodywork at the beginning of 1950. Thomas Tilling Ltd also purchased twelve Regals (T 307-318), one of which (T 317) lasted until 1953 first as an Accident Demonstration Unit and later as a trainer. London Transport also acquired sixty-three other Regals from a variety of sources but none of these survived in their original form at the beginning of 1950. In 1938, thirty-one of the withdrawn coaches were fitted with oil engines and 1935 Weymann 30-seat bodies salvaged from R-class chassis which were scrapped. These were classified 11T11 and most remained in stock until 1953 when they were replaced by RFs.

In 1936 the LPTB purchased fifty Weymann bodied Regals for Green Line service (T 403-452; classified 9T9). These were London's first Regals with oil engines, preselective gearboxes and fluid flywheels. The 9T9s were demoted to bus work in 1939. As part of its large 1938/39 replacement programme London Transport ordered 266 AEC Regals (the 10T10 class) to replace all pre-1936 Green Line coaches. These employed the new AEC pot cavity 8.8 litre oil engine, which had been inspired by the similar engines supplied by Leyland in the STD class. The bodywork was of composite construction, the first run of such bodies built in the shops at Chiswick. The first 150 had thirty seats but the last 116

Two of the 1T1s had their original square cabs replaced by the rounded version as used on most of the LTs and STs: T 34, the subject of this photograph, in 1942 and T 45 in 1947. T 34 was converted to oil in January 1950 and was one of the eight that had not been renovated by Marshalls which remained at Kingston until the weight restriction on Walton Bridge was eased in 1953. F.G. Reynolds

were to a modified design with thirty-four seats. All 9T9s and 10T10s were converted to ambulances at the outbreak of war and later many were used by the American Red Cross as 'Clubmobiles' or transports. Twelve 10T10s and one 9T9 did not return from war service but the remainder re-entered passenger service in 1945/1946. With the arrival of RF class coaches in 1951/1952, the 10T10s were downgraded to bus work to replace older vehicles, having their heaters, side route board fittings, ash trays and linoleum floor coverings removed. Forty were painted red for Central Bus operation. Some 9T9s also worked in the Central Area for a time in 1949/1950 but these retained their green livery. The 9T9s and 10T10s were replaced by the RF and GS classes between 1951 and 1954.

In 1946 London Transport was allotted fifty crash gearbox AEC Regals with 'provincial' standard Weymann thirty-five seat bodywork, which were intended as a stop-gap until vehicles built to LT's own specification could be acquired. Seating capacity was later reduced to thirty-three and then in 1954, on twenty-six vehicles to thirty-two. They were first allocated to Uxbridge, Kingston and Muswell Hill garages and later to Southall. In 1948 a further thirty Regals were acquired for service expansion in the Country Bus department. They were standard 'provincial' Regal Mark IIIs but with a mechanical specification comparable to the double-deck RTs and their bodywork was a standard product from Mann Egerton of Norwich. They were originally allocated to Hemel Hempstead and Watford (Leavesden Road) garages and later to Garston, Crawley, Grays, Tring, Hatfield and Amersham. They were painted in the wartime livery of Lincoln green and white, although this style had otherwise been discontinued.

During 1949, eighteen of the 1T1s were thoroughly rebuilt and refurbished by

Marshalls of Cambridge in the same style as the single-deck LTs. These and eight surviving Regals which had not been rebuilt were fitted during 1949 with reconditioned oil engines salvaged from scrapped STLs. These twenty-six buses were allocated to Kingston garage for operation on routes 218 and 264 across Walton Bridge, which was then subject to a weight restriction. They were replaced by 10T10s in 1953 when a new temporary bridge was opened. The last 'General' T to be sold was T 31, believed to be the first bus to be purchased privately for preservation.

Eleven of the original 1/7T7/1 Green Line coach Regals, dating from 1930/1931 were still in stock at the beginning of 1950 but all were withdrawn during that year. Apart from the livery, the main difference to be detected on T 277 compared with its days as a coach is the one piece bus destination indicator box. Although remaining part of Country Bus stock, many of these buses were lent to the Central department during the severe post-war vehicle shortages. T 277 is seen when on loan and allocated to Kingston garage. F.G. Reynolds

The first AEC Regals bought by the LPTB for Green Line service were the fifty 9T9s, in 1936. In post-war years they were used as buses, in which guise T 440 is at Dartford garage. They were the first of the basic design which was then used on all single-deckers until 1939, differing from the later 10T10 in the treatment of the nearside wing and in having a bumper bar. F.W. Ivey

One of the most admired vehicles of all time was the 10T10, bought for Green Line duties in 1938/1939. The class introduced the integrated wing and bulkhead structure to a standard vehicle for the first time, its success leading to its adoption as standard on the RT family. T 468 is at Eccleston Bridge, the main London picking-up point for the coaches.
F.G. Reynolds

With the arrival of the RFs from 1951, the 10T10s were demoted to bus work, having their Green Line trappings like heaters, ash trays and linoleum floor coverings removed and their fleet names altered. T 480, which was not withdrawn until March 1954, is in this condition at Weybridge.
F.G. Reynolds

Forty Green Line Regals were repainted red to enable older single-deckers to be replaced more quickly. Now recoded 10T10/3, T 485 is at work from Kingston garage on route 201 at Hampton Court station.
F.G. Reynolds

The chassis of T 361 was originally an Amersham & District petrol engined coach but was converted to oil and given this 1935 Weymann bus body second-hand from R 22 in November 1938. It continued in service until June 1953 and was photographed at Chorleywood towards the end of its career. F.G. Reynolds

The 14T12s were standard provincial model AEC Regals with Weymann bodywork and were part of the early post-war 'stop-gap' intake of new vehicles. They were London's first motor buses with sliding vent windows, a feature which did not reappear until the arrival of the GS class in 1953. T 745 is at Esher, working from Kingston garage which was its first home in July 1946. G.W. Morant

The Mann Egerton bodied 15T13 was the closest London Transport got to having a single-deck RT but neither chassis nor body conformed to its standard. This photograph of T 785 shows the complete vehicle to be a handsome product which looked well in the wartime green and white colour scheme in which these vehicles were, surprisingly, finished when new. F.G. Reynolds

Chassis: AEC Regal 662/0662 or MkIII 0962/9621E (769-798)

Engine: AEC A140 6-cylinder 6.1 litre 95 bhp petrol (1-46 until 1950); AEC A145 6-cylinder 7.4 litre 95 bhp petrol (207, 219, 244, 262, 265, 270, 273, 277, 290, 292, 297); AEC A173 6-cylinder 7.7 litre direct injection 95 bhp oil (11T11 class; 719-768); AEC A171 6-cylinder 7.7 litre 95 bhp oil (1-46 from 1950; 403-452); AEC A180 6-cyl 8.8 litre direct injection 100 bhp oil (453-718); or A208 6-cylinder 9.6 litre direct injection 125 bhp oil (769-798).

Transmission: AEC D124 four speed crash (1-396 and 719-768); D132 direct selection preselective with fluid flywheel (403-718); or D140 air operated preselective with fluid flywheel (769-798).

Bodywork: LGOC (1-46); Weymann, Ransomes or Duple (T207 etc.); LPTB (453-718); Weymann (11T11 type, 403-452 and 719-768); Mann Egerton (769-798).

Capacity: B30F (1-452); DP30 or 34F (453-718); B32 or 33F (719-768); B31F (769-798).

L.T. codes: 1, 1/1 or 2/1T1 or 1/1 (1-46); 1/7T7/1 (207 etc.); 9T9 (403-452); 1/10 or 10T/T10 or 10/1 (453-718); 11T11 (see below); 14T12 (719-768); 15T13 (769-798)

Built: 1929 (1-46); 1930/31 (207 etc.); 1930/31 chassis/1935 body (11T11 type - marked * in list); 1936 (403-452); 1938/39 (453-718); 1946 (719-768); 1948 (769-798)

Number built: 780   Number in stock: 1.1.50: 452   31.12.54: 129

T		Date out of stock	T		Date out of stock	T		Date out of stock
1	UU6616	15.1.53	36	UU6651	25.2.53	*223	GK5491	21.5.52c
2	UU6617	15.1.53	37	UU6652	7.5.54	*226	GN2018	7.7.53
9	UU6624	25.2.53	40	UU6655	30.7.53	*232	GH3803	21.5.52
11	UU6626	27.2.53	41	UU6656	31.7.53	*234	GK3185	15.7.53
14	UU6629	30.7.53	42	UU6657	31.7.53	*236	GN2080	1.1.53
16	UU6631	24.2.53	44	UU6659	27.2.53	*237	GN2004	21.5.52c
17	UU6632	31.7.53	45	UU6660	10.4.52c	244	GH3888	1.5.50
22	UU6637	30.7.53	46	UU6661	23.2.53	*250	GN2069	10.7.53
23	UU6638	25.2.53	156	GF7251	6.11.52c	*253	GH3807	27.1.53
24	UU6639	26.2.53	207	GK5493	16.5.50	*255	GK5497	9.7.53
27	UU6642	30.7.53	*208	GH8096	14.5.52c	*261	GN2023	22.4.53
28	UU6643	26.2.53	*212	GK5492	10.7.53	262	GH3890	9.3.50
30	UU6645	10.8.53	*213	GN2016	14.5.52c	265	GH3823	22.3.50
31	UU6646	18.10.53	*214	GK3181	8.7.53	*266	GK3187	14.7.53
32	UU6647	30.7.53	*215	GK5488	23.4.53	*267	GH3824	15.7.53
33	UU6648	11.8.53	*216	GN2176	21.5.52c	270	GH3821	30.1.50
34	UU6649	24.2.53	219	GK5486	28.11.50p	*271	GH3822	8.7.53

c   Chassis only, body scrapped earlier
p   Retained by London Transport for preservation
*   11T11 type

T		Date out of stock	T		Date out of stock	T		Date out of stock
273	GN4683	3.2.50	453	ELP177	14.8.53	524	ELP248	18.5.53
*275	GK3177	9.7.53	454	ELP178	14.8.53	525	ELP249	28.8.53
*276	GH3825	24.4.53	455	ELP179	14.8.53	526	ELP250	11.8.53
277	GK3180	18.5.50	456	ELP180	13.8.53	527	ELP251	8.4.53
*280	GN4647	9.10.53	457	ELP181	11.11.53	528	ELP252	12.3.54
*283	GN2104	16.7.53	458	ELP182	14.8.53	529	ELP253	14.8.53
*285	GH8098	1.1.53	459	ELP183	7.8.53	530	ELP254	21.1.54
290	GN2106	15.3.50	461	ELP185	14.5.53	531	ELP255	21.1.54
292	GN2108	11.3.50	462	ELP186	14.5.53	532	ELP256	7.8.53
*296	GN4684	16.7.53	463	ELP187	1.9.53	533	ELP257	14.8.53
297	GN2107	28.2.50	464	ELP188	11.6.53	534	ELP258	13.11.53
*298	GN4672	26.3.53	465	ELP189	12.11.53	535	ELP259	11.11.53
317	GY8417	28.1.53	466	ELP190	24.8.53	536	ELP260	12.3.54
*359	KX7886	21.7.53	467	ELP191	14.8.53	537	ELP261	2.9.53
*361	KX7634	18.6.53	468	ELP192	26.5.53	538	ELP262	15.5.53
*362	KX7635	28.4.53	469	ELP193	14.8.53	539	ELP263	18.8.53
*364	KX6785	14.7.53	470	ELP194	30.8.54	540	ELP264	21.7.53
*396	PG7839	7.7.53	471	ELP195	14.4.53	541	ELP265	18.8.53
403	CLX551	14.3.52	472	ELP196	10.11.53	542	ELP266	2.9.53
404	CLX552	18.7.52	473	ELP197	7.8.53	543	ELP267	7.8.53
405	CLX553	17.7.52	474	ELP198	1.3.54	544	ELP268	18.5.53
406	CLX554	18.7.52	475	ELP199	24.8.53	545	ELP269	7.8.53
407	CLX555	18.7.52	476	ELP200	25.10.54	546	ELP270	30.3.53
408	CLX556	21.3.52	477	ELP201	24.3.53	547	ELP271	7.8.53
409	CLX557	10.3.52	478	ELP202	23.7.53	548	ELP272	19.1.54
410	CLX558	11.3.52	479	ELP203	13.4.53	549	ELP273	19.8.53
411	CLX559	30.4.53	480	ELP204	12.3.54	550	ELP274	28.8.53
412	CLX560	11.3.52	481	ELP205	7.8.53	551	ELP275	17.3.53
413	CLX561	18.7.52	482	ELP206	1.9.53	552	ELP276	19.8.53
414	CLX562	24.3.52	483	ELP207	2.4.53	553	ELP277	20.1.54
415	CLX563	12.3.52	484	ELP208	30.3.53	554	ELP278	28.5.53
416	CLX564	17.7.52	485	ELP209	12.3.54	555	ELP279	21.1.54
417	CLX565	24.3.52	487	ELP211	23.7.53	556	ELP280	8.7.53
418	CLX566	17.7.52	489	ELP213	19.8.53	557	ELP281	20.1.54
419	CLX567	4.4.52	490	ELP214	18.8.53	558	ELP282	30.3.53
420	CLX568	17.7.52	491	ELP215	24.8.53	559	ELP283	14.8.53
421	CLX569	29.4.53	492	ELP216	8.6.53	560	ELP284	15.5.53
422	CLX570	11.3.52	493	ELP217	30.8.54	561	ELP285	17.3.53
423	CLX571	6.3.52	494	ELP218	7.4.53	562	ELP286	4.5.53
424	CLX572	17.7.52	495	ELP219	24.3.53	563	ELP287	7.8.53
425	CLX573	4.4.52	496	ELP220	14.5.53	564	ELP288	24.3.53
426	CLX574	29.4.53	497	ELP221	7.8.53	565	ELP289	24.11.54
427	CLX575	4.4.52	498	ELP222	2.9.53	566	EYK201	8.6.53
428	CXX151	18.7.52	499	ELP223	15.4.54	567	EYK202	8.6.53
429	CXX152	21.3.52	500	ELP224	28.7.53	568	EYK203	11.5.54
430	CXX153	14.3.52	501	ELP225	19.1.54	569	EYK204	17.8.53
431	CXX154	21.3.52	502	ELP226	14.8.53	570	EYK205	16.11.54
432	CXX155	11.3.52	503	ELP227	13.7.53	571	EYK206	13.11.53
433	CXX156	4.4.52	504	ELP228	26.7.54	572	EYK207	30.3.53
434	CXX157	24.3.52	505	ELP229	28.8.53	573	EYK208	24.7.53
435	CXX158	6.3.52	506	ELP230	21.4.54	574	EYK209	18.8.53
436	CXX159	6.3.52	507	ELP231	24.7.53	575	EYK210	28.8.53
437	CXX160	22.1.53	508	ELP232	24.8.53	576	EYK211	18.8.53
438	CXX161	13.4.53	510	ELP234	19.1.54	577	EYK212	12.11.53
439	CXX162	6.3.52	511	ELP235	1.9.53	579	EYK214	24.5.54
440	CXX163	24.3.52	512	ELP236	14.8.53	580	EYK215	28.8.53
441	CXX164	4.4.52	513	ELP237	25.5.54	581	EYK216	18.8.53
442	CXX165	7.3.52	514	ELP238	11.8.53	582	EYK217	7.4.53
444	CXX167	14.4.53	515	ELP239	7.8.53	583	EYK218	26.5.53
445	CXX168	11.3.52	516	ELP240	19.1.54	584	EYK219	14.8.53
446	CXX169	14.3.52	517	ELP241	28.8.53	585	EYK220	7.8.53
447	CXX170	24.3.52	518	ELP242	1.3.54	588	EYK223	24.5.54
448	CXX171	10.3.53	519	ELP243	13.11.53	589	EYK224	22.9.53
449	CXX172	14.3.52	520	ELP244	11.5.54	590	EYK225	30.3.53
450	CXX173	1.5.53	521	ELP245	18.6.53	591	EYK226	11.8.53
451	CXX174	14.4.53	522	ELP246	30.8.54	592	EYK227	11.6.53
452	CXX175	21.3.52	523	ELP247	22.4.53	593	EYK228	

*   11T11 type

T

No.	Reg	Date out of stock
595	EYK230	28.4.54
596	EYK231	7.4.53
597	EYK232	13.11.53
598	EYK233	26.5.54
599	EYK234	20.1.54
600	EYK235	18.5.53
601	EYK236	28.8.53
602	EYK237	19.5.54
603	EYK238	7.4.53
604	EYK239	13.11.53
605	EYK240	20.1.54
606	EYK241	17.8.53
607	EYK242	
608	EYK243	20.1.54
609	EYK244	26.10.54
610	EYK245	27.5.54
611	EYK246	23.12.54
612	EYK247	25.10.54
613	EYK248	
614	EYK249	14.8.53
615	EYK250	25.5.54
616	EYK251	26.10.54
617	EYK252	
618	EYK253	20.1.54
619	EYK254	
620	EYK255	26.5.54
621	EYK256	
622	EYK257	22.1.54
623	EYK258	24.5.54
624	EYK259	
625	EYK260	24.11.54
626	EYK261	
627	EYK262	27.5.54
628	EYK263	
629	EYK264	
630	EYK265	4.11.54
631	EYK266	
632	EYK267	1.3.54
633	EYK268	4.11.54
634	EYK269	
635	EYK270	
636	EYK271	
637	EYK272	
638	EYK273	27.7.51c
639	EYK274	
640	EYK275	9.11.54
641	EYK276	
642	EYK277	
643	EYK278	24.11.54
644	EYK279	10.6.53
645	EYK280	
646	EYK281	
647	EYK282	
648	EYK283	19.1.54
649	EYK284	1.3.54
650	EYK285	
651	EYK286	12.11.53
652	EYK287	8.1.54
653	EYK288	12.3.54
654	EYK289	
655	EYK290	15.5.53
656	EYK291	15.4.54
657	EYK292	1.3.54
658	EYK293	25.5.54
659	EYK294	
660	EYK295	11.11.54
661	EYK296	

T

No.	Reg	Date out of stock
662	EYK297	
663	EYK298	28.10.54
664	EYK299	25.10.54
667	EYK302	
668	EYK303	
669	EYK304	
671	EYK306	
672	EYK307	28.8.53
673	EYK308	
674	EYK309	11.11.53
675	EYK310	26.5.54
676	EYK311	
677	EYK312	20.1.54
678	EYK313	9.11.54
679	EYK314	
680	EYK315	
682	EYK317	
683	EYK318	
684	EYK319	
685	EYK320	24.5.54
686	EYK321	24.5.54
687	EYK322	27.5.54
688	EYK323	
689	EYK324	1.3.54
690	EYK325	25.10.54
691	EYK326	10.11.54
692	EYK327	
693	EYK328	
694	EYK329	27.8.54
695	EYK330	6.10.53c
696	EYK331	9.11.54
697	EYK332	
698	EYK333	28.10.54
699	EYK334	22.10.54
700	EYK335	4.11.54
701	EYK336	18.6.54
702	EYK337	23.12.54
703	EYK338	7.8.53
704	EYK339	1.3.54
705	EYK340	
706	EYK341	
707	EYK342	
708	EYK343	1.4.54
709	EYK344	11.11.54
710	EYK345	1.9.53
711	EYK346	
712	EYK347	8.1.54
713	EYK348	24.11.54
714	EYK349	
715	EYK350	21.7.53
716	EYK351	
717	EYK352	
718	EYK353	22.10.54
719	HGF809	
720	HGF810	
721	HGF811	
722	HGF812	
723	HGF813	
724	HGF814	
725	HGF815	
726	HGF816	
727	HGF817	
728	HGF818	
729	HGF819	
730	HGF820	
731	HGF821	
732	HGF822	

T

No.	Reg
733	HGF823
734	HGF824
735	HGF825
736	HGF826
737	HGF827
738	HGF828
739	HGF829
740	HGF830
741	HGF831
742	HGF832
743	HGF833
744	HGF834
745	HGF835
746	HGF836
747	HGF837
748	HGF838
749	HGF839
750	HGF840
751	HGF841
752	HGF842
753	HGF843
754	HGF844
755	HGF845
756	HGF846
757	HGF847
758	HGF848
759	HGF849
760	HGF850
761	HGF851
762	HGF852
763	HGF853
764	HGF854
765	HGF855
766	HGF856
767	HGF857
768	HGF858
769	HLX439
770	HLX440
771	HLX441
772	HLX442
773	HLX443
774	HLX444
775	HLX445
776	HLX446
777	HLX447
778	HLX448
779	HLX449
780	HLX450
781	HLX451
782	HLX452
783	HLX453
784	HLX454
785	HLX455
786	HLX456
787	HLX457
788	HLX458
789	HLX459
790	HLX460
791	HLX461
792	HLX462
793	HLX463
794	HLX464
795	HLX465
796	HLX466
797	HLX467
798	HLX468

c   Chassis only, body scrapped earlier

The 4Q4 did not take advantage of the ability to have an entrance ahead of the front axle but had one in the position then favoured by the Country Bus department. The characteristic downward sloping roofline of the Birmingham Railway Carriage and Wagon Company body is well displayed in this view of Q 25 at Three Bridges. Alan B. Cross

Q

The AEC 'Q' was first introduced experimentally by the London General Omnibus Company in 1932 with single-deck Q 1 and was for a short period in 1935/36 London Transport's standard single-deck bus. There were five double-deckers (Q 2-5 and 188) but the 232 production vehicles were all single-deckers. London Transport's first order for large saloons was for one hundred centre entrance Qs for the Country Bus department (Q 6-105; coded 4Q4), to which two were added shortly afterwards (Q 187/188). These had Birmingham Railway Carriage & Wagon Company Ltd bodywork seating thirty-seven, two of whom were alongside the driver. These two were found to obstruct the driver's view so the seats were removed during 1936 and replaced by a full width driver's cab. The first London Transport saloons for Central buses were eighty Qs with a shorter wheelbase so that a doorless entrance could be placed ahead of the front axle. The thirty-seven seat bodywork was supplied by Park Royal and the vehicles were classified 5Q5. Only fifty-three were red, because the last twenty-seven to be built were diverted to the Country Bus department to release a like number of 4Q4s modified for Green Line service at the end of 1936. These were reclassified 1/4Q4/1 and retained this coding when they were returned to bus service in 1938. Four of the Country Bus 5Q5s were transferred to Central Buses in 1938, a further nine in 1942 and the remainder in 1948/49. The last fifty Qs were also by Park Royal but were long wheelbase thirty-two seat centre entrance Green Line coaches coded 6Q6 with full width driver's cabs.

The five double-deckers and Q 1 were withdrawn from service in 1939 and 1945 respectively. In common with all Green Line coaches, the 6Q6s were converted to public ambulances at the outbreak of the Second World War and remained as such until being restored as coaches between October 1945 and October 1948. One 6Q6 did not return from ambulance duties, as Q 217 was destroyed in July 1944 while at Elmers End when the garage was hit by a flying bomb. Otherwise all production Qs were still in service at the beginning of 1950.

The only Qs to have a true front entrance were the eighty Park Royal bodied 5Q5s, intended for Central area service and therefore built without platform doors. Q 139, in the post-war 'all red' livery, is at Bromley-by-Bow, its thirty-seven seats providing much valued capacity on busy route 208. The unusual arrangement of having the route number stencil behind glass had its drawbacks, as can be seen in this photograph where the number has partly disappeared behind a reflection. C. Carter

In 1948, seven 4Q4s were repainted red and transferred to Central Buses but were returned to Country Buses the following year. Five retained their red livery and four of these (Q 8, 44, 53, 65) were among fourteen 4Q4s transferred to Central Buses in 1950, initially to cover a shortage of single-deckers during the conversion of Ts and LTs to oil. A further five of these (Q 6, 16, 20, 21, 26) were repainted red. The five which remained green were Q 10, 13, 15, 67, 69. Three more were transferred during 1952 (Q 18, 42, 64).

Withdrawal of the 4Q4s began in January 1952, when TFs released from coach service by new RFs replaced them at St Albans, and was completed in April 1953 when those at Reigate were replaced by bus RFs. The 6Q6s were withdrawn from coach and country bus service in January 1952 but were relicensed in March 1952 at Muswell Hill garage in place of single-deck LTs on route 212 to resolve a long running dispute with drivers. They retained their Green Line colours but the fleetname was altered to London Transport. They were replaced in September and October the same year when the first red RFs entered service. Some of the 5Q5s were withdrawn in December 1952 but most were replaced by RFs in February and March 1953, the last being at Sidcup garage.

Many withdrawn Qs were exported to Cyprus, Gold Coast, Libya, Malaya, Malta and Yugoslavia but none was sold for further PSV service in the UK as this was forbidden by the British Transport Commission at that time. Those remaining in the UK were either used as contractors' or welfare vehicles, or were eventually scrapped. One which stayed in the LT area was Q 69 which was sold to the Gravesend Old People's Welfare Committee who continued to operate it in its Lincoln green and white colours. In 1952 Q75 was converted by London Transport into a mobile gas unit and allocated for Civil Defence training duties, renumbered Q1035CD. It too retained its Country Bus green and white livery and had its destination indicators and the lower halves of its saloon windows painted over, but otherwise its external appearance was not changed. It was the only Q still in stock at the end of 1954.

The 6Q6 Green Line version had a slightly cumbersome looking front end but was otherwise a handsome design, as illustrated by Q 190 at Hoddesdon. The square grille on the front dash served no purpose but the LPTB seemed to think it was a necessary embellishment for coaches as the 4Q4s modified for Green Line had similar grilles inserted. Alan B. Cross

Three months after being withdrawn from Green Line service, twenty-four 6Q6s were resurrected for service at Muswell Hill garage in place of single-deck LTs on routes 210 and 244. This photograph of Q 232 near Finsbury Park shows the only change which was made for this purpose, the substitution of the 'London Transport' fleet name for 'Green Line'. Alan B. Cross

Chassis: AEC 'Q' 0762   Engine: AEC A170 6-cylinder 7.7 litre 95 bhp oil
Transmission: AEC D133 4-speed direct selection preselective with fluid flywheel
Bodywork: Birmingham Railway Carriage & Wagon Co.Ltd (6-105, 186, 187); Park Royal
    (remainder).
Capacity: B35C (6-105, 186, 187); B37F (106-185); DP32C (189-238);
L.T.code: 4Q4 (6-105, 186, 187); 5Q5 (106-185); 6Q6 (189-238)
Built: 1935/36   Number built: 238   Number in stock: 1.1.50: 231;   31.12.54: 1

Q		Date out of stock	Q		Date out of stock	Q		Date out of stock
6	BXD527	20.5.53	17	BXD538	16.9.53	28	BXD549	7.9.53
7	BXD528	31.8.53	18	BXD539	1.5.53	29	BXD550	6.7.53
8	BXD529	15.5.53	19	BXD541	4.9.53	30	BXD551	26.8.53
9	BXD530	24.8.53	20	BXD540	18.5.53	31	BXD552	19.6.53
10	BXD531	20.3.53	21	BXD542	18.5.53	32	BXD553	19.6.53
11	BXD532	19.6.53	22	BXD543	3.9.53	33	BXD554	14.5.52c
12	BXD533	25.8.53	23	BXD544	18.8.53	34	BXD555	10.3.53
13	BXD534	6.5.53	24	BXD545	11.9.53	35	BXD556	30.4.52c
14	BXD535	23.4.52c	25	BXD546	28.8.53	36	BXD557	7.7.53
15	BXD536	7.4.53	26	BXD547	5.5.53	37	BXD558	20.8.53
16	BXD537	19.5.53	27	BXD548	30.4.52c	38	BXD559	16.9.53

c   Chassis only, body scrapped earlier

Q		Date out of stock	Q		Date out of stock	Q		Date out of stock
39	BXD560	1.9.53	105	CGJ210	27.8.53	171	CLE194	19.3.53
40	BXD561	28.8.53	106	CLE129	1.10.53	172	CLE195	12.3.53
41	BXD562	7.5.52c	107	CLE130	27.11.53	173	CLE196	21.7.53
42	BXD563	18.5.53	108	CLE131	26.5.53	174	CLE197	29.1.54
43	BXD564	2.9.53	109	CLE132	10.7.53	175	CLE198	7.5.53
44	BXD565	18.5.53	110	CLE133	13.4.53	176	CLE199	25.9.53
45	BXD566	7.5.52c	111	CLE134	23.11.53	177	CLE200	31.7.53
46	BXD567	1.9.53	112	CLE135	22.9.53	178	CLE201	23.7.53
47	BXD568	7.5.52c	113	CLE136	25.3.53	179	CLE202	27.11.53
48	BXD569	19.6.53	114	CLE137	23.9.53	180	CLE203	15.9.53
49	BXD570	8.7.53	115	CLE138	12.3.53	181	CLE204	28.4.54
50	BXD571	26.4.54	116	CLE139	10.4.53	182	CLE205	3.2.54
51	BXD572	24.8.53	117	CLE140	24.11.53	183	CLE206	7.7.53
52	BXD573	7.5.52c	118	CLE141	5.5.53	184	CLE207	18.6.53
53	BXD574	14.5.53	119	CLE142	6.5.53	185	CLE208	18.9.53
54	BXD575	8.7.53	120	CLE143	24.9.53	186	CLE127	11.9.53
55	BXD576	8.10.53p	121	CLE144	25.3.53	187	CLE128	29.4.53
56	CGJ161	25.8.53	122	CLE145	6.10.53	189	CXX382	27.3.53
57	CGJ162	30.4.52c	123	CLE146	6.10.53	190	CXX383	8.9.53
58	CGJ163	14.5.52c	124	CLE147	25.3.53	191	CXX384	24.4.53
59	CGJ164	14.5.52c	125	CLE148	25.9.53	192	CXX385	22.4.53
60	CGJ165	19.8.53	126	CLE149	28.9.53	193	CXX386	9.10.53
61	CGJ166	3.9.53	127	CLE150	25.3.53	194	CXX387	27.4.53
62	CGJ167	6.7.53	128	CLE151	25.3.53	195	CXX388	8.10.53
63	CGJ168	2.9.53	129	CLE152	1.5.53	196	CXX389	9.4.53
64	CGJ169	18.5.53	130	CLE153	23.4.54	197	CXX390	2.4.53
65	CGJ170	19.5.53	131	CLE154	22.9.53	198	CXX391	20.5.53
66	CGJ171	10.3.53	132	CLE155	29.1.54	199	CXX392	26.5.53
67	CGJ172	18.3.53	133	CLE156	19.3.53	200	CXX393	17.4.53
68	CGJ173	31.12.52	134	CLE157	2.2.54	201	CXX394	2.4.53
69	CGJ174	23.7.52	135	CLE158	24.4.53	202	CXX395	19.5.53
70	CGJ175	26.8.53	136	CLE159	25.11.53	203	CXX396	21.4.53
71	CGJ176	27.8.53	137	CLE160	1.5.53	204	CXX397	4.5.53
72	CGJ177	8.9.53	138	CLE161	26.4.54	205	CXX398	30.3.53
73	CGJ178	19.8.53	139	CLE162	15.7.53	206	CXX399	30.4.53
74	CGJ179	31.12.52	140	CLE163	29.4.53	207	CXX400	26.5.53
75	CGJ180	*	141	CLE164	23.11.53	208	CXX401	10.6.53
76	CGJ181	13.2.53	142	CLE165	5.8.53	209	CXX402	9.4.53
77	CGJ182	11.9.53	143	CLE166	24.9.53	210	CXX403	19.5.53
78	CGJ183	10.3.53	144	CLE167	18.9.53	211	CXX404	10.4.53
79	CGJ184	18.8.53	145	CLE168	19.3.53	212	CXX405	10.6.53
80	CGJ185	10.9.53c	146	CLE169	26.11.53	213	CXX406	19.6.53
81	CGJ186	5.5.53	147	CLE170	3.2.54	214	DGX220	19.5.53
82	CGJ187	20.3.53	148	CLE171	25.11.53	215	DGX221	28.5.53
83	CGJ188	14.1.54	149	CLE172	19.5.53	216	DGX222	27.2.53
84	CGJ189	30.4.53	150	CLE173	10.6.53	218	DGX224	24.4.53
85	CGJ190	19.5.53	151	CLE174	10.4.53	219	DGX225	7.5.53
86	CGJ191	21.8.53	152	CLE175	2.12.53	220	DGX226	8.9.53
87	CGJ192	18.3.53	153	CLE176	18.6.53	221	DGX227	22.4.53
88	CGJ193	7.9.53	154	CLE177	5.5.53	222	DGX228	23.4.53
89	CGJ195	6.2.53	155	CLE178	13.4.53	223	DGX229	26.11.53
90	CGJ194	31.8.53	156	CLE179	13.3.53	224	DGX230	27.4.53
91	CGJ196	7.4.53	157	CLE180	28.9.53	225	DGX231	28.5.53
92	CGJ197	20.5.53	158	CLE181	8.5.53	226	DGX232	7.5.53
93	CGJ198	4.9.53	159	CLE182	23.11.53	227	DGX233	9.4.53
94	CGJ199	26.3.53	160	CLE183	25.11.53	228	DGX234	19.5.53
95	CGJ200	20.3.53	161	CLE184	13.3.53	229	DGX235	19.6.53
96	CGJ201	18.6.53	162	CLE185	19.3.53	230	DGX236	4.6.53
97	CGJ202	9.9.53	163	CLE186	13.4.53	231	DGX237	26.3.53
98	CGJ203	7.5.52c	164	CLE187	13.4.53	232	DGX238	22.4.53
99	CGJ204	19.8.53	165	CLE188	28.9.53	233	DGX239	2.2.54
100	CGJ205	24.4.53	166	CLE189	23.4.54	234	DGX240	2.2.54
101	CGJ206	21.8.53	167	CLE190	11.3.53	235	DGX241	6.10.53
102	CGJ207	1.5.53	168	CLE191	10.7.53	236	DGX242	9.10.53
103	CGJ208	13.5.53	169	CLE192	13.11.53	237	DGX243	4.6.53
104	CGJ209	8.9.53	170	CLE193	20.8.53	238	DGX244	31.7.53

c Chassis only, body scrapped earlier
p Retained by London Transport for preservation　　* Converted to service vehicle 1035CD in 1952

Short Bros bodied C 60 was one of the original Country Bus batch delivered in 1935, coded 2C2, and its appearance had changed little when photographed near the end of its life with London Transport at Rickmansworth on the Loudwater Estate route 336A. It later saw service in Ceylon. F.G. Reynolds

C

The Leyland Cub was chosen by London Transport in 1935 as its standard one-man bus and was used to replace the many different types of small bus inherited from Independent operators. Ninety-eight buses were eventually owned, including the prototype C 1 and one acquired from Charles Russett and Sons of St Albans (C 76 – withdrawn in 1938). Of the remainder, the first seventy-four were Country Area buses bodied by Short Bros of Rochester (C 2-75) in 1935 and twenty-two were Central buses, bodied by Weymann in 1936 (C 77-98). There were also eight Park Royal bodied forward control 1½-deckers built in 1936 for the Inter-Station service (C 106-113). The intervening numbers (99-105, plus 114) were allocated to eight Leyland Cub lorries (numbered C99L etc in the Service Vehicle fleet).

The number of small buses required gradually diminished as traffic increased and larger buses were needed, particularly during the war when thirty-one Cubs were withdrawn. Thirty went to the Belgian Economic Mission for relief work in continental Europe in November 1945 and some of these were still at work with private operators in the early 1950s. In the immediate aftermath of the war many Cubs were used to cover the severe vehicle shortages in the double-deck fleet but they also opened up a number of new routes. The surviving buses were replaced by the GS class in 1953-54.

C 106-113 were allocated to Old Kent Road garage when in Inter-Station service but this facility was withdrawn on 16th September 1939 as one of the early wartime cuts. The Cubs were then put on loan to ENSA (Entertainments National Service Association). The Inter-Station service resumed in December 1943 to help in the movement of large numbers of service people across the capital but was reduced in frequency and converted to double-deck in 1950, when these buses had the honour of being the last petrol driven vehicles in LT passenger service. The Inter-Station Cubs were used in ordinary bus service between 1947 and 1949 when they were used to cover for the severe shortages in the double-deck fleet. For a time in 1951, eight were hired to British European Airways, after which all were sold.

C 95 was one of eleven survivors from the Weymann bodied 1/2C2/1 Central Bus version of the Cub to be repainted green for Country Bus service. It is at Onslow Street bus station Guildford, in the standard all-over green livery borne by few of this type. This version of the Cub did not have a front bumper bar.
Ernie Roberts

Chassis: Leyland Cub KPO3 (106-113: SKPZ2)
Engine: Leyland 6-cylinder 4.4 litre direct injection 65 bhp oil (77-98 - 4.7 litres; 106-113 4.7 litre petrol)
Transmission: Leyland 4-speed crash
Bodywork: Short Bros (2-74); Weymann (77-98); Park Royal (106-113)
Capacity: B20F (106-113 DP20F)   L.T. codes: 2C2 (22-74); 1/2C2 (77-98); 3C3 (106-113)
Built: 1935 (2-74) or 1936   Number built: 106   Number in stock: 1.1.50: 74; 31.12.54: 21

C		Date out of stock	C		Date out of stock	C		Date out of stock
2	BXD631	6.9.54	36	BXD661		70	BXD695	3.9.54
3	BXD627	6.9.54	37	BXD662	2.9.54	73	BXD698	6.9.54
4	BXD628		38	BXD663	20.8.54	74	BXD699	3.9.54
7	BXD630	1.9.54	39	BXD664	16.9.54	77	CLE105	
8	BXD633	7.9.54	40	BXD665	1.9.54	78	CLE106	
11	BXD636	2.9.54	41	BXD666		81	CLE109	
13	BXD638	2.9.54	42	BXD667	27.5.54	82	CLE110	
14	BXD639	3.9.54	44	BXD669		88	CLE116	28.3.51c
15	BXD640	2.9.54	45	BXD670	6.9.54	90	CLE118	
16	BXD641	6.9.54	47	BXD672	6.9.54	91	CLE119	
17	BXD642	2.11.54	49	BXD674	6.9.54	92	CLE120	
18	BXD643	7.9.54	50	BXD675		93	CLE121	
19	BXD644	6.9.54	52	BXD677	24.7.52c	94	CLE122	24.9.54
20	BXD645	7.9.54	53	BXD678		95	CLE123	
21	BXD646		56	BXD681	6.9.54	97	CLE125	28.3.51c
22	BXD647	2.9.54	57	BXD682	17.8.54	98	CLE126	
23	BXD648	3.9.54	58	BXD683	7.9.54	106	CLX543	30.4.53
24	BXD649	3.9.54	59	BXD684		107	CLX544	14.7.52
25	BXD650		60	BXD685	6.9.54	108	CLX545	12.5.53
26	BXD651	16.9.54	61	BXD686	6.9.54	109	CLX546	23.1.53
28	BXD653	3.9.54	63	BXD688	16.8.54	110	CLX547	12.5.53
30	BXD655	16.8.54	64	BXD689	27.8.53c	111	CLX548	24.8.53
31	BXD656		65	BXD690	7.9.54	112	CLX549	21.4.53
32	BXD657	2.9.54	66	BXD691	6.9.54	113	CLX550	21.4.53
34	BXD659	7.9.54	69	BXD694				

c Chassis only, body scrapped earlier

CR 14, at Oxted, was one of only five of the class still in service at the beginning of 1950, although most of the remainder were still in stock. It was one of the last three to be withdrawn in November 1953. J. H. Aston

CR

The CR was a revolutionary new version of the Cub chassis designed by Leyland in conjunction with London Transport in 1937. The standard Leyland 4.7 litre engine (4.4 litre on CR 1) was placed transversely at the rear of the chassis, along with the gearbox and radiator. A half-cab layout was adopted, with the passenger doorway immediately behind the front wheels, the area above the nearside wheel not being used. The first production CRs entered service in September 1939, and forty-four had been licensed by June 1941. All were delicensed soon afterwards and remained in store until 1946, except CR 18 which was one of the buses lost in the bombing of Bull Yard, Peckham in 1940. From 1946 they were put into service as reliefs on various routes. Some were used by Country Buses for post-war route development but the majority were withdrawn in 1949. Five, painted green, remained in service for a few more years, the last being withdrawn in November 1953.

Chassis: Leyland REC
Engine: Leyland 6-cylinder 4.7 litre indirect injection 65 bhp oil, mounted transversely.
Transmission: Leyland 4-speed crash (helical third gear)
Bodywork: LPTB   Capacity: B20F   Built: 1939   L.T.code: 2CR2
Number built: 49   Number in stock: 1.1.50: 47   31.12.54: 4

CR		Date out of stock	CR		Date out of stock	CR		Date out of stock
2	FXT108	26.1.53	19	FXT125	6.7.51	35	FXT141	26.1.53
3	FXT109	21.9.51	20	FXT126	13.5.52	36	FXT142	21.9.51
4	FXT110		21	FXT127	6.7.51	37	FXT143	1.11.51c
5	FXT111	6.7.51	22	FXT128	15.11.51	38	FXT144	15.11.51
6	FXT112		23	FXT129	13.5.52	39	FXT145	6.7.51
7	FXT113	4.1.52	24	FXT130	13.5.52	40	FXT146	29.4.53
8	FXT114	4.1.52	25	FXT131	4.1.52	41	FXT147	7.4.53
9	FXT115	10.3.53	26	FXT132	13.5.52	42	FXT148	1.4.53
10	FXT116		27	FXT133	10.3.53	43	FXT149	17.12.53
11	FXT117	24.10.51	28	FXT134	7.11.51c	44	FXT150	21.9.51
12	FXT118	15.11.51	29	FXT135	15.11.51	45	FXT151	4.1.52
13	FXT119	17.12.53	30	FXT136	13.5.52	46	FXT152	20.4.53
14	FXT120	25.3.54p	31	FXT137	15.11.51	47	FXT153	21.9.51
15	FXT121	1.4.53	32	FXT138		48	FXT154	1.4.53
16	FXT122	6.7.51	33	FXT139	22.4.53	49	FXT155	12.11.51
17	FXT123	29.12.53	34	FXT140	3.12.54			

c Chassis only, body scrapped earlier
p Retained by London Transport for preservation

The design of the Weymann bodywork on the AEC Renown private hire coaches of 1937 was based on the 9T9, but the built-up nearside wing assembly was omitted and a curved panel inserted instead. Other differences included an openable roof, the downward sweep of the rear mudguards and the inclusion of the autovac on the front bulkhead. LTC 15 is parked in the yard at the rear of Camberwell garage. J.H. Aston

LTC

The LTC class was purchased in 1937 to replace the life expired fleet of Private Hire coaches, mainly T class AEC Regals. The AEC Renown chassis was chosen in order to reduce wheel arch intrusion in the saloon and petrol engines were specified for quiet running. They differed from the LT class Renowns in having fully floating rear axles. Their Weymann 30-seat bodywork was similar to the 9T9 but without a rear destination indicator, built-up bonnet and wing assembly or bumper bar. They were fitted with sliding roof, radio and individual coach seats arranged in staggered pairs.

On the outbreak of war in September 1939, the LTCs were converted to public ambulances and remained as such until December 1945. In the early post-war years, when Private Hire was still restricted, some LTCs were used as buses or Green Line coaches to cover shortages in the scheduled fleet, including an official allocation at Hertford for a time in 1947/1948. Their seats were changed to standard tubular framed type at some time after the war and their petrol engines were replaced by 8.8 litre oil units salvaged from scrapped LTs in 1949/1950. The LTCs were replaced by new Private Hire RFs once the Festival of Britain was over in October 1951, although six were licensed for the summer season in 1952.

Chassis: AEC Renown 663
Engine: AEC A180 6-cylinder 8.8 litre 130bhp oil
Transmission: AEC D132 4-speed direct acting preselective with fluid flywheel
Bodywork: Weymann   Capacity: C30F
L.T.code: 1LTC1   Built: 1937/1938
Number built: 24   Number in stock: 1.1.50: 24; 31.12.54: Nil.

LTC		Date out of stock	LTC		Date out of stock	LTC		Date out of stock
1	EGO505	6.2.53	9	EGO513	4.2.53	17	EGO521	17.8.53
2	EGO506	18.6.54	10	EGO514	4.2.53	18	EGO522	10.8.53
3	EGO507	28.9.53	11	EGO515	5.8.53	19	EGO523	28.7.53
4	EGO508	5.8.53	12	EGO516	25.9.52	20	EGO524	6.2.53
5	EGO509	17.8.53	13	EGO517	6.8.53	21	EGO525	2.2.53
6	EGO510	29.9.53	14	EGO518	17.8.53	22	EGO526	9.10.53
7	EGO511	4.8.53	15	EGO519	29.9.53	23	EGO527	6.8.53
8	EGO512	4.8.53	16	EGO520	21.1.53	24	EGO528	5.8.53

TF 9, the only one of the twelve 2TF3 coaches of 1939 to avoid being bombed into oblivion, is outside Broadcasting House in Portland Place on the private hire duties for which it was built. F.G. Reynolds

TF

The prototype TF 1, which was taken into stock on 10th July 1937, was a revolutionary new design by Leyland Motors, incorporating an underfloor engine for the first time and including air operated brakes and gearbox. The Leyland body was similar in many respects to the contemporary Chiswick designs but with swept down front and rear saloon windows, streamlined mudguards and an unusual driver's cab with its windscreen rising high into the front dome to accommodate a high driving position. To allow the inclusion of a sliding door, the entrance was behind the front axle and the area ahead of the nearside bulkhead was effectually a wide wing. There were two production batches: twelve Private Hire coaches (TF 2-13) with Park Royal 33-seat bodywork; and seventy-five Green Line coaches with LPTB (Chiswick) 34-seat bodywork (TF 14-88). The basic layout was the same as on TF 1 but significant changes included a more conventional driving position and cab, a straight window line and the incorporation of a radiator and filler cap in the nearside wing. TF 1 was rebuilt with the same type of cab and radiator in 1940. The Private Hire coaches also differed in having glass cant panels for sightseeing, a sliding roof, radio, an offside emergency exit and no rear destination indicator.

The production TFs were delivered during 1939 but saw little service as the Green Line coaches were withdrawn for use as public ambulances on the outbreak of war. The Private Hire coaches were used by Country Buses for a time but were delicensed in November 1939. TF 1 and TF 9 were relicensed in October 1940 for limited private hire work but the remaining eleven Private Hire coaches were destroyed when Bull Yard, Peckham, where they were in store, was bombed on 22nd October 1940. TF 1 was sold in January 1946 but the rest returned to service between December 1945 and July 1948. The Green Line coaches had been allocated entirely to Romford (London Road) in 1939 but were now allocated to Dorking, Grays, Luton, St Albans and, later, Epping where they continued until replaced by RFs in 1952. Most were then downgraded to bus work until again replaced by RFs during 1953, when they were sold. TF 77 was transferred to London Transport preserved stock in April 1954.

The Chiswick-built thirty-four seat bodywork of the 2TF2 was based on the 10T10 but had a straight waistline and an entirely different front end, both determined by the underfloor position of the engine. TF 19 is at Stevenage 'White Lion' on 5th April 1952, shortly after being displaced from Green Line work by the new RF class. Alan B. Cross

Chassis: Leyland Tiger FEC
Engine: Leyland 8.6 litre direct injection 94 bhp oil, horizontal.
Transmission: AEC D132 air-operated direct selection preselective with fluid flywheel.
Bodywork: LPTB (TF 9: Park Royal)   Capacity: DP34F (TF 9: C33F).
L.T.code: 2TF2 (TF 9: 2TF3)
Built: 1939   Number built: 88   Number in stock: 1.1.50: 76   31.12.54: Nil.

TF		Date out of stock	TF		Date out of stock	TF		Date out of stock
9	FJJ610	2.12.53	39	FJJ650	17.9.52c	65	FJJ762	17.7.53
14	FJJ615	19.8.53	40	FJJ651	24.9.52c	66	FJJ763	3.9.53
15	FJJ616	28.8.53	41	FJJ652	28.8.53	67	FJJ764	28.5.53
16	FJJ617	16.6.53	42	FJJ653	27.7.53	68	FJJ765	27.5.53
17	FJJ618	19.8.53	43	FJJ654	24.8.53	69	FJJ766	3.9.53
18	FJJ629	24.8.53	44	FJJ655	14.10.53	70	FJJ767	14.7.53
19	FJJ630	20.8.53	45	FJJ656	27.7.53	71	FJJ768	13.7.53
20	FJJ631	16.10.53	46	FJJ657	21.8.53	72	FJJ769	28.8.53
21	FJJ632	22.5.53	47	FJJ658	21.8.53	73	FJJ770	21.5.52c
22	FJJ633	28.5.52c	48	FJJ659	14.10.53	74	FJJ771	19.8.53
23	FJJ634	24.8.53	49	FJJ660	16.10.53	75	FJJ772	7.7.53
24	FJJ635	7.7.53	50	FJJ661	16.10.53	76	FJJ773	18.6.53
25	FJJ636	15.7.53	51	FJJ662	25.8.53	77	FJJ774	9.4.54p
26	FJJ637	31.7.53	52	FJJ663	12.10.53	78	FJJ775	13.7.53
27	FJJ638	21.5.53	53	FJJ664	3.9.53	79	FJJ776	13.7.53
28	FJJ639	25.8.53	54	FJJ665	17.9.53	80	FJJ777	12.10.53
29	FJJ640	25.8.53	55	FJJ666	16.10.53	81	FXT41	14.10.53
30	FJJ641	21.8.53	56	FJJ667	16.6.53	82	FXT42	1.10.53
31	FJJ642	15.7.53	57	FJJ668	16.6.53	83	FXT43	21.8.53
32	FJJ643	17.9.52c	58	FJJ669	14.10.53	84	FXT44	28.8.53
33	FJJ644	24.8.53	59	FJJ670	16.6.53	85	FXT45	13.10.53
34	FJJ645	25.8.53	60	FJJ671	25.8.53	86	FXT46	3.9.53
35	FJJ646	17.9.53	61	FJJ672	17.9.53	87	FXT47	1.10.53
36	FJJ647	21.5.53	62	FJJ673	13.7.53	88	FXT48	16.10.53
37	FJJ648	26.5.53	63	FJJ674	4.6.53			
38	FJJ649	21.5.53	64	FJJ761	14.10.53			

c Chassis only, body scrapped earlier
p Retained by London Transport for preservation

The thirty-one 1TD1s had Leyland Tiger PS1 chassis similar in specification to the 4STDs and Weymann bodywork identical to that on the 14T12s. Originally the exclusive allocation for route 212 at Muswell Hill, they were replaced by RFs in 1953 and transferred mostly to Kingston but also to Loughton. When it was seen at Ealing Broadway on 16th February 1952, TD 29 was in temporary exile from Muswell Hill. Alan B. Cross

TD

In 1946, following the delivery of the 14T12s and as part of the same 'stop-gap' programme, London Transport was allotted thirty-one of the new Leyland Tiger PS1 model which had a mechanical specification the same as the 4STD3s. They were fitted with 'provincial' standard Weymann bodywork identical to the Ts but with thirty-three seats from the outset. The seating capacity was reduced to thirty-two in 1954. All thirty-one were allocated to Muswell Hill garage, where they replaced 14T12s on route 212 between December 1946 and March 1947. They were replaced in turn by RFs in 1952 and transferred to Kingston and Loughton. A repeat order for one hundred similar chassis was placed in 1948 and put into service between October 1948 and October 1949. These had Mann Egerton bodywork identical to that supplied on the 15T13s except that no door was fitted to the passenger entrance. These were used to replace the oldest Ts and single-deck LTs at nine Central Area garages.

Chassis: Leyland Tiger PS1
Engine: Leyland 6-cylinder 7.4 litre direct injection 100 bhp oil
Transmission: Leyland 4-speed constant mesh
Bodywork: Weymann (1-31); or Mann Egerton   Capacity: B32F (1-31); or B31F
Built: 1946/47 (1-31); 1948   L.T.codes: 1TD1 (1-31) or 1/1TD2   Number built: 131
Number in stock: 1.1.50: 131   31.12.54: 131

The second batch of Tigers, coded 1/1TD2, also had bodies identical to others mounted on AEC Regal chassis, in this case the Mann Egerton model used on the 15T13s, although the sliding platform door was omitted in deference to the Metropolitan Police who felt it would slow down boarding and alighting. Kingston's TD 82, at Littleton Common approaching Esher, has acquired a chromium radiator shell from a 1TD1 in place of the polished aluminium type normally associated with the later PS1s.
F.G. Reynolds

TD		TD		TD		TD		TD		TD	
1	HGF959	23	HGF981	45	JXC238	67	JXC260	89	JXC282	111	JXC304
2	HGF960	24	HGF982	46	JXC239	68	JXC261	90	JXC283	112	JXC305
3	HGF961	25	HGF983	47	JXC240	69	JXC262	91	JXC284	113	JXC306
4	HGF962	26	HGF984	48	JXC241	70	JXC263	92	JXC285	114	JXC307
5	HGF963	27	HGF985	49	JXC242	71	JXC264	93	JXC286	115	JXC308
6	HGF964	28	HGF986	50	JXC243	72	JXC265	94	JXC287	116	JXC309
7	HGF965	29	HGF987	51	JXC244	73	JXC266	95	JXC288	117	JXC310
8	HGF966	30	HGF988	52	JXC245	74	JXC267	96	JXC289	118	JXC311
9	HGF967	31	HGF989	53	JXC246	75	JXC268	97	JXC290	119	JXC312
10	HGF968	32	JXC225	54	JXC247	76	JXC269	98	JXC291	120	JXC313
11	HGF969	33	JXC226	55	JXC248	77	JXC270	99	JXC292	121	JXC314
12	HGF970	34	JXC227	56	JXC249	78	JXC271	100	JXC293	122	JXC315
13	HGF971	35	JXC228	57	JXC250	79	JXC272	101	JXC294	123	JXC316
14	HGF972	36	JXC229	58	JXC251	80	JXC273	102	JXC295	124	JXC317
15	HGF973	37	JXC230	59	JXC252	81	JXC274	103	JXC296	125	JXC318
16	HGF974	38	JXC231	60	JXC253	82	JXC275	104	JXC297	126	JXC319
17	HGF975	39	JXC232	61	JXC254	83	JXC276	105	JXC298	127	JXC320
18	HGF976	40	JXC233	62	JXC255	84	JXC277	106	JXC299	128	JXC321
19	HGF977	41	JXC234	63	JXC256	85	JXC278	107	JXC300	129	JXC322
20	HGF978	42	JXC235	64	JXC257	86	JXC279	108	JXC301	130	JXC323
21	HGF979	43	JXC236	65	JXC258	87	JXC280	109	JXC302	131	JXC324
22	HGF980	44	JXC237	66	JXC259	88	JXC281	110	JXC303		

Serious replacement of the pre-war single-deck fleet did not start until 1951 when the RF class of AEC Regal IVs began to arrive. In preparation, the demonstrator prototype UMP227 was borrowed from AEC intermittently between May 1950 and September 1951 for trial operation, mostly on route 355 from St Albans garage, but here seen working from Reigate. The chassis design and specification was, other than being 27ft 6ins long, identical to the production model, but its Park Royal body bore a strong resemblance to those supplied on Q chassis before the war.

The first twenty-five RFs were the unique short-wheelbase private hire coaches, coded 1RF1/2, which were adorned with a new livery of Lincoln green and grey with red lettering and fleet numbering, and were the first vehicles to be fitted as standard with quarter-drop wind-down opening windows. RF 2 is parked outside the New Victoria cinema in Vauxhall Bridge Road, Victoria, when in almost mint condition.
Roy Marshall

RF

Replacement of the bulk of London Transport's pre-war single-deckers was delayed until the worst of the much larger double-deck fleet had been withdrawn and did not start until 1951. The standard single-decker was to be the AEC Regal IV, a model which was launched by AEC in 1949. Trials carried out by London Transport during 1950 with the demonstrator UMP227 proved successful and an order was placed for 700 chassis with bodywork by Metro-Cammell Carriage & Wagon Co. Ltd. The bodywork order was placed in substitution for 550 RTL bodies which were transferred to Park Royal. The standard AEC chassis was modified for London Transport in a number of respects, including the addition of Pilot Injection, a system designed to reduce diesel knock. At the time the orders were placed the regulations restricted the length of single-deckers to 27ft 6ins but the permitted length was increased to thirty feet in 1950. The orders were then altered to a mixture of short and long wheelbase, as not all routes were then approved for the longer vehicle. Approval was forthcoming later and the order was amended so that 675 were thirty-footers. The change in regulations was too late to affect the first twenty-five which were the only production Regal IVs built to the smaller dimensions.

Priority was given to the Green Line in the single-deck replacement programme and, when new, the first thirty-foot RFs had the appearance demonstrated by RF 29 at Victoria in April 1952.
E.J. Smith

All 675 thirty-foot RFs had the same general appearance, with only the liveries or the coach fittings providing any variety. The 2RF2 Central bus version was unique in having no platform doors but was otherwise identical to the Country buses. RF 391 was one of twenty-four at Norbiton and Sutton which were fitted experimentally with a new type of semaphore signal, which can be seen as a black line behind the driver's signalling window.

The bodywork for all seven hundred was of basically the same design but there were four major variants. RF 1-25 were the short wheelbase vehicles and were intended for Private Hire and touring work. They had tubular framed seats to Green Line specification, glass observation windows in the side roof panels and public address equipment. RF 26-288 were thirty foot long Green Line coaches with all thirty-nine seats facing forwards; RF 289-513 were forty-one seat Central Area buses and were the only RFs built without platform doors; RF 514-700 were Country Buses, identical to the Central version except for having platform doors. Three of the latter (RFs 517, 647 and 700) were modified for one-man operation before entering service in March 1954 and RF 649 was added in October 1954. The RFs were the first standard London Transport buses other than a few RTs to have quarter drop, rather than half drop, opening saloon windows.

The first Private Hire coaches were licensed in time for the Festival of Britain in May 1951, the Green Line coaches between October 1951 and November 1952, the Central buses between September 1952 and March 1953 and finally the Country buses between March and December 1953. A further seventy-nine were authorised by the British Transport Commission but by 1953 reduced vehicle requirements made these unnecessary and the authority was never taken up.

RF 571 on the single afternoon journey to Nazeing Gate on route 342 shows the 2RF2/2 Country type in its original condition, complete with conductor wearing a Gibson ticket issuing machine. J.H. Aston

Three Country Bus Regal IVs were made suitable for experimental one-man operation in 1954, their driver's cabs being extensively remodelled to include ticket-issuing and change-giving machines and a glass partition on top of the cab door. They were recoded 2RF5. The complete enclosure of the cab created a need for an emergency exit and this was provided by incorporating the driver's signalling window into a single frame which could be pushed out in one piece. This changed it into a three piece arrangement with an opening section in the middle, as shown on RF 517 in early experimental service on Epsom local route 419. Michael Rooum

Chassis: AEC Regal IV 9821LT   Engine: AEC A219 9.6 litre horizontal 125 bhp
Transmission: AEC D140 4-speed air operated preselective with fluid flywheel
Bodywork: Metro-Cammell   Capacity: DP35F (1-25); DP39F (26-288); B41F (289-516, 518-646, 648-699); B39F OMO (517, 647, 700)
Original L.T. codes: 1RF1/2 (1-25); 2RF2/1 (26-288); 2RF2 (289-513); 2RF2/2 (514-516, 518-646, 648-699); 2RF5 (517, 647, 700)
Built: 1951-1953   Number built: 700   Number in stock: 1. 1.50: Nil   31.12.54: 700

RF		Date into stock	RF		Date into stock	RF		Date into stock
1	LUC201	4.4.51	69	LYF420	30.11.51	137	MLL524	23.1.52
2	LUC202	16.4.51	70	LYF421	4.12.51	138	MLL525	31.1.52
3	LUC203	19.4.51	71	LYF422	3.12.51	139	MLL526	29.1.52
4	LUC204	19.4.51	72	LYF423	14.12.51	140	MLL527	29.1.52
5	LUC205	23.4.51	73	LYF424	3.12.51	141	MLL528	31.1.52
6	LUC206	2.5.51	74	LYF425	11.12.51	142	MLL529	29.1.52
7	LUC207	27.4.51	75	LYF426	11.12.51	143	MLL530	29.1.52
8	LUC208	2.5.51	76	LYF427	11.12.51	144	MLL531	31.1.52
9	LUC209	3.5.51	77	LYF428	10.12.51	145	MLL532	1.2.52
10	LUC210	2.5.51	78	LYF429	10.12.51	146	MLL533	1.2.52
11	LUC211	3.5.51	79	LYF430	10.12.51	147	MLL534	1.2.52
12	LUC212	3.5.51	80	LYF431	14.12.51	148	MLL535	1.2.52
13	LUC213	7.5.51	81	LYF432	10.12.51	149	MLL536	1.2.52
14	LUC214	11.5.51	82	LYF433	10.12.51	150	MLL537	5.2.52
15	LUC215	10.5.51	83	LYF434	14.12.51	151	MLL538	8.2.52
16	LUC216	7.5.51	84	LYF435	10.12.51	152	MLL539	5.2.52
17	LUC217	10.5.51	85	LYF436	14.12.51	153	MLL540	8.2.52
18	LUC218	11.5.51	86	LYF437	11.12.51	154	MLL541	5.2.52
19	LUC219	11.5.51	87	LYF438	17.12.51	155	MLL542	8.2.52
20	LUC220	15.5.51	88	LYF439	17.12.51	156	MLL543	8.2.52
21	LUC221	15.5.51	89	LYF440	11.12.51	157	MLL544	9.2.52
22	LUC222	18.5.51	90	LYF441	17.12.51	158	MLL545	8.2.52
23	LUC223	15.5.51	91	LYF442	17.12.51	159	MLL546	9.2.52
24	LUC224	18.5.51	92	LYF443	20.12.51	160	MLL547	9.2.52
25	LUC225	18.5.51	93	LYF444	20.12.51	161	MLL548	9.2.52
26	LYF377	17.9.51	94	LYF445	20.12.51	162	MLL549	13.2.52
27	LYF378	5.10.51	95	LYF446	21.12.51	163	MLL550	9.2.52
28	LYF379	5.10.51	96	LYF447	20.12.51	164	MLL551	13.2.52
29	LYF380	12.10.51	97	LYF448	20.12.51	165	MLL552	15.2.52
30	LYF381	19.10.51	98	LYF449	21.12.51	166	MLL553	15.2.52
31	LYF382	12.10.51	99	LYF450	21.12.51	167	MLL554	15.2.52
32	LYF383	19.10.51	100	LYF451	21.12.51	168	MLL555	19.2.52
33	LYF384	5.11.51	101	LYF452	21.12.51	169	MLL556	19.2.52
34	LYF385	29.10.51	102	LYF453	28.12.51	170	MLL557	19.2.52
35	LYF386	22.10.51	103	LYF454	27.12.51	171	MLL558	22.2.52
36	LYF387	12.11.51	104	LYF455	27.12.51	172	MLL559	22.2.52
37	LYF388	2.11.51	105	LYF456	27.12.51	173	MLL560	23.2.52
38	LYF389	5.11.51	106	LYF457	27.12.51	174	MLL561	22.2.52
39	LYF390	5.11.51	107	LYF458	28.12.51	175	MLL562	23.2.52
40	LYF391	5.11.51	108	LYF459	28.12.51	176	MLL563	23.2.52
41	LYF392	19.11.51	109	LYF460	28.12.51	177	MLL564	26.2.52
42	LYF393	6.11.51	110	LYF461	1.1.52	178	MLL565	28.2.52
43	LYF394	12.11.51	111	LYF462	28.12.51	179	MLL566	26.2.52
44	LYF395	12.11.51	112	LYF463	1.1.52	180	MLL567	26.2.52
45	LYF396	19.11.51	113	LYF464	1.1.52	181	MLL568	29.2.52
46	LYF397	19.11.51	114	LYF465	1.1.52	182	MLL569	28.2.52
47	LYF398	19.11.51	115	LYF466	1.1.52	183	MLL570	29.2.52
48	LYF399	12.11.51	116	LYF467	17.1.52	184	MLL571	4.3.52
49	LYF400	19.11.51	117	LYF468	15.1.52	185	MLL572	11.3.52
50	LYF401	22.11.51	118	LYF469	1.1.52	186	MLL573	6.3.52
51	LYF402	23.11.51	119	LYF470	11.1.52	187	MLL574	29.2.52
52	LYF403	22.11.51	120	LYF471	11.1.52	188	MLL575	29.2.52
53	LYF404	23.11.51	121	LYF472	11.1.52	189	MLL576	6.3.52
54	LYF405	26.11.51	122	LYF473	15.1.52	190	MLL577	4.3.52
55	LYF406	27.11.51	123	LYF474	16.1.52	191	MLL578	6.3.52
56	LYF407	26.11.51	124	LYF475	15.1.52	192	MLL579	7.3.52
57	LYF408	26.11.51	125	LYF476	17.1.52	193	MLL580	11.3.52
58	LYF409	27.11.51	126	MLL513	21.1.52	194	MLL581	14.3.52
59	LYF410	26.11.51	127	MLL514	16.1.52	195	MLL582	7.3.52
60	LYF411	26.11.51	128	MLL515	16.1.52	196	MLL583	12.3.52
61	LYF412	30.11.51	129	MLL516	23.1.52	197	MLL584	14.3.52
62	LYF413	30.11.51	130	MLL517	21.1.52	198	MLL585	12.3.52
63	LYF414	30.11.51	131	MLL518	23.1.52	199	MLL586	14.3.52
64	LYF415	4.12.51	132	MLL519	21.1.52	200	MLL587	18.3.52
65	LYF416	4.12.51	133	MLL520	23.1.52	201	MLL588	14.3.52
66	LYF417	3.12.51	134	MLL521	25.1.52	202	MLL589	18.3.52
67	LYF418	30.11.51	135	MLL522	25.1.52	203	MLL590	14.3.52
68	LYF419	30.11.51	136	MLL523	25.1.52	204	MLL591	21.3.52

RF		Date into stock	RF		Date into stock	RF		Date into stock
205	MLL592	18.3.52	273	MLL810	8.8.52	341	MLL978	30.10.52
206	MLL593	19.3.52	274	MLL811	7.8.52	342	MLL979	30.10.52
207	MLL594	21.3.52	275	MLL812	8.8.52	343	MLL980	31.10.52
208	MLL595	21.3.52	276	MLL813	18.8.52	344	MLL981	3.11.52
209	MLL596	21.3.52	277	MLL814	13.8.52	345	MLL982	31.10.52
210	MLL597	19.3.52	278	MLL815	25.8.52	346	MLL983	30.10.52
211	MLL598	24.3.52	279	MLL816	18.8.52	347	MLL984	31.10.52
212	MLL599	24.3.52	280	MLL817	14.8.52	348	MLL985	3.11.52
213	MLL600	27.3.52	281	MLL818	25.8.52	349	MLL986	5.11.52
214	MLL601	26.3.52	282	MLL819	5.9.52	350	MLL987	5.11.52
215	MLL602	26.3.52	283	MLL820	14.8.52	351	MLL988	5.11.52
216	MLL603	28.3.52	284	MLL821	25.8.52	352	MLL989	6.11.52
217	MLL604	27.3.52	285	MLL822	1.9.52	353	MLL990	12.11.52
218	MLL605	29.3.52	286	MLL823	1.9.52	354	MLL991	6.11.52
219	MLL606	29.3.52	287	MLL824	14.10.52	355	MLL992	7.11.52
220	MLL607	28.3.52	288	MLL825	26.9.52	356	MLL993	7.11.52
221	MLL608	1.4.52	289	MLL926	1.9.52	357	MLL994	11.11.52
222	MLL609	8.4.52	290	MLL927	12.9.52	358	MLL995	7.11.52
223	MLL610	3.4.52	291	MLL928	5.9.52	359	MXX1	11.11.52
224	MLL611	1.4.52	292	MLL929	12.9.52	360	MXX2	11.11.52
225	MLL612	8.4.52	293	MLL930	5.9.52	361	MXX3	13.11.52
226	MLL763	5.4.52	294	MLL931	12.9.52	362	MXX4	14.11.52
227	MLL764	4.4.52	295	MLL932	18.9.52	363	MXX5	12.11.52
228	MLL765	3.4.52	296	MLL933	18.9.52	364	MXX6	18.11.52
229	MLL766	5.4.52	297	MLL934	18.9.52	365	MXX7	13.11.52
230	MLL767	4.4.52	298	MLL935	26.9.52	366	MXX8	14.11.52
231	MLL768	15.4.52	299	MLL936	26.9.52	367	MXX9	17.11.52
232	MLL769	15.4.52	300	MLL937	2.10.52	368	MXX10	17.11.52
233	MLL770	15.4.52	301	MLL938	2.10.52	369	MXX11	18.11.52
234	MLL771	15.4.52	302	MLL939	2.10.52	370	MXX12	21.11.52
235	MLL772	15.4.52	303	MLL940	3.10.52	371	MXX13	21.11.52
236	MLL773	22.4.52	304	MLL941	3.10.52	372	MXX14	21.11.52
237	MLL774	18.4.52	305	MLL942	3.10.52	373	MXX15	26.11.52
238	MLL775	18.4.52	306	MLL943	6.10.52	374	MXX16	26.11.52
239	MLL776	25.4.52	307	MLL944	6.10.52	375	MXX17	24.11.52
240	MLL777	22.4.52	308	MLL945	7.10.52	376	MXX18	24.11.52
241	MLL778	24.4.52	309	MLL946	7.10.52	377	MXX19	28.11.52
242	MLL779	25.4.52	310	MLL947	8.10.52	378	MXX20	26.11.52
243	MLL780	24.4.52	311	MLL948	8.10.52	379	MXX21	1.12.52
244	MLL781	25.4.52	312	MLL949	9.10.52	380	MXX22	3.12.52
245	MLL782	29.4.52	313	MLL950	10.10.52	381	MXX23	26.11.52
246	MLL783	24.4.52	314	MLL951	10.10.52	382	MXX24	28.11.52
247	MLL784	15.5.52	315	MLL952	14.10.52	383	MXX25	2.12.52
248	MLL785	29.4.52	316	MLL953	15.10.52	384	MXX26	28.11.52
249	MLL786	6.5.52	317	MLL954	14.10.52	385	MXX27	3.12.52
250	MLL787	6.5.52	318	MLL955	16.10.52	386	MXX28	3.12.52
251	MLL788	16.5.52	319	MLL956	16.10.52	387	MXX29	4.12.52
252	MLL789	17.5.52	320	MLL957	16.10.52	388	MXX30	2.12.52
253	MLL790	16.5.52	321	MLL958	17.10.52	389	MXX277	9.12.52
254	MLL791	15.5.52	322	MLL959	17.10.52	390	MXX278	5.12.52
255	MLL792	27.5.52	323	MLL960	17.10.52	391	MXX279	4.12.52
256	MLL793	17.5.52	324	MLL961	17.10.52	392	MXX280	3.12.52
257	MLL794	20.5.52	325	MLL962	20.10.52	393	MXX281	5.12.52
258	MLL795	27.5.52	326	MLL963	20.10.52	394	MXX282	9.12.52
259	MLL796	9.6.52	327	MLL964	22.10.52	395	MXX283	10.12.52
260	MLL797	17.5.52	328	MLL965	21.10.52	396	MXX284	9.12.52
261	MLL798	20.5.52	329	MLL966	21.10.52	397	MXX285	9.12.52
262	MLL799	23.5.52	330	MLL967	9.10.52	398	MXX286	10.12.52
263	MLL800	23.5.52	331	MLL968	22.10.52	399	MXX287	12.12.52
264	MLL801	6.6.52	332	MLL969	23.10.52	400	MXX288	11.12.52
265	MLL802	27.5.52	333	MLL970	23.10.52	401	MXX289	12.12.52
266	MLL803	6.6.52	334	MLL971	24.10.52	402	MXX290	12.12.52
267	MLL804	6.6.52	335	MLL972	24.10.52	403	MXX291	12.12.52
268	MLL805	9.6.52	336	MLL973	27.10.52	404	MXX292	11.12.52
269	MLL806	9.6.52	337	MLL974	24.10.52	405	MXX293	12.12.52
270	MLL807	13.8.52	338	MLL975	24.10.52	406	MXX294	12.12.52
271	MLL808	7.8.52	339	MLL976	27.10.52	407	MXX295	16.12.52
272	MLL809	7.8.52	340	MLL977	30.10.52	408	MXX296	17.12.52

RF

No.	Reg.	Date into stock
409	MXX297	17.12.52
410	MXX298	16.12.52
411	MXX299	22.12.52
412	MXX389	19.12.52
413	MXX390	19.12.52
414	MXX391	23.12.52
415	MXX392	19.12.52
416	MXX393	22.12.52
417	MXX394	23.12.52
418	MXX395	22.12.52
419	MXX396	31.12.52
420	MXX397	5.1.53
421	MXX398	23.12.52
422	MXX399	31.12.52
423	MXX400	30.12.52
424	MXX401	30.12.52
425	MXX402	30.12.52
426	MXX403	1.1.53
427	MXX404	1.1.53
428	MXX405	5.1.53
429	MXX406	31.12.52
430	MXX407	1.1.53
431	MXX408	2.1.53
432	MXX409	2.1.53
433	MXX410	12.1.53
434	MXX411	7.1.53
435	MXX412	7.1.53
436	MXX413	12.1.53
437	MXX414	9.1.53
438	MXX415	9.1.53
439	MXX416	9.1.53
440	MXX417	12.1.53
441	MXX418	15.1.53
442	MXX419	15.1.53
443	MXX420	13.1.53
444	MXX421	21.1.53
445	MXX422	13.1.53
446	MXX423	21.1.53
447	MXX424	15.1.53
448	MXX425	21.1.53
449	MXX426	22.1.53
450	MXX427	21.1.53
451	MXX428	22.1.53
452	MXX429	22.1.53
453	MXX430	27.1.53
454	MXX431	30.1.53
455	MXX432	22.1.53
456	MXX433	29.1.53
457	MXX434	27.1.53
458	MXX435	29.1.53
459	MXX436	29.1.53
460	MXX437	29.1.53
461	MXX438	30.1.53
462	MXX439	27.1.53
463	MXX440	2.2.53
464	MXX441	29.1.53
465	MXX442	2.2.53
466	MXX443	30.1.53
467	MXX444	30.1.53
468	MXX445	6.2.53
469	MXX446	9.2.53
470	MXX447	3.2.53
471	MXX448	3.2.53
472	MXX449	5.2.53
473	MXX450	10.2.53
474	MXX451	5.2.53
475	MXX452	9.2.53
476	MXX453	6.2.53
477	MXX454	9.2.53
478	MXX455	10.2.53
479	MXX456	11.2.53
480	MXX457	11.2.53
481	MXX458	16.2.53
482	MXX459	13.2.53
483	MXX460	13.2.53
484	MXX461	16.2.53
485	MXX462	17.2.53
486	MXX463	17.2.53
487	MXX464	20.2.53
488	MXX465	23.2.53
489	MXX466	24.2.53
490	MXX467	25.2.53
491	MXX468	23.2.53
492	MXX469	20.2.53
493	MXX470	25.2.53
494	MXX471	20.2.53
495	MXX472	20.2.53
496	MXX473	27.2.53
497	MXX474	3.3.53
498	MXX475	24.2.53
499	MXX476	2.3.53
500	MXX477	2.3.53
501	MXX478	27.2.53
502	MXX479	3.3.53
503	MXX480	25.2.53
504	MXX481	6.3.53
505	MXX482	11.3.53
506	MXX483	11.3.53
507	MXX484	13.3.53
508	MXX485	6.3.53
509	MXX486	6.3.53
510	MXX487	17.3.53
511	MXX488	13.3.53
512	MXX489	17.3.53
513	MXX490	11.3.53
514	NLE514	20.3.53
515	NLE515	26.3.53
516	NLE516	25.3.53
517	NLE517	20.3.53
518	NLE518	25.3.53
519	NLE519	27.3.53
520	NLE520	27.3.53
521	NLE521	26.3.53
522	NLE522	1.4.53
523	NLE523	30.3.53
524	NLE524	2.4.53
525	NLE525	1.4.53
526	NLE526	30.3.53
527	NLE527	31.3.53
528	NLE528	2.4.53
529	NLE529	31.3.53
530	NLE530	7.4.53
531	NLE531	7.4.53
532	NLE532	7.4.53
533	NLE533	10.4.53
534	NLE534	13.4.53
535	NLE535	10.4.53
536	NLE536	13.4.53
537	NLE537	10.4.53
538	NLE538	16.4.53
539	NLE539	14.4.53
540	NLE540	16.4.53
541	NLE541	14.4.53
542	NLE542	16.4.53
543	NLE543	17.4.53
544	NLE544	17.4.53
545	NLE545	20.4.53
546	NLE546	20.4.53
547	NLE547	21.4.53
548	NLE548	17.4.53
549	NLE549	23.4.53
550	NLE550	21.4.53
551	NLE551	23.4.53
552	NLE552	29.4.53
553	NLE553	23.4.53
554	NLE554	28.4.53
555	NLE555	28.4.53
556	NLE556	1.5.53
557	NLE557	29.4.53
558	NLE558	1.5.53
559	NLE559	28.4.53
560	NLE560	1.5.53
561	NLE561	5.5.53
562	NLE562	5.5.53
563	NLE563	5.5.53
564	NLE564	7.5.53
565	NLE565	7.5.53
566	NLE566	15.5.53
567	NLE567	11.5.53
568	NLE568	8.5.53
569	NLE569	8.5.53
570	NLE570	15.5.53
571	NLE571	12.5.53
572	NLE572	12.5.53
573	NLE573	11.5.53
574	NLE574	18.5.53
575	NLE575	29.5.53
576	NLE576	21.5.53
577	NLE577	18.5.53
578	NLE578	21.5.53
579	NLE579	28.5.53
580	NLE580	26.5.53
581	NLE581	26.5.53
582	NLE582	8.6.53
583	NLE583	28.5.53
584	NLE584	27.5.53
585	NLE585	27.5.53
586	NLE586	5.6.53
587	NLE587	29.5.53
588	NLE588	29.5.53
589	NLE589	5.6.53
590	NLE590	8.6.53
591	NLE591	5.6.53
592	NLE592	10.6.53
593	NLE593	10.6.53
594	NLE594	10.6.53
595	NLE595	15.6.53
596	NLE596	15.6.53
597	NLE597	17.6.53
598	NLE598	10.6.53
599	NLE599	18.6.53
600	NLE600	24.6.53
601	NLE601	15.6.53
602	NLE602	17.6.53
603	NLE603	18.6.53
604	NLE604	26.6.53
605	NLE605	15.6.53
606	NLE606	24.6.53
607	NLE607	24.6.53
608	NLE608	17.6.53
609	NLE609	3.7.53
610	NLE610	26.6.53
611	NLE611	7.7.53
612	NLE612	1.7.53

RF

RF		Date into stock	RF		Date into stock	RF		Date into stock
613	NLE613	2.7.53	643	NLE643	14.8.53	673	NLE673	11.9.53
614	NLE614	6.7.53	644	NLE644	24.8.53	674	NLE674	16.9.53
615	NLE615	26.6.53	645	NLE645	20.8.53	675	NLE675	18.9.53
616	NLE616	1.7.53	646	NLE646	24.8.53	676	NLE676	16.9.53
617	NLE617	2.7.53	647	NLE647	19.8.53	677	NLE677	25.9.53
618	NLE618	3.7.53	648	NLE648	19.8.53	678	NLE678	18.9.53
619	NLE619	6.7.53	649	NLE649	24.8.53	679	NLE679	22.9.53
620	NLE620	8.7.53	650	NLE650	19.8.53	680	NLE680	29.9.53
621	NLE621	7.7.53	651	NLE651	25.8.53	681	NLE681	22.9.53
622	NLE622	9.7.53	652	NLE652	25.8.53	682	NLE682	25.9.53
623	NLE623	9.7.53	653	NLE653	26.8.53	683	NLE683	29.9.53
624	NLE624	8.7.53	654	NLE654	26.8.53	684	NLE684	9.10.53
625	NLE625	14.7.53	655	NLE655	28.8.53	685	NLE685	8.10.53
626	NLE626	9.7.53	656	NLE656	27.8.53	686	NLE686	8.10.53
627	NLE627	10.7.53	657	NLE657	2.9.53	687	NLE687	16.10.53
628	NLE628	10.7.53	658	NLE658	27.8.53	688	NLE688	9.10.53
629	NLE629	10.7.53	659	NLE659	28.8.53	689	NLE689	16.10.53
630	NLE630	14.7.53	660	NLE660	31.8.53	690	NLE690	21.10.53
631	NLE631	16.7.53	661	NLE661	31.8.53	691	NLE691	21.10.53
632	NLE632	16.7.53	662	NLE662	4.9.53	692	NLE692	21.10.53
633	NLE633	17.7.53	663	NLE663	2.9.53	693	NLE693	30.10.53
634	NLE634	17.7.53	664	NLE664	4.9.53	694	NLE694	30.10.53
635	NLE635	7.8.53	665	NLE665	4.9.53	695	NLE695	12.11.53
636	NLE636	7.8.53	666	NLE666	10.9.53	696	NLE696	23.11.53
637	NLE637	11.8.53	667	NLE667	4.9.53	697	NLE697	23.11.53
638	NLE638	11.8.53	668	NLE668	10.9.53	698	NLE698	11.11.53
639	NLE639	7.8.53	669	NLE669	10.9.53	699	NLE699	4.12.53
640	NLE640	14.8.53	670	NLE670	11.9.53	700	NLE700	10.12.53
641	NLE641	11.8.53	671	NLE671	11.9.53			
642	NLE642	19.8.53	672	NLE672	16.9.53			

RFW

In May 1950 the British Transport Commission gave London Transport authority to operate contract carriage services up to a one hundred mile radius from 55 Broadway, for which purpose the Executive purchased fifteen luxury coaches, five of which had been diverted by the BTC from a Tilling group company. The chassis was the eight foot wide version of the Regal IV, built to the newly authorised length of thirty feet. They were standard 9821E models but with some modifications for London Transport. The thirty-nine seat bodies supplied by Eastern Coach Works were of a rather austere design but interior furnishings and fittings were to full coach standards. They had glass observation panels at cant level, a swing passenger door and no destination indicators. All fifteen entered service in May and June 1951 and were allocated to both Central and Country garages.

Chassis: AEC Regal IV 9821E   Engine: AEC A219 9.6 litre horizontal 125 bhp
Transmission: AEC D140 4-speed air operated preselective with fluid flywheel
Bodywork: Eastern Coach Works   Capacity: C39F   L.T.code: 3RF3   Built: 1951
Number built: 15   Number in stock: 1.1.50: Nil   31.12.54: 15

RFW

RFW		Date into stock	RFW		Date into stock	RFW		Date into stock
1	LUC376	27.4.51	6	LUC381	7.5.51	11	LUC386	25.5.51
2	LUC377	30.4.51	7	LUC382	11.5.51	12	LUC387	7.5.51
3	LUC378	7.5.51	8	LUC383	11.5.51	13	LUC388	29.5.51
4	LUC379	30.4.51	9	LUC384	11.5.51	14	LUC389	29.5.51
5	LUC380	30.4.51	10	LUC385	7.5.51	15	LUC390	18.5.51

The fifteen RFWs were purchased to fulfil the Executive's new but short-lived concession to operate private hire and tours outside the statutory London Passenger Transport area. The Eastern Coach Works bodies were to full coach standard and these were London Transport's only eight-foot wide Regal IVs. They were finished in the same livery as the RF1/2s but had no other outward similarities, as these official views of RFW 4 and RFW 11 show. L.T. Museum

Eastern Coach Works twenty-six seat bodywork was specified for the Guys which were used to replace the C and CR classes in 1953, incorporating sliding vent windows in a bus built to London Transport design for the first time. GS 31 is seen at Guildford. J. H. Aston

GS

To replace its fleet of small twenty-seat Leyland Cub one-man buses London Transport chose a modified version of the Guy Vixen chassis incorporating some Otter parts and a special bonnet made by Briggs Motor Bodies of Dagenham. The Perkins oil engine was specified and transmission was through a normal clutch and crash gearbox. The Eastern Coach Works bodies were built to a design which had many characteristics of contemporary LT practice but with standard ECW internal finishings and with sliding vent, rather than wind-down opening windows. The seating capacity of twenty-six took advantage of new regulations which allowed one-man operation of buses up to that capacity. The first GSs went into service at Chelsham in October 1953 and the remainder were allocated in small numbers all around the fleet. Some were used to replace full size single-deckers on lightly trafficked routes.

Chassis: Guy Vixen   Engine: Perkins P6 indirect-injection 65 bhp
Transmission: 4-speed crash
Bodywork: Eastern Coach Works   Capacity: B26F   L.T.code: 1GS1   Built: 1953
Number built: 84   Number in stock: 1.1.50: Nil   31.12.54: 84

Just over a month after being delivered to London Transport, GS 5 is seen working from Leatherhead garage on the short local route 481 at Epsom station. The elegant lines of the ECW body fitted well into the Executive's post-war family. Alan B. Cross

GS		Date into stock	GS		Date into stock	GS		Date into stock
1	MXX301	8.10.53	29	MXX329	6.11.53	57	MXX357	2.12.53
2	MXX302	2.10.53	30	MXX330	12.11.53	58	MXX358	9.12.53
3	MXX303	8.10.53	31	MXX331	12.11.53	59	MXX359	9.12.53
4	MXX304	12.10.53	32	MXX332	6.11.53	60	MXX360	9.12.53
5	MXX305	12.10.53	33	MXX333	13.11.53	61	MXX361	16.12.53
6	MXX306	16.10.53	34	MXX334	11.11.53	62	MXX362	16.12.53
7	MXX307	23.10.53	35	MXX335	13.11.53	63	MXX363	18.12.53
8	MXX308	12.10.53	36	MXX336	17.11.53	64	MXX364	11.12.53
9	MXX309	12.10.53	37	MXX337	17.11.53	65	MXX365	11.12.53
10	MXX310	23.10.53	38	MXX338	17.11.53	66	MXX366	11.12.53
11	MXX311	20.10.53	39	MXX339	13.11.53	67	MXX367	16.12.53
12	MXX312	30.10.53	40	MXX340	26.11.53	68	MXX368	18.12.53
13	MXX313	16.10.53	41	MXX341	17.11.53	69	MXX369	23.12.53
14	MXX314	16.10.53	42	MXX342	13.11.53	70	MXX370	18.12.53
15	MXX315	20.10.53	43	MXX343	26.11.53	71	MXX371	18.12.53
16	MXX316	23.10.53	44	MXX344	26.11.53	72	MXX372	23.12.53
17	MXX317	4.11.53	45	MXX345	26.11.53	73	MXX373	22.12.53
18	MXX318	23.10.53	46	MXX346	26.11.53	74	MXX374	12.1.54
19	MXX319	23.10.53	47	MXX347	27.11.53	75	MXX375	1.1.54
20	MXX320	4.11.53	48	MXX348	26.11.53	76	MXX376	1.1.54
21	MXX321	4.11.53	49	MXX349	27.11.53	77	MXX377	22.12.53
22	MXX322	30.10.53	50	MXX350	9.12.53	78	MXX378	1.1.54
23	MXX323	30.10.53	51	MXX351	27.11.53	79	MXX379	12.1.54
24	MXX324	11.11.53	52	MXX352	11.12.53	80	MXX380	21.1.54
25	MXX325	11.11.53	53	MXX353	27.11.53	81	MXX381	14.1.54
26	MXX326	6.11.53	54	MXX354	2.12.53	82	MXX382	14.1.54
27	MXX327	11.11.53	55	MXX355	9.12.53	83	MXX383	12.1.54
28	MXX328	12.11.53	56	MXX356	11.12.53	84	MXX384	21.1.54

LOANED LIGHTWEIGHTS

The delivery of the seven hundred RFs did not exhaust the authority granted to London Transport by the BTC which allowed for the purchase of up to 779 new single-deckers to cover not only the replacement of pre-war single-deckers but also to allow for the expected growth of demand in later years. Estimates made in the early 1950s showed a need for seventy-four additional coaches by 1957 to meet extra demand for travel to the New Towns and other housing developments in the Country Area. Rather than place a repeat order for the RF, which was already an obsolete design, the Executive decided to try out examples of the new generation lightweight vehicles to help decide what should be ordered. Three vehicles were selected for the trials, an AEC Monocoach chassisless bus, a Bristol LS and a Leyland Tiger Cub. The Bristol LS, which was probably included to meet the BTC's standing instruction that products from the two government-owned factories should be given first consideration, went into service on route 447 at Reigate in April 1953. The other two joined it in July. They subsequently ran on Green Line route 711 and finally on Central Bus route 208, from Dalston garage. They were returned to their owners in April 1954. No orders were ever placed, as the expected increases in traffic did not materialise.

NLP 635
Chassis: AEC Monocoach integral Engine: AEC AH410 6.75 litre six cylinder horizontal
Transmission: AEC D140 4-speed air operated preselective with fluid flywheel
Bodywork: Park Royal Vehicles
Capacity: B44F
L.T. code: None allocated
Built: 1953   Number in stock: 1.1.50: Nil   31.12.54: Nil

PHW 918
Chassis: Bristol LS5G Engine: Gardner 5HLW five cylinder horizontal 94 bhp
Transmission: Five speed synchromesh
Bodywork: Eastern Coach Works
Capacity: B45F
L.T. code: None allocated
Built: 1953   Number in stock: 1.1.50: Nil   31.12.54: Nil

PTE 592
Chassis: Leyland Tiger Cub PSUC1/1 Engine: Leyland 0350 5.76 litre six cylinder
    horizontal 90 bhp
Transmission: RV16 four speed air operated direct-acting
Bodywork: Saunders Roe ('SARO')
Capacity: B44F
L.T. code: None allocated
Built: 1953   Number in stock: 1.1.50: Nil   31.12.54: Nil

	Date borrowed	Date returned
NLP 635	July 1953	April 1954
PHW 918	April 1953	April 1954
PTE 592	July 1953	April 1954

Three possible successors to the RF from the new generation of lightweight single-deckers were tried out for a year between April 1953 and April 1954, their first assignment being on Reigate's route 447, followed by Green Line route 711 and Central Bus route 208. The AEC participant was an integral Park Royal bodied Monocoach with the registration NLP635 which came, surprisingly for a demonstrator, from a London Transport series. Like the other two it was finished in Green Line colours with appropriate lettering but there was apparently no room for a bullseye on the elaborately decorated dash panel. The rear view emphasises the high waist and relatively shallow roof, which spoilt the proportions of the otherwise attractive design. F.G. Reynolds

Leyland's contribution to the trials was PTE592, a Tiger Cub with a body by Saunders Roe, whose contemporary style was particularly handsome and stylish. It was also painted in Green Line colours which included the customary bullseye motif at the front. It was photographed outside Reigate garage. F.G. Reynolds

The third trial vehicle was the standard Tilling single-decker of the time, a Bristol LS with ECW bodywork, whose handsome, well proportioned lines are well caught in this photograph taken at the 'Red Lion', Reigate in April 1953. PHW918 carried a particularly prominent and large bullseye plaque immediately below the 'Bristol' scroll. Nothing came of these trials. D.W.K. Jones